THE AMERICAN 1930s

Beginning with the stock market crash of 1929 and ending with America's entry into the Second World War, the long Depression decade was a period of immense social, economic, and political turmoil. In response, writers as various as John Dos Passos, William Faulkner, Eugene O'Neill, Langston Hughes, Pearl S. Buck, and others looked to the past to make sense of the present. In this important new study of the 1930s, the distinguished cultural historian Peter Conn traces the extensive and complex engagement with the past that characterized the imaginative writing of the decade. Moving expertly between historical events and literature, Conn includes discussions of historical novels, plays and poems, biographies and autobiographies, as well as factual and imaginary works of history. Mapping the decade's extraordinary intellectual range with authority and flair, *The American 1930s* is a widely anticipated contribution to American literary studies.

PETER CONN is Professor of English at the University of Pennsylvania. He is the author of *The Divided Mind: Ideology and Imagination in America, 1898–1917* (Cambridge, 1983), *Literature in America: An Illustrated History* (Cambridge, 1989), and *Pearl S. Buck: A Cultural Biography* (Cambridge, 1996).

THE AMERICAN 1930s

A Literary History

PETER CONN

CAMBRIDGE
UNIVERSITY PRESS

CAMBRIDGE UNIVERSITY PRESS
Cambridge, New York, Melbourne, Madrid, Cape Town, Singapore, São Paulo, Delhi

Cambridge University Press
The Edinburgh Building, Cambridge CB2 8RU, UK

Published in the United States of America by Cambridge University Press, New York

www.cambridge.org
Information on this title: www.cambridge.org/9780521734318

First published 2009

Printed in the United Kingdom at the University Press, Cambridge

A catalogue record for this publication is available from the British Library

Library of Congress Cataloguing in Publication data
Conn, Peter J.
The American 1930s : a literary history / Peter Conn.
p.   cm.
Includes bibliographical references and index.
ISBN 978-0-521-51640-2 – ISBN 978-0-521-73431-8 (pbk.)
1. American literature–20th century–History and criticism.   2. Nineteen thirties.
3. Literature and history–United States–History–20th century.
4. America–In literature.   5. United States–Civilization–1918–1945.   I. Title.
PS221.C656 2009
810.9'35873917–dc22   2008039998

ISBN 978-0-521-51640-2 hardback
ISBN 978-0-521-73431-8 paperback

For Terry

Again

For our children
Steven, David, Alison, and Jennifer

And for our grandchildren
Nolan, Olivia, Mary, Zachary, and Alex

Contents

Illustrations

Acknowledgments

In the course of writing this book, I have accumulated a substantial list of obligations. Some of my colleagues, family members, and friends have read portions and drafts of the book. Others have offered companionship and needful distractions that have made the several years of work far more pleasant than they would otherwise have been.

I owe thanks to Roger Abrahams, Bob Barchi, Francis Barchi, Nina Baym, Omar Blaik, Angela Brintlinger, Ann Brownlee, David Brownlee, Art Casciato, Joel Conarroe, Steven Conn, Alison Conn, David Conn, Jennifer Conn, Patrice Razler Conn, Audrey Cotterell, Marta Dabezies, Michael delli Carpini, Joseph Farrell, Rich Gelles, Bonnie Gibson, Eduardo Glandt, Glen Gaulton, Gary Hack, Judy Ivy, Randy Ivy, Brian Kirk, Bill Koons, Linda Koons, Valarie Swain-Cade McCoullum, Afaf Meleis, James O'Donnell, Juan Parada, Susan Phillips, Jordan Pollinger, David Pope, Dina Portnoy, John Richetti, George Ritchie, Pat Rose, Arthur Rubenstein, Ray Ryan, Maartje Scheltens, Cathy Turner, Gerald Weales, Lawrence White, and Wendy White. Mike Fitts provided abundant hospitality. Wendy Steiner's suggestions made this book better than it would have been. Finally, I owe a particular debt of gratitude to Carton Rogers and the entire staff of the University of Pennsylvania libraries. I have worked in a great many libraries and archives over several decades; Penn's professional staff is by a long measure the finest I have ever encountered.

A cultural and political timeline

1929

October 25: "Black Friday," the beginning of the stock market crash
    November: Puccini's "Madame Butterfly" is the first opera broadcast on American radio

1930

1930 census reports a US population of 122,700,000
    Sigmund Freud's *Civilization and Its Discontents* published in an English translation
    Institute for Advanced Study established in Princeton, New Jersey
    April: the first Nancy Drew mystery book, *The Secret of the Old Clock*, by the pseudonymous Carolyn Keene
    April 6: Gandhi leads the "salt march" in violation of British law and initiates the civil disobedience movement in India
    June 17: Herbert Hoover signs the Smoot–Hawley Act, imposing the highest tariffs in US history
    November 4: Democrats win a majority in the House of Representatives

1931

March 3: Congressional resolution establishes "The Star Spangled Banner" as the US national anthem
    March 25: arrest of nine African-American youths – the "Scottsboro Boys" – for the alleged rape of two white women
    May 1: dedication of the Empire State Building, the tallest building in the world
    June 1: Supreme Court, in Near v. Minnesota, prohibits prior restraint of the press and affirms the freedom of the press

September 18: Japan invades Manchuria

October: First nonstop flight across the Pacific Ocean, from Saishiro, Japan to Wenatchee, WA (forty-one hours)

November: opening of the first museum of American art, the Whitney Gallery, in New York City

November 24: Al Capone sentenced to eleven years in prison for income tax evasion

December: annual emigration exceeds immigration for first time in US history

1932

February 10: "Modern Architecture: International Exhibition" opens at the Museum of Modern Art

March 1: kidnapping of Anne and Charles Lindbergh's baby son

July 28: Washington DC police and US Army troops attack and disband Bonus Army

July 30: Olympic Games open in Los Angeles

November 8: Franklin Roosevelt elected President, defeating incumbent Herbert Hoover by 22,800,000 to 15,700,000 votes

December 27: opening of Radio City Music Hall, with 6,200 seats the largest movie theater in the world

1933

Carl Jung's *Modern Man in Search of a Soul* published in an English translation

January 30: Adolph Hitler installed as German Chancellor

February 27: German Reichstag burns

March 4: Franklin D. Roosevelt inaugurated as President

March: Frances Perkins, appointed Secretary of Labor, is the first woman to serve in the US Cabinet

March 27: Japan withdraws from the League of Nations

May 18: Franklin Roosevelt signs legislation creating the Tennessee Valley Authority (TVA)

May 27: Chicago World's Fair "Century of Progress" opens

October 21: Germany withdraws from the League of Nations

November 16: USA and USSR establish diplomatic relations

December 5: approval of the twenty-first amendment to the US Constitution repeals prohibition

1934

Arnold Toynbee, volumes I–III of *A Study of History*

January 1: Francis Townsend launches his Old Age Revolving Pension Plan

February 1: 2,000 taxi drivers strike in New York City

February 9: "Man at the Crossroads," Diego Rivera's mural in Rockefeller Center, is destroyed when Rivera refuses to eliminate a portrait of Lenin

March 24: Tydings–McDuffie Act establishes commonwealth status for the Philippines and sets a timetable for independence

May 23: Bonnie Parker and Clyde Barrow shot to death by police

July: Southern Tenant Farmers Union is established in Arkansas

September 19: the Soviet Union is admitted to the League of Nations

October 16: commencement of the Communist "Long March" in China

1935

May: Works Progress Administration (WPA) formed

July 5: Franklin Roosevelt signs the National Labor Relations Act

August 14: Franklin Roosevelt signs the Social Security Act

September 8: Huey Long assassinated by Dr. Carl Weiss

September 15: promulgation of the Nuremburg racial laws in Germany

October 3: Italy invades Ethiopia

September 30: Franklin Roosevelt dedicates Boulder Dam (renamed Hoover Dam in 1947)

1936

John Maynard Keynes, *The General Theory of Employment, Interest and Money*

Walter Benjamin, "The Work of Art in the Age of Mechanical Reproduction"

March 7: Germany reoccupies the Rhineland

June: Mary McLeod Bethune named Director of Negro Affairs in the National Youth Administration, the first black woman to receive a major federal appointment

July 18: Francisco Franco leads a military rebellion against the elected government of Spain

August 1: Olympic Games open in Berlin

August: Moscow show trials begin

September: sit-down strikes, through May 1937, involve 500,000 workers

October 25: Mussolini and Hitler sign Rome–Berlin Axis agreement

November 3: Franklin Roosevelt re-elected, defeating Republican Alf Landon by 27,700,000 to 16,700,000 votes

December 7: "Fantastic Art, Dada, Surrealism" exhibition opens at the Museum of Modern Art

December 11: Edward VIII abdicates the British throne

December 12: Chiang Kai-shek taken prisoner by his own generals in Xi'an and forced to agree to a united front with Communists against the Japanese

1937

February 16: Dupont patents nylon

March 17: "Photography: 1839–1937" exhibition opens at the Museum of Modern Art, the museum's first exhibition of photography

April 26: German planes bomb the Basque town of Guernica

May 6: German airship *Hindenburg* crashes at Lakehurst, New Jersey

May: Texas Democrat Martin Dies named first chairman of House Un-American Activities Committee

July 2: Amelia Earhart disappears on a round-the-world flight

July 7: Japan invades China proper

July 19: Nazi exhibition of "Degenerate Art" opens in Munich

December 12: US gunboat *Panay* is sunk by Japanese planes in Chinese waters

1938

January 16: Benny Goodman plays in the first jazz concert at Carnegie Hall

February: Walt Disney releases *Snow White and the Seven Dwarfs*

March 18: Mexican government nationalizes foreign oil concessions

June: "Superman" debuts in the first issue of *Action Comics*

September 29: Munich Pact between Germany and Great Britain

October 3: German occupation of Czech Sudetenland

November 9: *Kristallnacht* (Night of Broken Glass) and anti-Semitic riots in Germany

November 11: Irving Berlin's "God Bless America" released
November: nuclear fission achieved by German scientists

1939

March 2: Eugenio Pacelli elected Pope Pius XII

April 1: Franco's forces capture Madrid: the end of the Spanish Civil War

May 2: New York Yankee first baseman Lou Gehrig ends fourteen-year, 2,130 game streak

August 2: Albert Einstein writes to Franklin Roosevelt urging US research toward the construction of an atomic bomb

August 24: Germany and the Soviet Union sign a Non-Aggression Treaty

September 1: Germany invades Poland

September 3: Britain declares war on Germany

1940

1940 census reports a US population of 131,670,000

May 10: Winston Churchill takes office as British Prime Minister

Olympic Games, scheduled for Tokyo and Helsinki, canceled

June 22: Germany invades the Soviet Union

July: German air force begins bombing "Blitz" of England

July 4: opening of the American Negro Exposition (Chicago), to celebrate the seventy-fifth anniversary of the Emancipation Proclamation

August 21: assassination of Leon Trotsky in Mexico City

September 12: discovery of the Lascaux cave paintings

September 16: USA initiates first peacetime military draft

September 27: Germany, Japan, and Italy sign the Axis (Tripartite) Pact

October 25: Benjamin O. Davis, Sr. is the first African-American promoted to the rank of general in the US Army

November 5: Franklin Roosevelt re-elected, defeating Republican Wendell Willkie by 27,300,000 to 22,300,000 votes

1941

March 17: the National Gallery of Art opens in Washington, DC

December 7: Japan attacks Pearl Harbor

Introduction: History and literary history

"If it's not art, it's at least history."[1]

Thomas Hart Benton

Bounded by the traumas of the Wall Street Crash and the attack on Pearl Harbor, the period that historians refer to as the long decade of the thirties is a narrative anchored in the economic and political emergency of those years. With the exception only of the Civil War, Americans faced in the Depression the most wrenching and divisive domestic crisis in their history. An economic structure that had seemed unshakable simply collapsed, and neither experts nor ordinary citizens were ever sure why.

Theories have multiplied, and the argument continues to this day. The Depression was caused by the economic imbalances and war debts imposed by the Treaty of Versailles, by an unusually sharp decline in the business cycle, by stock market speculation and irresponsible purchases on margin, by the market's crash, by the unequal distribution of income, by high tariffs and other restrictions on international trade, by agricultural overproduction, by the counter-productive efforts of many governments to balance national budgets, by some or all of these in numberless combination.[2]

The tremors of what Edmund Wilson called "the great earthquake" shook every American city and village. Individual stock prices fell by as much as 90 percent; the market as a whole lost two-thirds of its value.

---

[1] Cited in Emily Braun and Thomas Branchick, *Thomas Hart Benton: The America Today Murals* (Williamstown, MA: Williams College Museum of Art, 1985), p. 11.

[2] For a survey of these debates, see the first two chapters of John Garraty, *The Great Depression: an Inquiry into the Causes, Course, and Consequences of the The Worldwide Depression of the Nineteen-Thirties, as Seen by Contemporaries and in the Light of History* (New York: Harcourt Brace Jovanovich, 1986). Among the scores of books on the Depression, this volume is indispensable for its consistently international and comparative focus. For a useful and more recent comparative analysis, though limited to three countries, see Wolfgang Schivelbush, *Three New Deals: Reflections on Roosevelt's America, Mussolini's Italy, and Hitler's Germany, 1933–1939*, Jefferson Chase, trans. (New York: Metropolitan Books, 2006).

Between October 1929 and March 1933, more than 5,000 banks failed, and 600,000 homeowners saw their mortgages foreclosed. The worst drought in a century turned much of the Midwest to dust: 35 million acres of cropland had been completely destroyed, and another 100 million acres – an area the size of Pennsylvania – lost their topsoil.

By 1932, the third year of the Depression, more than 10 million persons were unemployed – almost 20 percent of the work force. In big-industry towns, such as Chicago and Detroit, the numbers out of work reached nearly 50 percent – 624,000 in Chicago alone. Many of those who kept their jobs were reduced to working part-time, or on split shifts. "Investors had ceased to invest and workers had ceased to work."[3] Nothing like this level of unemployment had ever been seen in the USA before, not even in the long slump following the Panic of 1893, which had lingered through the last years of the nineteenth century.

Furthermore, for nearly a decade, the devastated economy responded only fitfully to New Deal reform programs. The severity and duration of the Depression seemed to define it as an essentially new phenomenon. Though the cyclical nature of the market economy had brought regular alternations of prosperity and contraction – boom and bust as they were universally called – the failure of the 1930s appeared to be more systemic, more fundamental, and more intractable than anything in previous American or indeed global experience. British economist John Maynard Keynes said the nearest parallel to the hard times of the thirties "was called the Dark Ages and it lasted 400 years."[4]

In fact, however, the situation was more complicated. Not everyone lost a job, and not all the indicators were doom-laden. The unemployed were a minority of the work force, even in the worst years of the Depression, and the majority of those who lost jobs found new ones. "It is important to keep in mind," John Garraty reminds us, "that during the Great Depression, people who had full-time jobs were usually better off, at least economically, than they had been before 1929" (*The Great Depression*, p. 86) because the cost of living fell faster than wages. Even in the ravaged Dust Bowl, hundreds of thousands of men, women and children – two-thirds of the 1930 population – clung to their homesteads.[5]

[3] See David M. Kennedy, *Freedom From Fear: The American People in Depression and War, 1929–1945* (New York: Oxford University Press, 1999), pp. 133, 163, 87.
[4] Cited in William Manchester, *The Glory and the Dream* (Boston: Little, Brown, 1974), p. 31.
[5] Timothy Egan, *The Worst Hard Time: The Untold Story of Those Who Survived the Great American Dust Bowl* (Boston: Houghton Mifflin Company, 2006), pp. 9–10. According to Egan, John Steinbeck told only "part of the story."

Despite the hard times, "[b]y 1937, fifty-two million people in fifteen million cars were spending an estimated five billion dollars on motor travel." To be sure, migrants like Steinbeck's Joads, seeking escape from misery, drove some of those cars, but recreational tourism increased notably during the decade.[6] Catering to those tourists, thousands of new motels sprouted next to roads and highways across America in the thirties.[7] Commercial air traffic increased twelve-fold in the 1930s, reaching one billion passenger miles by the end of the decade.[8] Book sales slumped, but millions of Americans spent tens of millions of dollars on movie tickets.

Available data indicate that the health of Americans did not diminish during the 1930s, and the trend toward increased longevity continued: life expectancy rose from 57.1 years in 1929 to 63.7 years in 1939 (Garraty, *The Great Depression*, pp. 86, 104). In December 1933, the Metropolitan Life Insurance Company placed a full-page ad in *Current History* and other publications, headlined: "The United States of America enjoyed better health and had a lower death rate during the year 1932 and in 1933 than ever before in its history." To give a single local example, of added significance because it is taken from the South: statistics published in Georgia in 1939 showed that the death rate from malaria in that impoverished state had declined markedly in the preceding ten years.[9]

While these encouraging reference points do not subtract from the scale of anxiety and deprivation during the thirties, they usefully suggest that the decade encompassed a striking diversity of experience. Some Americans recoiled in disappointment and anger, and sought alternative structures and explanations. At the same time, others embraced all the more fervently the essential rightness and continued relevance of traditional national propositions. One study indicated that only a few citizens reacted with either apathy or protest: "Established values and desires persisted," even among the unemployed.[10]

---

[6] Lloyd Morris, *Not So Long Ago* (New York: Random House, 1949), p. 386. For an informative history of the subject, see Marguerite Shaffer, *See America First: Tourism and National Identity, 1880–1940* (Washington, DC: Smithsonian Institution Press, 2001).

[7] Bill Stott, "Introduction" to Archie Hobson, ed., *Remembering America: A Sampler of the WPA American Guide Series* (New York: Columbia University Press, 1985), p. 2. Hobson's anthology includes upwards of 500 selections from the Guides.

[8] Sean D. Cashman, *America in the Twenties and Thirties: the Olympian Age of Franklin Delano Roosevelt* (New York: New York University Press, 1989), pp. 30–31.

[9] *Georgia: A Guide to Its Towns and Countryside* (Athens: University of Georgia Press, 1939), p. 53.

[10] Cited in Terry A. Cooney, *Balancing Acts: American Thought and Culture in the 1930s* (New York: Twayne Publishers, 1995), p. 5.

Thus, while many of the victims of the Depression directed their anger toward the government or "conditions," sometimes to the point of violence, others blamed themselves. As many contemporary observers pointed out, a commitment to self-reliance survived among countless men and women who continued to believe in the efficacy of initiative and hard work and considered poverty a proof of moral turpitude. Since up to a quarter of the work force was idled, such a belief could engender enormous emotional pain.

Many of those who lost jobs or homes expressed feelings of "guilt and self-recrimination" (Kennedy, *Freedom from Fear*, p. 174). In doing the travel and research for *My America* (1938), Louis Adamic interviewed scores of people who felt personally responsible for their unemployment and impoverishment.[11] Journalist Lorena Hickok, reporting to Harry Hopkins on the conditions she was observing, quoted a young woman who refused either aid or encouragement: "Oh, don't bother. . . . If, with all the advantages I've had, I can't make a living, I'm just no good, I guess."[12] On his travels around the country in the mid-thirties, Sherwood Anderson met a man who told him: "I failed. I failed. It's my own fault."[13] From Dale Carnegie's *How to Win Friends and Influence People* (1936) to its host of imitators, Depression-era books and articles insisted that "failure is personal, not social, and success can be achieved by some adjustment, not in the social order but in the individual personality."[14]

Blaming themselves or blaming the system, "Middletown Faces Both Ways." The title of the final chapter of Robert and Helen Lynd's *Middletown in Transition* (1937) summarized the national mood. Every revolutionary manifesto can be matched by a call to re-affirmation. In 1932, Malcolm Cowley, Langston Hughes, Edmund Wilson, and the other intellectuals who published *Culture and the Crisis* demanded a revolution and supported William Z. Foster, the Communist candidate for President. A couple of years later, on the other hand, regionalist painter Grant Wood, in his *Revolt Against the City* (1935), argued, "during boom times conservatism is a thing to be ridiculed, but under unsettling conditions it becomes a virtue."[15] Wood detected, in the opinion of one

---

[11] Louis Adamic, *My America, 1928–1938* (New York: Harper & Brothers, 1938), pp. 283ff.
[12] Richard Lowitt and Maurine Beasley, eds., *One Third of a Nation: Lorena Hickok Reports on the Great Depression* (Urbana: University of Illinois Press, 1981), p. 223.
[13] Sherwood Anderson, *Puzzled America* (New York: Charles Scribner's Sons, 1935), p. 46.
[14] See Warren I. Susman, *Culture as History: The Transformation of American Society in the Twentieth Century* (New York: Pantheon Books, 1984), p. 165.
[15] Grant Wood, *Revolt against the City* (Iowa City: Clio Press, 1935), p. 29.

scholar, a "powerful yearning for security" as the dominant mood of the time.[16] Looking back on the 1930s from a village called Grafton in upstate New York, ex-Communist Granville Hicks decided that the Depression had "changed no one's views," in part because the majority of his neighbors understood the slump to be a "natural catastrophe, in no wise different from a drought or a hurricane."[17]

Those diverse understandings led to diverse imaginative expressions, in effect a debate over the meaning of America. The task of the pages that follow is to provide a through line for exploring that rich heterogeneity, by tracing one of the main subjects to which the decade's writers turned again and again: the past. The writing of the 1930s comprises an extensive and complex engagement with the past, in myriad forms: the memoirs and biographies of influential individuals, and the factual and imaginary histories of the United States and other nations.

By mapping the contours of the thirties' engagement with the past, I propose to document the decade's extraordinary intellectual range. The search for what was frequently called "a usable past" reached into government programs, scholarship, and popular culture.[18] The 1930s, after all, were the years in which the National Archives opened, most of the volumes of the *Dictionary of American Biography* were published, the Historical Records Survey and the Historic American Buildings Survey were initiated, and the Index of American Design was established, tasked with recording the artifacts of the nation's past.[19] The twelve-volume

---

[16] Steven Biel, *American Gothic: A Life of America's Most Famous Painting* (New York: W. W. Norton & Company, 2005), p. 109. Numerous historians have concluded that "security" was the irreducible central theme of the New Deal, whatever the apparent incoherence and right and left turns of Franklin Roosevelt's particular choices.

[17] Granville Hicks, *Small Town* (New York: Fordham University Press, 2004 [1946]), pp. 117–118.

[18] Van Wyck Brooks first used the durable phrase "usable past," in *America's Coming of Age* (1915). As that date accurately indicates, the 1930s were not the first years in which Americans turned toward the past as a subject for study and imaginative exploration. Hawthorne's novels have been described with the same term. My point about the rediscovery of the past in the thirties is twofold: (1) the turbulent circumstances of the Depression stimulated an especially vigorous engagement with history, which is worth recovering because (2) since the end of the 1930s, decades of scholarly and critical absorption in the political literature of the decade has tended to obscure this large and informative body of retrospective texts.

[19] Two major works of historical restoration – or re-creation – were also completed in the 1930s. The first phase in the rebuilding of Colonial Williamsburg, announced by its patron, John D. Rockefeller, Jr., in 1928, was accomplished in the 1930s. Another Rockefeller-funded project, the Cloisters, with its thousands of medieval artifacts housed in a reconstructed European monastery, opened in Manhattan in 1938.

History of American Life, edited by Arthur M. Schlesinger, appeared in installments from 1928 through 1944.

Americans, in Eric Foner's view, "have always looked to history for a sense of national cohesiveness," especially in times of crisis, when cohesiveness is under siege.[20] It is not surprising that many Americans turned to the past in response to the turbulence of the Depression decade. The historian David Lowenthal has argued that the recovered past – even if recovered only in the form of mythology – "legitimates and fortifies the present order against subsequent mishap or corruption."[21]

These statements are helpful, though both claim too much and distinguish too little. While the retrospection of American writers in the 1930s was sometimes nostalgic, they frequently revived the past to criticize American values and institutions. In historical novels, poems and films, biographies and autobiographies, historical monographs and folklore studies, in painting, music, and photography, men and women of the thirties discovered a kaleidoscope of pasts shaped by a wide variety of political and cultural commitments. Some of these writers considered themselves radical, others conservative; still others were uninterested in politics at all. The conflicting pasts offered vehicles to defend competing views of the present and future.

Thus, to see the thirties exclusively as "the red decade" is to reduce a complex palette to a monotone. In this book, I want to argue against the current, widely shared scholarly assumption that the 1930s were largely characterized in cultural terms by Left aesthetics and politics. In fact, the United States in the 1930s was – as it has always been, and despite the pressures of the Depression – a place of enormous ideological and imaginative complexity, and the uses to which writers put the past can assist in recovering the heterogeneity of intellectual life in the decade. The French writer André Maurois, after several visits to the USA in the thirties, summarized his "total impression" of the country at the end of the decade:

This is an immense country made up of overpopulated islands sprinkled among the prairies, the forests, and the deserts. Among these islets of skyscrapers there is hardly any common life. The newspapers of Minneapolis are not read in Cincinnati. The great man of Tulsa is unknown in Dallas. The Negro of Georgia, the Swede of Minnesota, the Mexican of San Antonio, and the German

[20] Eric Foner, *Who Owns History? Rethinking the Past in a Changing World* (New York: Hill and Wang, 2002), p. 150.
[21] David Lowenthal, *The Past is a Foreign Country* (New York: Cambridge University Press, 1985), p. 41.

of Chicago, Marquand's patricians, and Steinbeck's tramps are all citizens of the United States, but there is slight resemblance among them.[22]

A number of the texts discussed in this book, apart from their contribution to American diversity, are worth recovering and reading on their own terms. Questions of literary value and valuation have become a rich and vexed subject in the past several decades. Are literary reputations constructed by the collaboration of critics, publishers, academics, and editors, or do they rise above fashion and conspiracy by asserting their own eminence? I am less interested in that argument than in the opportunity to describe a more populous artistic 1930s, more inclusive and hence more interesting.

Consequently, *The American 1930s* includes prize-winning books and bestsellers, novels as well as poetry, and quite a few volumes of non-fiction as well. The relevance of so much of the decade's writing to my argument can be taken as a simple but serviceable measure of the vital currency of the past in the 1930s.[23] Beyond that, as William St. Clair has recently reminded us, literary history should take at least some account of "books that were actually read, and were admired in their generation."[24] Especially for works not likely to be familiar to most readers, I have tried to provide enough detail to make their diverse purposes and achievements clear. The pages that follow offer a set of what might be called case studies in the literary thirties.

Some years ago, Peter Novick offered an important admonition about the writing of history:

As cultural historians multiply, cultural epochs get cut finer and finer: where once we had the Age of the Baroque and the Siècle des Lumières, we now have characterizations of the culture of decades: "iconoclasm" for the 1920s; "radicalism" for the 1930s. But there was no shortage of superstition in the Age of Reason; plenty of traditionalism and complacency in the decades of iconoclasm and radicalism.[25]

---

[22] André Maurois, *Etats-Unis 39: Journal d'un voyage en Amérique*. The passage cited is printed in Oscar Handlin, ed., *This Was America: True Accounts of People and Places, Manners and Customs, as Recorded by European Travels to the Western Shore in the Eighteenth, Nineteenth, and Twentieth Centuries* (Cambridge, MA: Harvard University Press, 1949), p. 566. No translator is credited. Maurois's catalogue sounds a bit like Mark Twain's demand, in his *Essays on Paul Bourget*, that "the native novelist" must attend to the villages of each region and state, along with the lives of Indians, miners, Irish, Germans, Italians, Swedes, Catholics, Methodists, Baptists, and Jews, not excluding the moonshiners, the train robbers, the "Idiots and Congressmen." The serious point that both writers were emphasizing is the irreducible diversity of the nation's people, and the need for novelists – and their critics – to attend to as much of that diversity as possible.

[23] I have included a list of bestselling and prize-winning work in the appendix.

[24] See William St. Clair, "But What Did We Actually Read?," *TLS* (May 12, 2006), pp. 13–15.

[25] Peter Novick, *That Noble Dream: The "Objectivity Question" and the American Historical Profession* (Cambridge: Cambridge University Press, 1988), p. 133.

Or, in the more vernacular formulation of journalist Robert Bendiner, whose family lived a hand-to-mouth existence through the American thirties: "It has always seemed to me fatuous to fix a single label on a whole decade – as though the Nineties were gay for immigrant ladies in the garment sweatshops of Manhattan or the Twenties stood for hot jazz in the mind of Calvin Coolidge."[26]

These comments usefully warn against the reduction of entire decades to two or three hackneyed adjectives. At the same time, the advantages of working within the confines of a relatively brief period such as the 1930s are substantial: among them precisely the opportunity to enrich our understanding by documenting the breadth and even the internal contradictions of the decade. Part of that cultural breadth consists in the patterns of continuity that link the 1930s to the history that had come before. As Oscar Cargill shrewdly observed, many years ago, "nothing precisely ceased or began on October 29, 1929."[27] By connecting the 1930s to earlier American pasts, this book provides a fuller description of the cultural life of the Depression decade. That in turn offers at least the beginnings of an alternative literary history of the 1930s.

The focus is on fiction and non-fiction writing, but I also include some comment on the decade's history painting, as a way of further widening the scope of the analysis. The 1930s was among the busiest of all American decades for the production of historical pictures: highbrow and lowbrow, populist and elitist, serious and comic. Such works demonstrate that painters, like writers, found in the past a means of responding to the dislocations of the present moment.

Let me conclude these preliminary comments with a final distinction. Some of the texts I shall be discussing, for example the novels of John Dos Passos and the plays of Clifford Odets, deployed history in direct response to the political and economic events of the 1930s. Other historically engaged work, for instance the novels of William Faulkner and the plays of Eugene O'Neill, would probably have been produced whether the Depression had occurred or not. The point is that all the novels, plays, and paintings here contributed to the thick texture of "pastness" that helped to define the decade, and they participated thereby in the debate over the meaning of America.

---

[26] Robert Bendiner, *Just Around the Corner: A Highly Selective History of the Thirties* (New York: Harper & Row, Publishers, 1967), p. xi.

[27] Oscar Cargill, *Ideas on the March* (New York: The Macmillan Company, 1941), p. xi. Cargill's remark has particular relevance to the subject of this study. The widespread interest in the past that writers of the Depression decade displayed intensified and expanded the surge of interest in American history – one result of postwar nationalism – that had also marked the writing of the 1920s.

CHAPTER I

Farewell to the twenties

For the 1930s, the twenties were the years of the near past, and they were instantly codified and mythologized. An unsigned editorial in the January 1930 issue of *The Bookman* announced that "it is apparent that the 'twenties had a flavor and a spirit of their own, a composite personality that will figure in history as a distinct entity, a 'period.'" The prevailing images captured the decade's alleged glamour, ill-distributed but undeniable affluence, and assorted revolts – chiefly against the village and sexual repression. But onlookers of all persuasions also welcomed the end of what they considered an era of triviality and excess.

Speaking from the left, Edmund Wilson wrote that he found the economic perturbations "not depressing but stimulating. One couldn't help being exhilarated at the sudden unexpected collapse of that stupid gigantic fraud."[1] Albert Jay Nock, a libertarian gadfly and incorrigible snob who had written influentially on subjects from education to religion, made much the same point from a different direction. In a diary entry in 1932, Nock noted: "The Dark Ages must have been a grand gorgeousness of gaiety and sparkle compared with the intellectual life of the last fifteen years."[2]

The Depression's reconstruction of the 1920s began with the First World War, which had shaped many of the characteristic gestures and moods of that earlier decade. In four years of stalemated carnage, the war had killed 10 million men, women, and children, soldiers and civilians, participants and bystanders, and truncated an entire European generation. Although America entered the war relatively late, and fought for only eighteen months, the political and imaginative consequences were profound. John Dos Passos's *Three Soldiers* (1921), E. E. Cummings's *The*

---

[1] Edmund Wilson, *The Shores of Light: A Literary Chronicle of the Twenties and Thirties* (New York: Farrar, Straus and Giroux, 1952), p. 498.

[2] Albert Jay Nock, *A Journal of These Days, June 1932 – December 1933* (New York: William Morrow & Company, 1934), p. 80.

Enormous Room (1922), Willa Cather's Pulitzer Prize winning *One of Ours* (1922), Ernest Hemingway's *The Sun Also Rises* (1926) and *A Farewell to Arms* (1929), William Faulkner's *Soldier's Pay* (1926), were only the more prominent texts that engaged the war and its aftermath.

The war continued to loom behind the thirties as the preeminent catastrophe of the twentieth century. By the thirties, it had been transformed from current events into history, and as such it continued to provide an important subject for imaginative writing. By one count, upwards of forty novels with World War I as their subject were published in the USA in the 1930s – far fewer than those published in the 1920s, and fewer than those published in the thirties in Great Britain, but a significant number.[3] The first section of this chapter will survey several of those novels, which collectively made a singular contribution to the literature of remembrance in the 1930s.

Perhaps more successfully than any other writer of the 1930s, John Dos Passos found a prose that combined modernist technique with political statement. After graduating from Harvard in 1916 he went to Europe, intending to study architecture in Spain but shortly thereafter volunteering to serve as a medic and driver in the legendary Norton–Harjes Volunteer Ambulance Service on the Western Front. The war catalyzed his opposition to the institutional straitjackets of modern life. Dos Passos had waged his private campaign against the war in several previous novels and stories, including *One Man's Initiation – 1917* (1920) and *Three Soldiers*.

Dos Passos's *Nineteen Nineteen* (1932) was the preeminent war novel of the 1930s. Revisiting the carnage he had seen firsthand, Dos Passos captures the nastiness, the tedium, the intermittent horror, and above all the sheer stupidity that propelled men repeatedly into meaningless death. In the novel's final pages, an embittered set piece called "The Body of an American" indicts the misguided and ultimately murderous patriotism that made World War I possible. Dos Passos recreates the ceremony that took place in Arlington National Cemetery on November 11, 1921, when President Warren G. Harding presided over the burial of the Unknown Soldier. Presidential rhetoric and newspaper headlines are juxtaposed against the grisly anatomical realities of "John Doe's" mutilated body:

The blood ran into the ground, the brains oozed out of the cracked skull and were licked up by the trenchrats, the belly swelled and raised a generation of bluebottle flies...

---

[3] Philip E. Hager and Desmond Taylor, eds., *The Novels of World War I: an Annotated Bibliography* (New York: Garland, 1981).

and Mr. Harding prayed to God and the diplomats and the generals and the brasshats and the politicians and the handsomely dressed ladies out of the society column of the Washington Post stood up solemn

and thought how beautiful sad Old Glory God's Country it was to have the bugler play taps and the three volleys made their ears ring.[4]

Dos Passos might have written this scene whether the economy had crashed in 1929 or not; his outrage had its source in his personal experience of the war, and the passage of time never healed his psychological wounds or mollified his anger. At the same time, the Depression seemed to confirm his diagnosis of the fundamental distortions that had corrupted America's national values. The field of his polemic was history and his task, throughout the entire *U.S.A.* trilogy, was skeptical revision.

William March (born William Edward Campbell in Mobile, Alabama in 1893) served with exceptional distinction on the Western Front; his battlefield actions earned the US Distinguished Service Cross and the French Croix de Guerre. After the war, he co-founded the Waterman Steamship Corporation and served as vice-president for over a decade, living mostly in New York and traveling in Europe. After he retired, March returned to the South, living in New Orleans and writing the one book for which he remains known, *The Bad Seed* (1954).[5]

In 1933, March published *Company K*, an extraordinary fictional account of the war's human devastation. Departing in its design from conventional narration, the novel consists of over 100 separate statements by the men and officers of a single infantry company. Most of these chapters are only a page or two in length, some only a couple of paragraphs. Private Joseph Delaney, who opens the book with a kind of prologue on March's behalf, talks about pinning all the stories to "a huge wheel," and spinning the wheel to tell the story of the war. These are the fragments of modernist practice, not shored against ruin, but displayed to demonstrate the absolute futility of war.

The chapters alternate sensational set pieces with images of the boredom, bad food, and bullying that defined the typical soldier's day in the trenches: maggoty meat; ill-fitting boots that rub a man's feet raw to the point of infection; decomposing bodies lifted out of their shallow graves by rain or artillery shells; omnipresent filth and stench. The sustained, low-grade despair is heightened to terror by the intervals of action. Two

---

[4] John Dos Passos, *Nineteen Nineteen* (New York: New American Library, 1969 [1932]), p. 466.
[5] For biographical details, see Roy S. Simmonds, *The Two Worlds of William March* (Tuscaloosa: University of Alabama Press, 1984).

famished soldiers eat a blood-soaked loaf of bread they take from the body of a dead German. A soldier with his foot torn nearly in half is denied morphine, which is reserved for officers. Several of the chapters are narrated by dead men, after they've been killed by mustard gas, or machine guns, or friendly fire. In the novel's most scarifying sequence, a sadistic American captain orders the illegal execution of twenty-two German prisoners. One of the enlisted men assigned to the job deserts rather than comply with the order, but the others do as they're told. One of them searches the bodies for souvenirs, in particular Iron Crosses, which bring 150 francs on the open market.

Like other anti-war writers, March reserves some of his most bitter prose for the war's corruption of language. A private assigned to write condolence letters gives every man "a glorious, romantic death with appropriate last words," but then, as he starts the thirtieth letter, decides to tell the truth:

Dear Madam:
     Your son, Francis, died needlessly in Belleau Wood. You will be interested to hear that at the time of his death he was crawling with vermin and weak from diarrhea. His feet were swollen and rotten and they stank. He lived like a frightened animal, cold and hungry. Then, on June 6th, a piece of shrapnel hit him and he died in agony, slowly. You'd never believe that he could live three hours, but he did. He lived three full hours, screaming and cursing by turns. He had nothing to hold on to, you see: He had learned long ago that what he had been taught to believe by you, his mother, who loved him, under the meaningless names of honor, courage, and patriotism, were all lies.[6]

Herbert Gorman published two dozen books in the course of a long and prolific career. He held a number of newspaper jobs as reporter and editor with the *New York Times* and *Herald Tribune,* and published a couple of volumes of poetry when he was in his twenties. He went on to write biography (Longfellow, Hawthorne), criticism (Hawthorne, Thornton Wilder), and a sequence of novels, most of them based on recreations of the American or European past. For a number of years, Gorman had the rather remarkable distinction of having been chosen by James Joyce as his authorized biographer. He published two biographies of Joyce, *James Joyce, His First Forty Years* (1926), and *James Joyce* (1939).[7]

---

[6] William March, *Company K* (New York: Arbor House, 1984 [1933]), p. 63.
[7] After suffering from Joyce's continual interference, Gorman allegedly "swore that he would never again choose as a subject a living man." Stan Gebler Davies, *James Joyce: A Portrait of the Artist* (New York: Stein & Day, 1975), p. 7.

Gorman had an abiding interest in French history and his sprawling fictional representations of the French Revolution and the Franco-Prussian War will be discussed below. In 1934, he published *Suzy*, which takes place in London and Paris during the First World War. *Suzy* is a combination of thriller and historical romance whose characters include a sensationalized Mata Hari. The novel is told mainly through the point of view of the title character, a young American woman.[8] Susan Dillworthy is descended from Henry James's heroines, a woman who exchanges her New World innocence for a deepening engagement with the complexity of Europe. Her adventures range from the melodramatic (she assists in the capture of Mata Hari) to the amorous (she is briefly married to an aristocratic French officer who dies in the trenches).

Suzy is unusual among American novels of World War I in several ways. Where most are set on the battlefield, and feature military, male protagonists, this one places a woman at the center of a largely civilian scene. The changes that affect Paris, the symbolic center of Western civilization and Enlightenment values, measure Europe's brightest achievements against the continental self-destruction entailed by war. Deploying his considerable talent for evoking amply detailed and textured settings, Gorman dramatizes the costs of war through its impact on the town houses, bistros, churches, and streets of the city. The scenes are less dramatic than the explosions of trench warfare, but also less predictable.

Miles behind the front lines, Suzy is nevertheless a sophisticated witness to Europe's most destructive war. Through her observations and experiences, the novel dramatizes the irrevocable changes that overtook twentieth-century society as the result of the four years of relentless killing. She concludes that the war told the truth about the hollowness of European civilization, and the peace will bring only a temporary respite. As the fighting reaches its exhausted end, Suzy decides that heroic ideals were "only a form of propaganda," and that Christianity has proven "a complete failure."[9] The ancient Baron D'Eze, the father of Suzy's dead husband, declines into despair: "It was insanity to talk of a better world"; the marching of soldiers' feet was a metaphor for "the regimented millions of the world, passing and passing" (p. 431).

---

[8] A much-altered cinematic version of the novel was produced in 1936. The MGM film, starring Cary Grant, Franchot Tone, and Jean Harlow in the title role, listed Herbert Gorman and Dorothy Parker as principal writers. Germany's most famous spy was also the subject of a mostly fanciful film, *Mata Hari*, produced by MGM in 1932 and starring Greta Garbo.

[9] Herbert S. Gorman, *Suzy* (New York: Farrar & Rinehart, 1934), pp. 421, 432.

Year by year, the military and diplomatic events of the thirties traced
an arc of accelerating danger and threat in Asia, Europe, and Africa. The
Japanese occupied Manchuria, renaming it Manchukuo, in 1931. Six years
later, Japan invaded China proper, commencing a war that would last for
eight years. Hitler was installed as German Chancellor in January 1933,
and ingested one European country after another through the rest of the
decade. Germany occupied the Rhineland in 1936 and the Sudetenland in
1938, and annexed Austria in the same year. In 1935, Mussolini invaded
Ethiopia, using bombs and poison gas. Despite paltry protests from
the League of Nations and several European powers, Italy occupied
Addis Ababa and annexed all of Ethiopia by May 1936. Later that year,
Francisco Franco and his Nationalist army revolted against the Popular
Government of Spain. After three years of warfare, and with assistance
from Hitler and Mussolini, Franco established his control over the
country, took Madrid, and commenced nearly forty years of dictatorship.

The prospects of another foreign war met the revulsion of an invig-
orated isolationism. In September 1934, Senator Gerald Nye (R, ND), an
agrarian and isolationist, opened a Congressional investigation into the
origins of World War I. Nye's Senate Munitions Committee, as it was
called, pursued charges that the United States had been manipulated into
war by the arms industry. These were the "merchants of death," in Nye's
view; he summoned more than 200 witnesses, among them J. P. Morgan,
Jr., and Pierre du Pont, to make his point. Long before the hearings
ended, Nye predicted, "when the Senate investigation is over, we shall see
that war and preparation for war is not a matter of national honor and
national defense, but a matter of profit for the few."[10]

In 1935, upwards of 150,000 young men and women participated in
what they called "A Student Strike Against War."[11] Re-affirming its desire
to avoid entanglement, the US Congress passed Neutrality Acts in 1935
and 1936, which prohibited the supply of military equipment of any
kind to belligerents outside the Western Hemisphere. Louis Ludlow, a
Democratic representative from Indiana, led a campaign in 1935 for a

[10] David M. Kennedy, *Freedom from Fear: The American People in Depression and War, 1929–1945*
(New York: Oxford University Press, 1999), pp. 388, 394. As Kennedy points out, numerous
journalists and academics in the 1930s also traced the origins of the Great War to the greed of arms
merchants and bankers, and argued for American neutrality in any new European conflict. See
Walter Millis's *Road to War* (1935) and Charles Tansill's *America Goes to War* (1938).
[11] Rita James Simon, *As We Saw the Thirties: Essays on Social and Political Movements of the Decade*
(Urbana: University of Illinois Press, 1967), p. 171. The episode recalls the famous debate in the
Oxford Union in February 1933 when the motion, "This House will under no circumstances fight
for King and Country," was carried by 275 votes to 153.

constitutional amendment requiring a national referendum on any declaration of war unless the country was subject to direct attack.

Resistance to the prospect that the USA might be swept into yet another global conflict inspired several anti-war novels: history as jeremiad and prophecy. Two of the decade's last novels of World War I used the brutality and ultimate pointlessness of that conflict to warn Americans away from any similar adventure.

Among the American writers who had served in the First World War, Hervey Allen was one of the few who took part in front-line combat. He was gassed and shell-shocked, experiences that had a profound effect on his literary work. In the early twenties, while living in South Carolina, Allen published several volumes of poetry, based by turns on the traumas of war and the contemporary South. His first prose books included *Toward the Flame: A War Diary* (1925), and *Israfel* (1926), a pioneering biography of Edgar Allan Poe.

It Was Like This: Two Stories of the Great War was completed in the fall of 1939, after the commencement of the Second World War in Europe. In his "Introduction," Allen said that he was attempting to reconstruct the experience of war from the vantage point of the ordinary soldier. The first of the stories, "Report to Major Roberts," is nothing more than an adventure story, in which an intrepid young American officer accomplishes heroic deeds behind German lines. However, the second story, "Blood Lust," provides a genuinely devastating answer to the question: "How does it feel to kill a man?"[12] The tale's hero is a mild-mannered, allegorically named soldier, William Henry Virgin. Gradually hardened and coarsened by months of blood, hunger, ceaseless noise, and exhaustion, Virgin learns that killing a man feels like nothing much at all. In the story's climactic scene, he decapitates a German guard with a sickle. Crawling to safety, he finds himself face to face with the upper half of his company commander. The horrors leave him merely empty, without either remorse or fear. Political abstractions produce the inevitable and sheer barbarism that transforms human beings into brutes.

Dalton Trumbo grew up in Grand Junction, Colorado, dropped out of college to help with family expenses, and spent eight years working in a bakery before turning to writing. He sold his first story, "The Wolcott Case," to *International Detective Magazine* in 1933. At about the same time he began working as a scriptwriter, first at Warner Brothers, then at

---

[12] Hervey Allen, *It Was Like This: Two Stories of the Great War* (New York: Farrar and Rinehart Incorporated, 1940), p. 6.

Columbia, MGM, and RKO. By the end of the decade, Trumbo had written nine screenplays, including an adaptation of Christopher Morley's *Kitty Foyle* (1940), for which he and co-writer Donald Ogden Stewart received Academy Award nominations.

Along with his scripts, Trumbo also published three novels in the 1930s. *Eclipse* (1935), quite skillfully chronicles the step-by-step decline of an honorable businessman named John Abbott from prosperity to lonely poverty. *Eclipse* was published in London; nineteen American publishers turned it down.[13] Trumbo did better with his next novel, *Washington Jitters* (1936), which was simultaneously accepted by Alfred Knopf, and optioned for a stage version by Moss Hart and George S. Kaufman. In the event, the book's sales were poor, the reviews were mediocre, and Kaufman and Hart decided not to proceed with the play.[14]

Washington Jitters is a broader and more superficial satire than *Eclipse*. The plot resembles something a left-wing Capra would have concocted: Henry Hogg, an admirable and apolitical Everyman, finds himself mistaken for a senior New Deal official (coordinator of the Agricultural Survey Program). His candor, integrity, and instinctive common sense immediately make him a national sensation, and his success becomes the balance on which Trumbo can weigh other politicians and find them wanting. Trumbo himself said of the novel: "Nobody knows better than I that *Jitters* has absolutely no literary merit" (Cook, *Dalton Trumbo*, p. 96).

Trumbo's most important novel was his third. *Johnny Got His Gun* (1939) remains one of the most widely read and influential anti-war novels in American fiction. Joe Bonham, a young veteran of the First World War, has lost both legs and both arms, along with his hearing, sight, taste, and smell – every sense except touch. He is, in his own description, "a dead man with a mind that could still think."[15] At the opening of "Book 1: The Dead," Joe has come to consciousness, first believing that he is just temporarily immobilized and sightless. One of the novel's achievements is to map Joe's slowly emerging awareness of the extent of his injuries, each revelation accompanied by a flashback to his childhood and young manhood. Trumbo invests Joe's story with the thick details of an individual life, and in doing so lifts his character above the simplifications of allegory.

---

[13] Bruce Cook, *Dalton Trumbo* (New York: Charles Scribner's Sons, 1977), pp. 79, 85.
[14] The novel was dramatized in 1938 by John Boruff and Walter Hart. Produced by the Theatre Guild, it ran for twenty-four performances.
[15] Dalton Trumbo, *Johnny Got His Gun* (Philadelphia: J. B. Lippincott, 1939), p. 153.

Trumbo had worked with Nathanael West on a film script, the immensely successful *Five Came Back* (1939). West's fascination with the grotesque, including dismemberment (see the black comedy of *A Cool Million*, discussed below) may have influenced Trumbo's choices in *Johnny*. One of the most bizarre episodes in the novel concerns a German soldier who suddenly appears, all alone, on the far side of the barbed wire of no-man's-land. After being killed with dozens of rounds of British and American rifle fire, he falls on the wire and remains there for days. Then the soldiers begin to notice that "when the wind was right that Hun was raising quite a stink." A British patrol manages to bury the dead German, but the next day a barrage happens to fall on the grave. The body "leaped into the air like in a slow motion picture and landed high and dry on the wire again . . ." The soldiers use the body for target practice: "That was when Corporal Timlon started calling him Lazarus." Another squad dodges German fire to re-bury the body – "it wasn't very tasty work because Lazarus had gotten to the runny stage" – and once again the German is blown out of his grave (pp. 191–196).

The imagery of Lazarus recurs in *Johnny*'s "Book 11: The Living," which begins by recounting a victory of sorts. Joe learns to communicate with the outside world by tapping his head on his pillow in Morse code. Eventually he proposes that his mutilated body be used as "an educational exhibit. People wouldn't learn much about anatomy from him but they would learn all there was to know about war" (p. 287). He could be taken around the country so people "could see the difference between a war that's in the newspaper headlines and liberty loan drives and a war that is fought out lonesomely in the mud somewhere between a man and a high explosive shell" (p. 287). Recalling the attacks on militarized language that Hemingway and Dos Passos had so often deployed, Joe wants to be taken to parliaments and congresses: "I want to be there when they talk about honor and justice and making the world safe for democracy . . ." (p. 294). After a delay that seems interminable, he gets his answer, tapped out in Morse code on his skin: "What you ask is against regulations" (p. 299).

That final defeat savagely contaminates Joe's triumphant image of himself as a man who has come back from the dead to tell the truth to the world. "Never before . . . had the dead spoken never since Lazarus and Lazarus didn't say anything. Now he would tell them everything. He would speak from the dead. He would talk for the dead" (p. 277). But, like the dead German on the barbed wire, he never will.

Trumbo, who had seen maimed veterans return to Grand Junction when he was a teenager, had already announced his revulsion from World

War I in his first novel. *Eclipse* includes a character named Hermann Vogel, a history teacher at Shale City High School and a world-weary philosopher. He recalls how Americans eagerly embraced the war, how "we sang *"Johnny Get Your Gun, Just a Baby's Prayer at Twilight, America, I Love You."*[16] Vogel calls the war "hell. The maddest thing God ever let happen . . . Ten million deaths – you could take your miserable Y.M.C.A swimming pool, John Abbott, and fill it twice a week for two years with the brains of men who had died in that war. So many gallons of brains – and the thoughts that must have been in them" (p. 91).

Trumbo's anti-war testimony was as efficiently muffled as Joe Bonham's. *Johnny Got His Gun* was published exactly one week before Germany invaded Poland. While it received a number of supportive reviews, the novel almost immediately disappeared; when it first re-emerged, after World War II, the book was misread as Communist propaganda, the work of a man by then blacklisted as one of the Hollywood Ten. Trumbo recovered from the blacklist, and he lived to see his novel embraced by a new generation of activists opposing the war in Vietnam. Like several other important books of the thirties – *Call It Sleep, Their Eyes Were Watching God, Let Us Now Praise Famous Men* – *Johnny Got His Gun* was neglected for decades, then re-discovered when it was needed. In a prefatory note he included with a 1970 re-issue of the novel, Trumbo offered a mordant set of calculations, incorporating some of the arithmetic Hermann Vogel had used thirty-five years earlier:

Numbers have dehumanized us. Over breakfast coffee we read of 40,000 American dead in Vietnam. Instead of vomiting, we reach for the toast. Our morning rush through crowded streets is not to cry murder but to hit that trough before somebody else gobbles our share. An equation: 40,000 dead young men = 3,000 tons of bone and flesh, 124,000 pounds of brain matter, 50,000 gallons of blood, 1,840,000 years of life that will never be lived, 100,000 children who will never be born.[17]

Not surprisingly, most of the responses to the war, like those discussed here, were testaments of disillusionment. The primary – and predictable – exception in the 1930s was John J. Pershing's *My Experiences in the World War* (1931). Pershing had served as Commander-in-Chief of the American Expeditionary Forces; the bulk of his two-volume memoir is taken up with the details of logistics and military strategy: the gargantuan task of

[16] Dalton Trumbo, *Eclipse* (London: Lovat, Dickson & Thompson, 1935), p. 94.
[17] Dalton Trumbo, "Addendum: 1970," in *Johnny Got His Gun* (New York: Bantam Editions, 1970), n.p.

training, transporting, and deploying over a million soldiers and all of their paraphernalia to battlefields more than 3,000 miles from their homes. Infusing the technical exposition, however, is an undiminished conviction about the rightness both of the war and its outcome. Dedicated to the Unknown Soldier, Pershing's memoir is a tribute to the valor and self-sacrifice of the Allied soldiers, and the effectiveness of their commanders. Dos Passos and Hemingway may have repudiated the abstract language of patriotism ("I was always embarrassed by the words sacred, glorious, and sacrifice," as Frederick Henry famously declared in *A Farewell to Arms*),[18] but Pershing defends an unreconstructed, triumphalist point of view: "Once realizing their obligations, the American people willingly sent their sons to battle; with unstinted generosity, they gave of their substance; and with fortitude bore the sacrifices that fell to their lot. They, too, served, and in their service inspired the armies to victory."[19] Note that, unlike most of the anti-war novels and poems against which it might be measured, *My Experiences* was one of the bestselling books of the early 1930s.

Several painters joined writers in returning to the scenes of World War I for subject matter. John Steuart Curry, for example, best known for his images of tornadoes over Kansas and his large Wisconsin landscapes, found several of his most powerful subjects in the war. "The Return of Private Davis from the Argonne" (1928–1940), a large canvas, four-and-a-half feet across, depicts a burial service in Winchester, Kansas, which Curry remembered from his childhood. In that rural setting, with rolling fields for background, a flag-draped coffin is being lowered into the ground. The hundred mourners, arrayed in crowded concentric circles, form a wall of grief, their individual features mostly submerged in communal emotion. Their loss and anger are mirrored in the premonitions of storm that hang in the big sky behind them. Every compositional element in the picture – the centrality of the coffin, the bright red-white-and-blue flag that contrasts with the universal drab of the mourners' clothing, the lines of focus created by the bowed heads – forces the eye continuously back to the scene of death at the center.

"Parade to War" (1938) portrays a file of soldiers marching off to World War I amid a cheering crowd of civilians. What might have been a kind of military set piece is transformed into a shocking anti-war statement: the

---

[18] Ernest Hemingway, *A Farewell to Arms* (New York: Charles Scribner's Sons, 1929), p. 185.
[19] John J. Pershing, *My Experiences in the World War* (New York: Frederick A. Stokes Company, 1931), p. xv.

Illustration 1. John Steuart Curry, "The Return of Private Davis from the Argonne"

Illustration 2. John Steuart Curry, "Parade to War"

heads of the soldiers have all been replaced with identical grinning skulls. Like other artists and writers who confronted the war in the thirties, Curry intended his gruesome group portrait as a warning that Americans would do well to stay out of European conflicts.

Two books, both published in the early 1930s, Frederick Lewis Allen's *Only Yesterday* (1931) and Malcolm Cowley's *Exile's Return* (1934), provide some of the prose and imagery in which contemporaries described the transition from the 1920s to the Depression.[20] *Only Yesterday* was Allen's chatty but well-informed history of the twenties. A long-time editor at *Harper's* magazine, Allen mined the decade's headlines and popular culture for most of his material, embellishing anecdotes about movies, gangsters, and fads with comments on economics and politics.

Here is the Red Scare of 1919 and the rise of the reinvigorated Ku Klux Klan, the ubiquitous mantra of Emile Coué ("every day, in every way, I'm getting better"), short skirts and bobbed hair and speakeasies, Aimee Semple McPherson and her International Church of the Foursquare Gospel, Teapot Dome and the rest of the Harding scandals, the Dempsey–Tunney fights, the Florida land boom, and Lindbergh's epic flight to Paris. Allen, who called himself a "retrospective journalist,"[21] found an enormous audience for his instant history of an era that already seemed distant: the book sold over a million copies in more than twenty printings.

Allen was writing in the first years of the Depression – indeed before the capital "D" became standard in distinguishing this above all other slumps and panics and downturns – while Herbert Hoover was still assuring the nation that "conditions" would soon return to normal and New York Governor Franklin Roosevelt was making plans for the 1932 election. The depth and duration of the crisis were still imponderable, but it was already clear, to quote a section heading from the chapter called "Crash!," that America had come to "the end of an era." The last chapter, "Aftermath: 1930–31," includes Allen's comments on what had already changed – and what seemed unchanged – by the economy's collapse.

---

[20] A third book deserves at least a mention here. As Edmund Wilson was the first to point out, Henry Miller's scabrously luminous *Tropic of Cancer* (1934) wrote "the epitaph for the whole generation of writers and artists that migrated to Paris after the war." See Wilson's "Twilight of the Expatriates," in *The Shores of Light: A Literary Chronicle of the Twenties and Thirties* (New York: Farrar, Straus and Giroux, 1952 [1938]), p. 706.

[21] Darwin Payne, *The Man of Only Yesterday: Frederick Lewis Allen, the Former Editor of Harper's Magazine, Author and Interpreter of His Times* (New York: Harper & Row, 1975), p. 100.

In what would become a commonplace of Depression-era commentary, Allen claimed to see evidence that Americans were becoming more serious under the pressures of hard times. He looked at women's clothes – "the skirt length had come down with the stock prices" – and found decorum rather than adolescence.[22] "Gone, too . . . was that hysterical preoccupation with sex which had characterized the Post-war Decade." From this he reached the general conclusion: "The revolution in manners and morals had at least reached an armistice" (p. 348).

About the intelligentsia Allen was conspicuously wrong: "The revolt of the highbrows had spent its force" (p. 350). He had in mind the satires of Sinclair Lewis against "the village virus," and H. L. Mencken's fulminations against "the booboisie." He was right about the retreat of that sort of metropolitan chauvinism, but he could not have anticipated the robust dissent that would occupy many writers and intellectuals in the years immediately ahead. The fifty writers who endorsed the Communist candidate for President in 1932 had moved far beyond a "revolt against the village," beyond mere condescension toward middle-class pieties and hypocrisy. Allen offers an inadvertent forecast of the forthcoming trends when he notes, almost in passing, "there was a new interest in the Russian experiment" (p. 355).

Religion, in Allen's opinion, had lost some of its prestige and church membership had leveled off, but there seemed to be less hostility toward faith and more interest, "even among the doubters, to find some ground for a positive and fruitful interpretation of life" (p. 352). As several of the books discussed below will demonstrate, Allen's obituary for religion was premature.

Assessing the world of public relations, Allen concluded that "the noble art of ballyhoo . . . had lost something of its vigor," and that there was a "decline in the hero racket" (pp. 353–354). Allen's observation that "post-war apathy toward politics and everything political continued apparently undiminished" seems slightly surprising in retrospect but was confirmed repeatedly over most of the decade. Aside from the politicians themselves, the journalists who covered them, and the intellectuals who tried to choreograph public debate, the populace at large remained rather detached from political events. Franklin Roosevelt loomed large as a personality, loved by millions, despised by other millions, but even he frequently puzzled over the general lethargy he found across the nation.

[22] Frederick Lewis Allen, *Only Yesterday: An Informal History of the Nineteen-Twenties* (New York: Harper & Brothers, 1931), p. 347.

There were exceptions, to be sure. In *Seeds of Revolt* (1933), Mauritz Hallgren gathered evidence of unrest from across the country: armed white farmers in Arkansas invading a store for food; unemployed men battling with police in Detroit; gangs of white longshoremen attacking African-American workers in Boston; a two-day siege of the County-City building in Seattle by several thousand unemployed men and women.[23] Despite episodes like these, the more general mood was torpor, tempered by anxiety. In 1937, Robert and Helen Lynd published *Middletown in Transition*, the sequel to *Middletown*, their landmark study of Muncie, Indiana (1929). Based on their firsthand observations, the Lynds concluded that there would be no revolution in America, certainly not from the left. (They did express some concern about the emergence of a right-wing dictator.)

Exile's Return usefully complements *Only Yesterday*. Where Frederick Lewis Allen tried to capture something of the twenties across the breadth of the citizenry and its shared preoccupations, Malcolm Cowley attended to the special case of the decade's writers and artists, people whose lives were bounded by "two cities and a state: New York, Paris, Connecticut."[24] Cowley was one of the busiest of the thirties' left-wing critics. As literary editor of the *New Republic* from 1929 to 1940, and in his own essays, he played a significant role in shaping the debates that roiled the decade.[25]

From its opening sections, which trace Cowley's migration from small-town Pennsylvania to Harvard, the First World War and New York, to his chapters on Greenwich Village and Left Bank bohemianism, Dada and Surrealism, to the expatriate adventurers in Paris, *Exile's Return* did much to codify the dark but alluring glamour of the twenties in the historical imagination. *Exile's Return* includes a long valedictory essay on the suicide of Harry Crosby, whose life and death summarized the price that the war and the twenties had exacted from writers and intellectuals.

Looking back two decades later, Cowley said of his "generation" (slippery term) that Gertrude Stein was right. It was "lost," first of all because "it was uprooted, schooled away and almost wrenched away from its attachment to any region or tradition."[26] As we will see repeatedly in

---

[23] Cited in Howard Zinn, *A People's History of the United States, 1492–Present*, revised edition (New York: HarperPerennial, 1995), pp. 380–381.

[24] The book's original subtitle was *A Narrative of Ideas*. Cowley changed that to *A Literary Odyssey of the 1920s* in the 1951 reprint and thereafter. He also added a prologue, "The Lost Generation."

[25] His most famous editorial work would come in the 1940s, with the *Portable Faulkner* anthology that he compiled for Viking in 1946. Though it did not unilaterally restore Faulkner to visibility, it made a strong contribution to the recuperation of Faulkner's literary reputation.

[26] Malcolm Cowley, "Prologue," *Exile's Return: A Literary Odyssey of the 1920s* (New York: The Viking Press, 1951), p. 9.

the pages that follow, this assessment, which generalized from a highly visible but infinitesimal sample, was a compound more of mythmaking than reportorial accuracy. Cowley continued, sounding a lot like Henry Adams lamenting his own unfitness for the twentieth century (or even the nineteenth): "It was lost because its training had prepared it for another world than existed after the war" (p. 9).

For Cowley, no single figure better exemplified the trajectory that led from the twenties to the thirties than F. Scott Fitzgerald. The symbolic correspondence was irresistible. When Fitzgerald died in 1940, at forty-four, of a heart attack precipitated by alcoholism, heavy smoking, and despair, his death sealed the thematic bond between the failures of his last years and the crisis of the thirties. As his meteoric and fairy tale success in the twenties had offered a glamorous emblem of the Jazz Age (a term he invented), so his precipitous decline rhymed with the dislocations and fears of the Depression.

The Great Gatsby (1925), Fitzgerald's single unarguable masterpiece, was the last novel he wrote until after the Crash of 1929 ended the "long spree" that he had done so much to define. He felt that uncanny links bound him to his era, links that held as strong in the bitter thirties as they had in the momentary gaiety of the twenties. His early triumph, he later wrote, had been "unnatural – unnatural as the Boom." He continued, "my recent experience" (by which bland phrase he meant alcoholism, a shattered marriage, and his wife Zelda reduced to mental invalidism, a blocked and perhaps even vanished talent, and at least two attempted suicides) "parallels the wave of despair that swept the nation when the Boom was over."[27]

In those dreadful last years, which ended with what he considered Hollywood hackwork, Fitzgerald produced just one completed novel, *Tender is the Night* (1934), along with a substantial fragment of another novel, *The Last Tycoon* (edited by Edmund Wilson and published posthumously in 1941), and a handful of good stories.

Eloquently elegiac, *Tender is the Night* follows the decline of an American psychiatrist, Dick Diver, from early promise into middle-aged mediocrity. Diver's doomed relationship with his wealthy, schizophrenic wife, Nicole Warren, had its obviously biographical sources, but that pain has been transmuted by means of an unusually complex sensitivity. While it suffers from a wobbly organization and an uncertain tone, the book contains, especially in its comic catalogs and descriptive passages, some

[27] F. Scott Fitzgerald, *The Crack-Up*, ed. Edmund Wilson (New York: J. Laughlin, 1945), p. 84.

of Fitzgerald's most splendid prose. Here is Nicole on a shopping expedition:

She bought colored beads, folding beach cushions, artificial flowers, honey, a guest bed, bags, scarfs, love birds, miniatures for a doll's house and three yards of some new cloth the color of prawns. She bought a dozen bathing suits, a rubber alligator, a traveling chess set of gold and ivory, big linen handkerchiefs . . . two chamois leather jackets of kingfisher blue and burning bush from Hermes . . . For her sake trains began their run at Chicago and traversed the round belly of the continent to California; chicle factories fumed and link belts grew link by link in factories; men mixed toothpaste in vats and drew mouthwash out of copper hogsheads; girls canned tomatoes quickly in August or worked rudely at the Five-and-Tens on Christmas Eve; half-breed Indians toiled on Brazilian coffee plantations and dreamers were muscled out of patent rights in new tractors – these were some of the people who gave a tithe to Nicole, and as the whole system swayed and thundered onward it lent a feverish bloom to such processes of hers as wholesale buying, like the flush of a fireman's face holding his post before a spreading blaze.[28]

Like Jay Gatsby's wonderful shirts, Nicole's clothes and adornments summon a lost universe of appetite and gratification. Cost is beside the point. *Tender*'s title and its epigraph are taken from Keats, a poet for whom Fitzgerald maintained an intense and lifelong devotion. Surely it was Keats's fascination with beauty and its loss that drew Fitzgerald to his poetry. For Fitzgerald, success was always shadowed by doubt, and youthful grace contained the seeds of decay. (He was just twenty-one when he shared his fear of old age with Edmund Wilson.)

Dick Diver has his origins in the American artist and expatriate Gerald Murphy, in Fitzgerald's fearful struggles, and in his fictional predecessor Jay Gatsby. Dick is intelligent, handsome, and possessed of a special gift for friendship. His charm is alchemical; everyone who comes into his orbit seems refreshed by the experience. "People believed he made special reservations about them, recognizing the proud uniqueness of their destinies, buried under the compromises of how many years. He won everyone quickly with an exquisite consideration and a politeness that moved so fast and intuitively that it could be examined only in its effect" (pp. 27–28). His parties escape triviality by producing, for himself and those around him, moments of coherence and connection. The novel's principal task is to trace the gradual but ineluctable disintegration of Dick's talents and hopes. His partner in this unraveling, his rich and

---

[28] F. Scott Fitzgerald, *Tender is the Night* (New York: Scribner's, 1934), pp. 54–55.

beautiful wife Nicole, has been condemned to an unmerited derangement by her father, who raped her when she was a child. This incestuous horror has made her permanently fragile, and susceptible at every moment to nervous and mental collapse.

The first third of *Tender* is rendered primarily from the point of view of Rosemary Hoyt, a young and recently famous Hollywood star, who is vacationing on the Riviera with her mother. As almost every reader of the novel, including Fitzgerald, pointed out, Rosemary's infatuation with Dick takes up too much space. Her initial prominence sets up expectations that the remainder of the book fails to fulfill; Rosemary moves to the margins of the novel, returning only intermittently.[29] Though a case can be made that the failed structure of the novel offers an apt corollary for the shattered lives of its characters, nonetheless the book ultimately suffers from its uncertain focus. In *The Great Gatsby*, Nick Carraway observes that "life is much more successfully looked at from a single window, after all."[30] That is not, in fact, the only way to write a novel, but it would probably have served Fitzgerald's purpose in *Tender* as it had in *Gatsby*.

At about the time of *Tender*'s publication, Fitzgerald shared his irreparable unhappiness in a letter to his editor, Maxwell Perkins: "The mood of terrible depression and despair is not going to become a characteristic and I am ashamed and felt very yellow about it afterward. But to deny that such moods come increasingly would be futile." And he confided to his notebook: "I left my capacity for hoping on the little roads that led to Zelda's sanitarium."[31]

Tender attracted small sales and mainly ambivalent reviews. Writing in the *New York Post*, Herschel Brickell spoke for the consensus when he declared the novel "both a delight and a disappointment."[32] The book and its author received an especially hostile reception from the left-leaning intelligentsia. Among such critics, Fitzgerald was deemed irrelevant, and was dismissed as a writer whose slender thread of talent was wasted on the parties and neuroses of the idle rich. Philip Rahv, still in his youthful and fiercely doctrinaire Marxist phase, condescended to *Tender* in the Communist *Daily Worker*: "Dear Mr. Fitzgerald, you can't hide

[29] In a sense, *Tender* was not really completed. Fitzgerald was never satisfied with the book, and continued to plan revisions for years after it was published. Subsequently, Malcolm Cowley produced an alternative version of the novel, based on Fitzgerald's notes.
[30] F. Scott Fitzgerald, *The Great Gatsby* (New York: Scribner Paperback Fiction, 1995 [1925]), p. 9.
[31] *The Notebooks of F. Scott Fitzgerald*, ed. Matthew J. Bruccoli (New York: Harcourt Brace Jovanovich, 1978), p. 204.
[32] Herschel Brickell, "A Welcome Return," *New York Post* (April 14, 1934), p. 13.

from a hurricane under a beach umbrella."[33] The hurricane Rahv had in mind was of course the Depression and its turmoil. His attack was both reductive and misdirected. The novel's action concludes in 1929, just before the Crash, its action moves to the USA for just one page, and none of its characters represents the working class. But Fitzgerald, dealing with a personal hurricane of exceptional destructiveness, did also convey something of the dead-end atmosphere of the Depression decade. *Tender* is a memorial to a vanished world.

In 1936, Fitzgerald accepted a scriptwriting job in Hollywood at $1,000 a week, later raised to $1,250. He disliked the work, and was not especially good at it; he received a credit on just one film, *The Three Comrades* (1938), adapted from an Erich Maria Remarque novel. One byproduct of Fitzgerald's Hollywood years was a series of seventeen stories featuring a washed-up screenwriter named Pat Hobby. Hobby is a raggedy, hard-drinking scoundrel, a man with three divorces, a dozen credits, and a house with a swimming pool in his once-prosperous past, back in the era of silent films. Now, forty-nine years old, he scrapes out a living with intermittent and low-paid work as a script doctor, along with five- and ten-dollar loans from his few remaining friends. He steals ideas and dialogue, lies reflexively, and abuses everyone he meets. He is, in Fitzgerald's own description, "a complete rat."[34]

Etched in bile, the stories have a macabre humor, with the joke always at Hobby's expense. He is exposed by turns as a plagiarist, a drunk, a liar, a coward, and a would-be blackmailer. In short, Pat Hobby is Fitzgerald's lurid comic nightmare. His success has curdled into failure, he has lost the respect of everyone around him, and – above all – he knows himself to be a fraud. It is significant that most of the stories end not merely with Hobby's failure but with his humiliation.

The Pat Hobby stories are entertaining, in a dispiriting sort of way, and revealing of Fitzgerald's estimate of himself in the last few years of his life. A more substantial product of that final period was the novel, *The Last Tycoon*. A long fragment, which was published posthumously after Edmund Wilson's editorial interventions, *Tycoon* dramatizes the career of Monroe Stahr, a movie producer of exceptional authority and influence, derived in part from the legendary MGM executive Irving Thalberg.

---

[33] Philip Rahv, "F. Scott Fitzgerald on the Riviera," *Daily Worker* (1934), reprinted in Arabel J. Porter and Andrew J. Dvosin, eds., *Philip Rahv, Essays on Literature and Politics, 1932–1972* (Boston: Houghton Mifflin, 1978), p. 24.

[34] Quoted in the "Introduction" by Arnold Gingrich, *The Pat Hobby Stories by F. Scott Fitzgerald* (New York: Charles Scribner's Sons, 1962), p. xv.

Along with his last fiction, Fitzgerald also wrote a series of autobio-graphical sketches, most of them for *Esquire*, which were collected and published after his death as *The Crack-Up* (1945). These are the sad, confessional chapters of a penitent's life, often startling in their candor, and taking a masochistic delight in clinically observed details of suffering and disintegration. One of them, "Auction – Model 1934," written with Zelda, seems to be little more than a list of the contents of fifteen packing cases, which contain all the objects, the treasures and junk, that the Fitzgeralds had collected in their life together. Each case is unpacked, item by item; each item is offered for sale at an imaginary auction and finds no buyers. Despite its bouncy tone, "Auction" is a devastating glimpse into lives coming apart. The catalog is a funeral of exhausted objects, standing in turn for the human exhaustion of Scott and Zelda Fitzgerald. As their success had been expressed in accumulation, so their collapse is told in a stripping away (*The Crack-Up*, pp. 56–62).

By 1931, Fitzgerald pronounced the twenties an era of "wasted youth," and "as dead as were the Yellow Nineties in 1902."[35] But he occasionally looked back with something like nostalgia to the excesses he had done so much to memorialize:

Sometimes . . . there is a ghostly rumble among the drums, an asthmatic whisper in the trombones that swings me back into the early twenties when we drank wood alcohol and every day in every way grew better and better, and there was a first abortive shortening of the skirts, and girls all looked alike in sweater dresses, and people you didn't want to know said "Yes, we have no bananas," and it seemed only a question of a few years before the older people would step aside and let the world be run by those who saw things as they were – and it all seems rosy and romantic to us who were young then, because we will never feel quite so intensely about our surroundings any more. ("Echoes of the Jazz Age," p. 465)

The Great Gatsby went out of print in 1939. When Fitzgerald died, the following year, Malcolm Cowley solicited a few memorial tributes that were published in *The New Republic*. But even those commentaries, by John Dos Passos, Budd Schulberg, and Glenway Wescott, were rather lackluster. This is what the *Chicago Daily News* said of Fitzgerald in its obituary: "When he died at 44, F. Scott Fitzgerald, hailed in 1922 as the protagonist and exponent of the Flapper Age, was almost as remote from contemporary interest as the authors of the blue-chip stock certificates of 1929. He was still writing good copy, but no one was mistaking a story

---

[35] F. Scott Fitzgerald, "Echoes of the Jazz Age," *Scribner's* (November, 1931), p. 459.

writer for the Herald of an Era" (quoted in Gingrich, ed., *The Pat Hobby Stories*, p. xx).

African-American writers in the 1930s also looked back at the 1920s as a time and place apart. In his autobiography, *The Big Sea* (1940), Langston Hughes wrote, "Harlem [in the twenties] was like a great magnet for the Negro intellectual, pulling him from everywhere."[36] Through all his early years, living in Kansas, Illinois, Ohio, and Mexico, Hughes dreamed of Harlem. When he finally got there, a young man of nineteen and already a published poet, he felt an inspiriting joy: "I can never put on paper the thrill of the underground ride to Harlem. I went up the steps and out into the bright September sunlight. Harlem! I stood there, dropped my bags, took a deep breath and felt happy again" (p. 81).

By the mid-1930s, the Harlem Renaissance, with its aesthetic and exotic overtones, was finished. While it remained the vital center of African-American culture in the 1930s, Harlem was devastated by the Depression. Harlem had always included overcrowded and troubled regions: while many residents of "Sugar Hill" lived comfortably, in the slums of "the Valley," death from tuberculosis was recorded at twice the rate of white New York, and there were similar data for infant mortality.[37] But all of Harlem suffered in the aftermath of the Crash. One modest source of revenue, white patronage of the clubs and restaurants, declined with hard times and with the passing of what had been called "the vogue of the Negro." Far more seriously, Harlem's economic infrastructure was strained to the breaking point. Black unemployment outpaced white joblessness; thousands of Harlemites were unable to afford rents and mortgage. The small but vibrant black middle class substantially disappeared. Average family income across all classes declined from about $1,800 to just over $1,000, a difference of over 40 percent.[38]

The decade's gathering desperation exploded in the Harlem Riot of 1935. A dispute in a Kress 5&10 Cent store on 125th Street on March 21 led to a day and night of violence, in which over 100 people, black and white, were injured, several seriously. At least one man died. Police made over 100 arrests; most of those jailed were African-Americans.

---

[36] Langston Hughes, *The Big Sea, an Autobiography* (New York: Alfred A. Knopf, 1940), p. 240
[37] The pages on Harlem in the WPA Guide to New York are a valuable source of demographic and economic information. *New York Panorama: A Comprehensive View of the Metropolis* (New York: Random House, 1938).
[38] See Clyde V. Kiser, "Diminishing Family Income in Harlem: A Possible Cause of the Harlem Riot," *Opportunity: Journal of Negro Life* (June, 1935), p. 175.

The *New York Times* reported the next day that "Harlem's sidewalks, stoops and apartment house windows were alive with resentful Negroes," and editorialized against disorder. Putting its emphasis elsewhere, the Communist *Daily Worker* ran a six-column headline: "Negro Harlem Terrorized."

The most serious urban outbreak of the Depression years, the Harlem Riot drew a line across the troubled history of the area, and provided a tragic climax for a withdrawal of talent that was already underway. James Weldon Johnson, Arna Bontemps, and W. E. B. Du Bois were among the African-American writers who left New York, Johnson to teach at Fisk in 1931, Bontemps to teach at a junior college in Alabama in 1931, Du Bois in 1933 to accept a professorship at Atlanta University. Zora Neale Hurston decamped for the South. In 1934, both Wallace Thurman and Rudolph Fisher died.[39]

Before his death, Thurman looked back through the displacements of the early 1930s and wrote a sardonic epitaph to the Renaissance. *Infants of the Spring* (1932), with no plot to speak of, retailed Thurman's skeptical opinions of several of the leading literary figures he had known in New York. Raymond Taylor, Thurman's fictional surrogate, has taken lodgings in a place he calls "Niggeratti Manor" while he tries to write his big novel. His housemates, barely disguised versions of Countee Cullen, Zora Neale Hurston, Langston Hughes, and other major Renaissance figures are harassed by the alternating praise and demands of white patrons, anxious about the value of their achievements in a racially deformed critical culture, and in many cases deluded by their own narcissism.

They prove to be, at best, as Fitzgerald once said of himself, indifferent caretakers of their talent. Thurman's victims were understandably irritated by his satire, and the novel had only a small *succès de scandale*. Among the more positive notices, Martha Gruening, a white woman long associated with civil rights work (she had been a staff member at the NAACP), credited Thurman with telling a needful portion of the truth: "about color snobbery within the color line, the ins and outs of 'passing' and other vagaries of prejudice" which "Negro writers, under the stress of propaganda and counter propaganda, have generally and quite understandably omitted from their picture."[40]

---

[39] See Ann Douglas, *Terrible Honesty: Mongrel Manhattan in the 1920s* (New York: Farrar, Straus and Giroux, 1995), pp. 468–469.
[40] Martha Gruening, "Two Ways to Harlem," *Saturday Review of Literature* (March 12, 1932), p. 585.

Perhaps the most comprehensive of the decade's farewells to the 1920s was a volume called *America Now* (1938), edited by Harold Stearns. Sixteen years earlier, Stearns had published a similar volume, *Civilization in the United States* (1922). The contrast between the two books is instructive. The thirty-three essays that Stearns collected in the first anthology anatomized the state of American society, in the aftermath of the First World War, under headings ranging from "The City" to "Poetry" to "The Alien" to "Nerves." The contributors to this minor classic of cultural history included Van Wyck Brooks, Lewis Mumford, Ring Lardner, and H. L. Mencken.

While there are differences in emphasis and disagreements over detail, the articles in Stearns's anthology are striking chiefly for their broad and gloomy consensus. With few exceptions, the essays are angry, even embittered, estimates of the American scene. "The most moving and pathetic fact in the social life of America today," Stearns wrote in the preface, "is emotional and aesthetic starvation."[41] Editor and contributors alike deemed America's air provincial, utilitarian, and thin. In short, in a critique that brings forward the earlier opinions of de Tocqueville, Hawthorne, Henry James, and others, "civilization" was assumed to be a misnomer for the social structures and values the United States had produced.

These are the testimonies of internal exiles. Van Wyck Brooks, in "The Literary Life," remarked on "the singular impotence" of America's "creative spirit" (p. 179). H. L. Mencken, the caustic critic of "the booboisie" and propagandist for tough-minded skepticism, fulminated against American politicians. Along with most other social critics in the twenties, the participants in Stearns's symposium identified three forces as primarily responsible for America's cultural impoverishment: Puritanism, the pioneer spirit, and business. The Puritan's hypocrisy and joyless bigotry, the pioneer's rootless wanderings and casual lawlessness, the businessman's philistinism and insatiable greed: these were the recurring targets of satire. In the mid-thirties, one scholar dismissed *Civilization* as merely "the index of a group who . . . declared [a] belief that the worst in American life came from its traditions and that the best was accidental." The authors wrote in fear of each other, "afraid of being caught approving of anything."[42]

[41] Harold E. Stearns, ed., *Civilization in the United States: An Inquiry by Thirty Americans* (New York: Harcourt, Brace and Company, 1922), p. vii.
[42] Percy H. Boynton, *Literature and American Life* (Boston: Ginn and Company, 1936), pp. 779–780.

In the cold light of the Depression and Europe's looming chaos, Stearns and his contributors changed their minds. *America Now* was designed as a significantly more upbeat sequel to the earlier volume. Several of the same writers appeared in the second volume, and many of the essays covered the same subjects: the law, music, the small town, business, and the intellectual life are among the topics covered in both volumes. The changes are also noteworthy: there are no articles in 1938 about the city, nerves, or philosophy; psychiatry has been added, along with the labor movement, radio, the movies, and war. Sex has been replaced by birth control, and the focus of "racial minorities" has been shifted with the inclusion of two essays, one on racial prejudice, and another on the Negro.

More important, the tone of the later volume has shifted considerably. Stearns contends in his introduction that "our civilization . . . has become less frivolous" and more mature.[43] In his essay, on "the intellectual life," he contrasts the quiet pragmatism of the USA favorably with the ideological excesses of European fascism and communism (p. 379). A consistently conciliatory attitude toward American society and culture marks many of the essays: this in spite of nearly a decade of economic distress and the increasingly inescapable shadow of another world war. Zechariah Chafee, Jr., in his essay on "the law" predicts an impending era of legal reform: "We know better where we are going, and we are on the way" (p. 330). One of the most optimistic of the book's essayists, Roger Burlingame, says near the end of his article on "invention" that "[i]t is possible, then, that notwithstanding all our moment's troubles, invention may yet fulfill the hope of civilization whatever that hope may be" (p. 235).[44]

Stearns was not the only writer to testify that America in the 1930s was a stronger and even more spiritually coherent nation than its detractors might suggest. The old muckraker and former socialist, Gustavus Myers,

[43] Harold E. Stearns. ed., *America Now: An Inquiry into Civilization in the United States by Thirty-Six Americans* (New York: The Literary Guild of America, Inc., 1938), p. ix.

[44] "Literature," by John Chamberlain, the most directly relevant essay in *America Now* to the purposes of this study, is unfortunately one of the most disappointing. Chamberlain begins with the proposition that the literature of the 1920s – the work of Fitzgerald, Hemingway, and Dreiser, and Cather – is marked above all by "shallowness," because it failed "to come to grips with the great issues of contemporary life" (p. 37). The work of the 1930s, on the other hand, is "feeble" (p. 37), because it is in thrall to shifting party lines. Chamberlain grudgingly concedes that Farrell and Wolfe can "project living-and-kicking character" (p. 46) but the only fiction he finally approves of is Dos Passos's *U.S.A.* Erskine Caldwell and William Faulkner "have their points, but they have not developed into major artists" (p. 47). The "proletarian school" has "failed to keep up with events" (p. 47).

argued against what he insisted was the mere "legend" that America was "a nation sodden with materialism."[45] On the contrary, according to Myers, a fair comparison of America's behavior with that of its critics reveals that inclinations toward good government, the impartial administration of justice, and financial probity are more often to be found in the USA than in most foreign countries. Certainly more than in Great Britain, Myers's particular target, and the source of most anti-American mythology: "Parrotwise, one English writer after another dwelt upon this or that horrendous aspect of American standardization" (p. 343). Instead of looking at the facts on the ground, the parrots had substituted cliché and condescension for observation and truthful analysis. More critically, Matthew Josephson, self-described fellow traveler and historian, announced that the writers of the twenties – himself included – had been a "misled generation; we return, literally, to face the American scene with our hopes and demands."[46] The record of that search occupies the next chapter of this book.

[45] Gustavus Myers, *America Strikes Back: A Record of Contrasts* (New York: Ives Washburn, Inc., 1935), p. vii.
[46] Cited in Steven Biel, *Independent Intellectuals in the United States, 1910–1945* (New York: New York University Press, 1992), p. 108.

CHAPTER 2

Looking for America: The presence of the past

To look for America in the 1930s was inevitably to search for its past. Whether explicitly or by implication, the many reports that the decade's journalists and travelers filed as they moved across the nation almost all sought the causes of current circumstance in the historical subsoil that lay beneath the country's urban streets and rural farms. Writers in unprecedented numbers traveled the country, by car or train, even on foot, interviewing, watching, listening, recording. They searched out the hidden lives of individual men and women as a way of discovering the meaning of the Depression for America's national life. They filled a shelf with their books and articles, many of them angry and disillusioned by turns.

Let Us Now Praise Famous Men (1941), barely noticed at the time of its belated publication, would eventually be judged one of the decade's most significant texts – "a classic of the thirties' documentaries genre," in the uncontroversial estimation of one scholar.[1] In 1936, James Agee and Walker Evans accepted a commission from *Fortune* magazine's publisher, Henry Luce, to write a series of articles on the condition of poor whites in the rural South.[2] Luce's assignment took Agee and Evans into the sad center of America's agricultural troubles. Upwards of one-third of all farming families, white and black – perhaps 9 million individuals – worked in the cotton fields of the South. With the exception of a few resident landlords, most of these men, women, and children were poor, many of them desperately poor. Between 1927 and 1932, the price of

---

[1] William Stott, *Documentary Expression and Thirties America* (Chicago: University of Chicago Press, 1986 [1973]), p. 266.

[2] By an extraordinary coincidence, Henry Luce had announced the launch of *Fortune* – an expensive magazine targeted on middle and upper management and editorially committed to "the generally accepted commonplace that America's greatest achievement has been Business" – in the October 21, 1929 issue of *Time* magazine. Despite the irony, *Fortune* survived the Depression and remains a major publication in Time Warner's corporate inventory.

cotton fell from twenty cents a pound to four cents – less than the cost of making the crop.[3]

The three families in *Famous Men* are called the Ricketts, the Gudgers, and the Woods. Every detail in their bleak lives is rendered with laboriously close attention. The meager furniture, the tattered clothing, the flyblown coops in which scrawny chickens are kept – each small, undistinguished item is reproduced with unexpected affection and even reverence, with a patience out of all proportion to the values usually assigned to such scenes and people. The nearly identical palings in a split-pine fence are described one by one, each tiny difference a matter of mystery and significance. The cheap calendars and magazine advertisements that decorate a fireplace wall are reproduced with the painstaking care of illustrations in a museum catalog. Agee's prose is preceded by a portfolio of Walker Evans's photographs, black-and-white images that have become virtually synonymous with the Depression's lower depths.

Agee's fierce concentration on the present is anchored in the past. He traces the rural white South's contemporary misery to its heritage of received opinion and traditional agricultural practices that have conspired to cripple both the minds and the bodies of its impoverished men and women. Agee sustains a pitiless dialogue between past and present: the families of *Famous Men* are the people who have been betrayed by the values and arrangements handed down by the past of their region. Simultaneously, Agee appeals to an older, religious past to confer dignity and even an aura of sanctity on his sharecroppers. *Famous Men* is drenched in the liturgical language of the Catholic Church: the book's sections are labeled with the parts of the mass, and the impoverished subjects are implicitly – sometimes explicitly – likened to the despised, suffering Christ.

More economically, Dorothea Lange used a similar typology and a similar appeal to the religious past in constructing the photograph "Migrant Mother" (1936), the single most familiar image produced by any visual artist in the Depression years. Lange herself gave the background to the picture's making, in an interview:

I saw and approached the hungry and desperate mother, as if drawn by a magnet. I do not remember how I explained my presence or my camera to her, but I do remember she asked me no questions. I made five exposures, working closer and closer from the same direction. I did not ask her name or her history. She told me her age, that she was thirty-two. She said that they had been living on frozen

---

[3] Monroe Lee Billington, *The Political South in the Twentieth Century* (New York: Charles Scribner's Sons, 1975), p. 58.

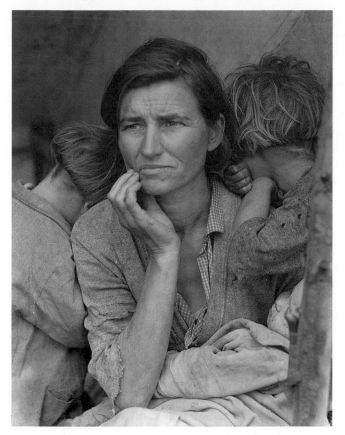

Illustration 3. Dorothea Lange, "Migrant Mother"

vegetables from the surrounding fields, and birds that the children killed. She had just sold the tires from her car to buy food. There she sat in that lean-to tent with her children huddled around her, and seemed to know that my pictures might help her, and so she helped me. There was a sort of equality about it.[4]

This offers a fair account of the circumstances of the event, a glance at the potential political authority of the photograph, and a slightly defensive claim of mutuality between photographer and subject. What Lange's comments do not explain, but what a glance at the image makes clear, is that the photograph derives much of its power from its religious

---

[4] The quotation, from the February, 1960 issue of *Popular Mechanics*, is posted on the Library of Congress Prints and Photographs website: www.loc.gov/rr/print/list/128_migm.html.

iconography. The migrant mother is posed in the manner of a Madonna, and thus becomes a latter-day symbol of suffering but saintly maternity. The woman is lifted out of the anonymous and topical, and her despair is suffused in the peculiar dignity of the religious past.

At about the same time that Henry Luce sent Agee and Evans to rural Alabama, he also dispatched a team of reporters to Rochester, Indiana, in this case to gather information on a small and presumably typical Midwestern city. The less controversial and less well-known result of that excursion was a single long article, titled simply "Pop. 3,518," which appeared in *Fortune*'s August, 1936 issue. Where Agee found southern poverty and torpor, *Fortune*'s reporters found Rochester to be generally comfortable, and its people content. Unlike Evans's monumental studies of deprivation, "Pop. 3,518" is illustrated with sunlit photographs of town buildings, alternating with folksy paintings by Maitland de Gogorza that were specially commissioned for the article. And unlike Agee's tortured prose, the writing in "Pop. 3,518" is straightforward and reportorial, untouched by self-consciousness or anything resembling emotional complexity:

Rochester, county seat of Fulton County, is fourteen blocks long and maybe eight wide, a ragged-edged rectangle laid flat on the level land, bounded on the north by the Erie tracks, cut into on the east by a branch of the Nickel Plate. It is small enough so that a man can walk the length of it, from Leiter's grain elevator to Mrs. Campbell's antique shop, in twelve minutes; cross it in ten, from the City Park through the fashionable district of the west side and the modest east-side section to the slums called Iceburg...[5]

It is a town with 1,500 church members, 1,010 telephone subscribers, and 1,200 car owners; homes have an average value of $2,500, and renters pay $17 a month. Though there are 236 unemployed, in general "business is good now," unions are non-existent, and the town is expected to vote for Alf Landon in the November election (pp. 142, 56). The people who live in Iceburg are "the shiftless, the improvident of the town," and they are propped up by County Poor Relief and the WPA (p. 145).

The town's culture is safely in the hands of the Woman's Club, which has persuaded the Carnegie Foundation to build a new library; the members of the Club keep an eye out for indecent books:

These censored books, which may still be read by inquiring adults, include: Sinclair Lewis's *Elmer Gantry*, Remarque's *All Quiet on the Western Front*, Hamsun's *Growth of the Soil*, *The Scientific Dream Book*, *Art in France*, Margaret

[5] "Pop. 3,518," *Fortune* (August, 1936), pp. 53–54.

Sanger's *Happiness in Marriage*, and Julia Peterkin's *Bright Skin*... The books most often stamped and passed out over the counter are western and detective stories, with Zane Grey leading all the rest... There is no copy of *War and Peace* on the shelves, no Hemingway, no Faulkner, no Caldwell, no Virginia Woolf. Thomas Wolfe is there, uncensored but seldom read. (p. 145)

Two reports from the summer of 1936 yield two different Americas: what Dos Passos, borrowing from Disraeli, would call "two nations." Rochester, Indiana, with its tidy streets and Saturday baseball games seems to occupy a different world than the disintegrating shacks and sickly children of Agee's sharecropping South. Above all, these two contrasting documents demonstrate the heterogeneity of America's experience in the thirties, and of the values that ordinary citizens attached to the meaning of the nation's history. Where the Alabama tenant farmers embody the financial and metaphorical bankruptcy of traditional beliefs, the people of Rochester, Indiana, continue to find solace and coherence in the patriotism and hierarchies bequeathed by the past.

Indiana was also the subject of one of the decade's most ambitious history paintings, Thomas Hart Benton's huge mural, "A Social History of Indiana" (1933). The Indiana mural was 12 feet high and stretched across more than 230 feet of canvas: Benton said he painted murals on this scale because he "could get more stuff in them."[6] The painting was the state's centerpiece exhibit at the Century of Progress Exposition in Chicago (a celebration of the city's founding in 1833). The work invoked history in technique as well as content: Benton chose the "difficult and archaic" egg tempera process as a tribute to the earlier masters of the genre.[7]

Completed in less than six months, the twenty-two panels of "Indiana" present a dual industrial and cultural history of the state, in parallel canvases that faced each other across the wide space of the Indiana Hall interior. Each sequence begins with an image of the Native peoples who originally occupied the territory; each then proceeds chronologically to a central scene commemorating the Civil War; each then concludes in the present. Mounted seamlessly, the panels move forward without

---

[6] From an interview printed in Matthew Baigell, ed., *A Thomas Hart Benton Miscellany: Selections from His Published Opinions, 1916–1960* (Lawrence: University Press of Kansas, 1971), p. 76.

[7] Nanette Esseck Brewer, "Benton as Hoosier Historian: Constructing a Visual Narrative in the Indiana Murals," in Kathleen A. Foster, *et al.*, eds., *Thomas Hart Benton and the Indiana Murals* (Bloomington: Indiana University Art Museum, 2000), p. 139.

interruption, exemplifying Benton's stated claim that he saw history "not as a succession of events but a continuous flow of action..."[8]

The industrial history moves from early settlement and farming, through the antebellum arrival of canals and railroads. Following the Civil War – pictured as a line of elderly men shuffling off to war, behind a woman weeping in the foreground – the paintings represent the transformation of Indiana from an agricultural into an industrial state: machines, electric power, steel plants. Cultural history commences with the ancient mound-building Native Americans, then recalls the early French missionaries, the leisure activities of frontier life, and early schools. In this case, the Civil War is evoked in a line of wounded veterans in the background returning to their small towns. The remaining panels represent reform movements, including the changing place of women.

Along with the undeniable nostalgia of swimming holes and county fairs, the Indiana murals contain a fair amount of skepticism and dissent. In addition to the central and sobering images of the Civil War, the panels also include a trapper corrupting an Native American with liquor, slaves seeking escape on the Underground Railroad, a striking miner poised to throw a rock at a rifle-toting company guard. In the tenth cultural panel, "Parks, the Circus, the Klan, the Press," Benton includes a crowd of hooded Ku Klux Klansmen, framed between a burning cross and an American flag. (Upwards of 40 percent of Indiana's white men paid KKK dues in the 1920s; the Klan was the largest social organization in the state [Foster, *et al. Thomas Hart Benton*, p. 72].)[9]

Hundreds of thousands of visitors saw the Indiana murals, and their clamorously divided opinions ensured Benton's notoriety. The crotchety but influential Thomas Craven devoted an entire chapter to Benton in his 1934 survey, *Modern Art*. In Craven's loudly reverent view, "[t]he rushing energy of America, the strength and vulgarity, the collective psychology, are embodied in his art." Craven argued that Benton's direct experience of life and his rejection of European modernism enabled him "to create

---

[8] Thomas Hart Benton, "A Dream Fulfilled," reprinted in Foster, *et al.*, *Thomas Hart Benton and the Indiana Murals*, following p. 32. Foster's essay in this collection, "Thomas Hart Benton and the Indiana Murals," is the best brief account of the creation, installation, and subsequent history of the paintings.

[9] In his eccentric, enjoyable memoir, Benton recalls the resistance his KKK and strike episodes elicited. See Thomas Hart Benton, *An Artist in America*, fourth revised edition (Columbia: University of Missouri Press, 1983 [1936]), pp. 253–254. "Parks, the Circus, the Klan, the Press" continues to provoke controversy. The Klan figures have been frequently vandalized; and in 2002 a group of African-American students demanded that the panel be removed from the classroom in which it is installed.

Illustration 4. Thomas Hart Benton, "Social History of Missouri"

the outstanding style in American painting, perhaps the only style."[10] *Time* magazine's editors contrived an even more convincing measure of Benton's celebrity; for the magazine's first full-color cover, in December 1934, they printed a Benton self-portrait.

He was soon commissioned by the leaders of his home state to create a "Social History of Missouri" (1936). Here again images of back-looking affection, including a salute to Twain's *Huckleberry Finn*, are counterpointed with darker scenes: a slave auction, the persecution of Mormons, a portrait of the corrupt boss Tom Pendergast, a lynching, and a railroad yard sunk in jobless vacancy. Those sections of the work – together with the naked bottom of a baby having its diaper changed – provoked a good deal of hostility from Benton's Missouri patrons. One scholar has called Benton "the last in the long didactic line of history painters that stretches back to the eighteenth-century Pennsylvania frontier and Benjamin West."[11] Benton welcomed that sort of label. Making larger claims for the truth of his images than the aesthetic value, Benton said: "If it's not art, it's at least history."[12] The comment could be directed at much Regionalist art.

The literary documentaries that have more or less survived – Theodore Dreiser's *Tragic America* (1931), Edmund Wilson's *American Jitters* (1932), Sherwood Anderson's *Puzzled America* (1935), in addition to Agee and Evans's *Famous Men* – are those that enumerated the deprivations of the period and offered harder or softer predictions of political upheaval.

Roots of America, by Charles Morrow Wilson, is an altogether different kind of book. *Roots*, published in 1936, the mid-most year of the Depression, reports on a present that legitimates the American past. Setting out his terms in the opening chapter, Wilson describes his subjects as "poor men, or comparatively so. Yet most of them are comparatively

---

[10] Thomas Craven, *Modern Art: The Men, the Movements, the Meaning* (New York: Simon and Schuster, 1934), p. 339. Benton was represented by more color plates – five – than any other American artist in Peyton Boswell, Jr., *Modern American Painting* (New York: Dodd, Mead & Company, 1940), a volume that gathered illustrations published in *Life* magazine's series, "Contemporary American Artists." Boswell exulted that "the band of Curry, Benton and Wood was like a Lewis and Clark expedition into the realm of the emotions." The American Scene triumvirate "let down the stifling barriers that the Academy, the Salon, and the School of Paris had put around art" (p. 60).

[11] Karal Ann Marling, "Thomas Hart Benton's Epic of the Useable Past," in R. Douglas Hurt and Mary K. Dains, eds., *Thomas Hart Benton: Artist, Writer and Intellectual* ([np]: The State Historical Society of Missouri, 1989), p. 117.

[12] Cited in Emily Braun and Thomas Branchick, *Thomas Hart Benton: The America Today Murals* (Williamstown, MA: Williams College Museum of Art, 1985), p. 11.

happy men . . ."[13] Wilson traveled across the entire country for his book, interviewing scores of men (and a few women). Amiably agrarian and populist in his orientation, Wilson selected a disproportionate number of his subjects from rural and agricultural areas: farmers, ranchers, small tradesmen, and artisans.[14] He finds that his informants are, on balance, conservative: "success in converting them to fascism, socialism, communism or any other codified *ism*" is quite unlikely (p. 8). He values what scholars would later call "history from the bottom up": transcribing the views of otherwise unremarkable and ordinary citizens. "The forgotten man," Wilson observes, deliberately recycling a favorite New Deal phrase, "is gradually becoming remembered, and he is anxious to do his part of the remembering" (p. 130).

Wilson talks with a New Hampshire auctioneer who tells him that very few auctions are part of bankruptcy proceedings (p. 40). A Vermont storekeeper points to his well-stocked shelves as "the real, visible, touchable life-story" of the people (p. 67). The Pueblo Indians of New Mexico are "the longest-settled American farmers, a people of peace and of good earth" (p. 212). Not surprisingly, Wilson's pastoral instincts recoil in the presence of modernity. Even so modern a subject as advertising has a history that was nobler in its past than its present: "In the old days," a sign painter in the Ozarks tells him,

most signs tried to tell people how to keep well, pick good bargains, shine up their homes, tend to their barnyards, dress up for Sundays and have nice dignified funerals. Nowadays the main idea seems to be to tell 'em how to set easy, have a good time, get a good taste in their mouths, and speed up their rate of travel.[15] (p. 204)

Like the more familiar Depression travelogues, *Roots of America* also includes a portfolio of photographs. However, unlike those in Lange's *American Exodus* or in *Let Us Now Praise Famous Men*, the pictures in *Roots* portray a sequence of reasonably well-fed, generally contented men, women, and children. Two smiling boys fish in a water hole, two men sit

---

[13] Charles Morrow Wilson, *Roots of America: A Travelogue of American Personalities* (New York: Funk & Wagnalls Company, 1936), p. 2.

[14] Since the Bureau of the Census was still using concentrations of 2,500 or more people as the divide between urban and rural, the percentage of Americans living in what might be regarded as genuine cities is hard to estimate. By one accounting, over half the population was living in villages and small towns in 1930. And, despite advances in mechanization, agriculture remained the largest single source of employment.

[15] In a generally favorable review of *Roots* in *The Mississippi Valley Historical Review*, Roy Marvin Robbins called Wilson "a faithful recorder" of his "plain people," and recommended the book "not only for entertainment, but also for an understanding and appreciation of . . . rural America" (December, 1936), pp. 446–447.

on a store's front porch, looking contented, a circus poster attracts the attention of three children – these are the images that document Wilson's thesis. There are photographs of work, but work that is productive and satisfying. Even the woman who sits on the stoop of her crude log cabin with her two babies beams, as if in response to the dour, defeated faces that appear in the pictures of Dorothea Lange or Walker Evans.

In an autobiographical aside early in the book, while reporting on a conversation with a New England farmer named Eben Whitaker, Wilson says: "I am a Vermont farmer living and working upon a rock-littered hillside. To both of us New England thrift is necessary. And it is more than that. In final essence it is a way of thinking and of living, a way that is sound and real and clean" (p. 19). The integrity of the past survives in the turbulence of the present.

A more soft-spoken version of that rural manifesto suffuses Margaret Ayer Barnes's *Years of Grace* (1930). A bestselling novel that won the 1931 Pulitzer Prize, *Years* traces the life of its heroine, Jane Ward, from her childhood in the 1880s through her early fifties. Barnes was already a successful playwright when the novel was published. In the 1920s, she and Edward Sheldon had co-written several long-running Broadway shows, including an adaptation of Edith Wharton's novel, *The Age of Innocence*. In part responding to Wharton's precedent, Barnes's novel also explores the conflict between sexual passion and marital duty.

After surviving a teenaged infatuation and then spending two years at Bryn Mawr, Jane Ward marries a pleasant, prosperous banker, Stephen Carver, with whom she has three children. By her mid-thirties, her life has resolved itself into a comfortable but predictable set of domestic obligations; she oscillates between contentment and spasms of resentment. She finds herself comparing what she has lost and gained, itemizing her good fortune – a faithful and admiring husband, three healthy and attractive children, a handsome house outside Chicago, financial security – and then concluding: "Still – suburban life was pretty awful. Narrow, confining, in spite of the physical asset of its wider horizons. Jane rose from her desk and walked to a western window . . . Jane was lucky to live there – lucky to have that picture to look out on, always, outside her window. Still –"[16] Into that suburban life drops the feckless but glamorous Jimmy Trent, a musician of considerable talent, sexually alluring and, melodramatically if inevitably, the husband of Jane's best friend. Jane is simultaneously aroused and resistant.

[16] Margaret Ayer Barnes, *Years of Grace* (Boston: Houghton Mifflin Company, 1930), p. 307.

The strength of *Years* lies in the adult seriousness with which Barnes lays out the choice Jane faces, and the implications of that choice. Urged by Jimmy to consult her own desire, Jane comes to realize that desire is meaningless outside the circle of obligation. She frankly acknowledges the power and even the beauty of sexual longing, but her identity and indeed her happiness consist in fidelity to her own commitments. Strongly influenced by Bryn Mawr President M. Carey Thomas, whose speeches she admired in college, Jane calls herself "a fighting feminist" (p. 183), and she sometimes disparages her values as "Victorian." In the end, however, she rests in the "durable satisfactions," as she calls them, of decency and deeply rooted affection (p. 452). She is not yielding to convention; rather, she is affirming her own integrity.

Years of Grace is a remarkably quiet book. In the course of its 600 hundred pages, there is one suicide, one death in battle (Jimmy, in the First World War), several deaths from old age, and two divorces (including one of Jane's daughters). The rest is a chronicle of ordinary events on ordinary days. It is Jane Ward's intelligence and self-awareness that infuse the novel with memorable depth. Set in the past, the novel offers a consolatory if tentative comment on the present and future: the strength of America's plain people can form a defense against crisis.[17]

Families under duress are also central to Thornton Wilder's *Our Town* (1938), in which the past offers insights into the power of integrity in a dangerous world. Perhaps the most popular play in American dramatic history, *Our Town* compels even critics who mistrust it to capitulate: literary historian C. W. E. Bigsby, for example, who methodically dissects the play's weaknesses, nonetheless concedes that it is "simply one of the most effective and affecting American plays."[18] It is regularly revived both on and off Broadway, and has been translated into dozens of languages.

Wilder had his first success as a novelist. *The Bridge of San Luis Rey* (1929), set in seventeenth-century Peru, is a meditation on the problem of evil provoked by the deaths of five people when the "finest bridge in all Peru" collapses. A bestseller and winner of the Pulitzer Prize, the novel identified Wilder's interest in philosophical problems, and in locations

---

[17] A quite different and more disillusioned conception of the past can be found in John Steinbeck's underrated *The Pastures of Heaven* (1932). A collection of related stories, *Pasture* opens in the colonial era, in which Spanish settlers and adventurers tore a richly fertile valley from its indigenous inhabitants. This primal violence begets a curse that continues to blight the farmers and merchants who live on that land in the twentieth century.

[18] C. W. E. Bigsby, *A Critical Introduction to Twentieth-Century America Drama, Volume 1, 1900–1940* (Cambridge: Cambridge University Press, 1982), p. 260.

rather remote from the here and now. He argued no particular theology, but he took spiritual questions seriously. He had almost no interest in economic analysis or class war. His next book, *The Woman of Andros* (1930), set on an imaginary island some 200 years before Christ, pre-cipitated one of the noisiest literary debates of the thirties.

Michael Gold was an enthusiastic Communist who had just published *Jews Without Money* (1930), a fictionalized autobiography that ends in a revolutionary conversion experience. Wilder's work exemplified just about every bourgeois vice Gold could imagine, and he said so in a notorious essay called "Wilder: Prophet of the Genteel Christ." Wilder has created a "museum," not a world, "an historic junkshop." He writes for "the genteel bourgeoisie," who seek only "comfort and status quo." Where are "the stockbroker suicides, the labor racketeers," the "passion and death of the coal miners?" Warming to his assignment, Gold launches a litany of abuse: Wilder's style is "a great lie. It is Death. Its serenity is that of a corpse." Wilder himself is the "Emily Post of culture." And a good deal more along those overheated lines.[19]

Gold's diatribe provoked a small tempest of angry letters on both sides of the confrontation, in which Wilder chose not to participate. Instead, he continued writing on his own terms. He did produce a novel that sent its hero across much of Depression America, but *Heaven's My Destination* (1935) is a funny picaresque adventure, not a proletarian protest. George Brush is an itinerant salesman, peddling religious texts from door to door, testing his dense naiveté against the various disappointments he meets, and holding on to his optimism despite accumulating evidence of human weakness. Candide in Iowa.

In *Our Town*, Wilder invented a new structure to examine the ques-tions that most engaged him. The play dramatizes life in Grovers Corners, a small New Hampshire town; the three acts are set on three summer days in the town's early twentieth-century history, in 1901, 1904, and 1913. Grovers Corners, based on the town of Peterborough, is divided between Franco-American Catholics and more prosperous Protestant Yankees, divisions that reach to residential neighborhoods and schooling as well.

A "Stage Manager" presides, a pipe-smoking combination of narrator and Greek chorus (by way of Pirandello), talking directly to the audience and the characters, and offering occasional homespun commentary. Wilder made clear that he wanted to affirm and at the same time transcend the

---

[19] Michael Gold, "Wilder: Prophet of the Genteel Christ," *New Republic* (October 22, 1930), pp. 266–267.

play's particular individuals. To that end, the stage is almost completely bare of furniture or props, and the arc of the drama is simplified: the play opens with an offstage birth, tells the story of a marriage, and ends in death. Though it is fairly thickly populated, *Our Town*'s main focus is on the Gibbs and Webb families, and especially on the romance between young George Gibbs and Emily Webb. Their marriage takes place at the center of the play, and Emily's death in childbirth provides the culminating calamity.

The Stage Manager's interventions, which include glimpses into the future, deliberately violate the conventions of realism; so too do questions that are shouted out by planted actors in the audience. Above all, the final act, in which Emily is permitted to return for one day from the grave and visit her family, rises to a kind of lyric fantasy. As she stands in her kitchen, unseen but watching, and filled with the pain of loss, Emily realizes, too late, that life demands our continual and amazed attention: "It goes so fast. We don't have time to look at one another."[20]

Sentimental? Only at first glance. Emily's speech is no more the play's authoritative last word than the bitter lines of Simon Stimson, the town drunk and notorious suicide: "That's what it was to be alive," he snarls. "To move about in a cloud of ignorance; to go up and down trampling on the feelings of those . . . of those about you" (p. 101). The play's pathos is anchored in an embrace of life's irreversible and headlong flight toward death. "*Our Town* is one of the toughest, saddest plays ever written," Edward Albee has said. "Why is it always produced as hearts and flowers?"[21] And Lanford Wilson has demanded: "Let's not be blinded by the homey cute surface from the fact that *Our Town* is a deadly cynical and acidly accurate play."[22] Grovers Corners is not as grim or joyless a place as Winesburg or Spoon River, but Wilder has no interest in rustic charm or smeary nostalgia. In a preface for a later edition of the play, Wilder wrote: "*Our Town* is not offered as a picture of life in a New Hampshire village; or as a speculation about the conditions of life after death . . . It is an attempt to find a value above all price for the smallest events in our daily life" (*Three Plays*, p. xii). Like all pastoral, *Our Town* sets up a dialogue between town and country that also links the present to the past.

---

[20] In Thornton Wilder, *Our Town*, in *Three Plays* (New York: Harper & Row, 1957), p. 100.
[21] Edward Albee, cited in Robert Hurwitt, "A Classic That's Ever Teetering Between Saccharine and Subversive," *San Francisco Chronicle* (September 16, 2005), E3.
[22] Lanford Wilson is also cited in Hurwitt's article.

The rural life Wilder dramatizes was vanishing even as he wrote: it was the preeminent place of America's disappearing past. The agricultural depression had begun in the 1920s, long before the Crash. Commencing in fact in the 1880s, the small family farm entered a decline that would continue through the twentieth century. In partial consequence, the symbolic allure of the independent farmer gained even more resonance. Not surprisingly, America's pastoral distrust of urban concentrations survived and even flourished as the facts on the ground moved away from life on the land. Two books by Ralph Borsodi, *This Ugly Civilization* (1929), and *The Flight from the City: the Story of a New Way to Family Security* (1933), signaled the continued attraction of the countryside, with its connotations of self-sufficiency and a humane scale of life.

A "back-to-the-land" movement gathered a bit of momentum, with endorsements alike from several New Deal policymakers and such groups as the National Catholic Rural Life Conference. Franklin Roosevelt, while still Governor of New York, said in a 1931 radio commentary: "Is it worthwhile for us to make a definite effort to get people in large numbers to move out of cities? . . . [T]o that question we must answer an emphatic YES."[23] He would keep answering yes throughout the first several years of his presidency, though with marginal results. In King Vidor's film *Our Daily Bread* (1934), a young and out-of-work city-dweller and his wife establish a collective farm, overcome a series of threats posed in turn by economics and sexual temptation, and achieve solidarity and a modest level of comfort.[24]

Along with the manifestoes and theoretical gestures, some urban Americans did attempt to make a living on the land. Dorothea Lange and Paul Taylor, in the "foreword" to *An American Exodus*, wrote, "in the face of industrial collapse in 1929 millions of Americans sought refuge in recoil

---

[23] Cited in John Garraty, *The Great Depression: an Inquiry into the Causes, Course, and Consequences of the The Worldwide Depression of the Nineteen-Thirties, as Seen by Contemporaries and in the Light of History* (New York: Harcourt Brace Jovanovich, 1986), p. 199.

[24] The pastoral impulse, always strong in American letters, was reflected in the critical success of 1930s novels that took rural experience – and either explicitly or by inference, the past – as their subject. The winners of the Pulitzer Prize for fiction in the thirties, to use one yardstick, included no fewer than seven such books, each of which in one way or another dramatized the success or failure of agrarian life: *The Good Earth* (1932), *The Store* (1933), *Lamb in His Bosom* (1934), *Now in November* (1935), *Gone With the Wind* (1937), *The Yearling* (1939), and *The Grapes of Wrath* (1940). One could add, H. L. Davis's *Honey in the Horn* (1936), which is set in the Oregon wilderness. All of these books are discussed in the pages that follow. Indeed, the only Pulitzer novel with an urban setting was John P. Marquand's *The Late George Apley*, the fictionalized history of a proper Bostonian, also discussed below.

to the land from which they had sprung."[25] Sherwood Anderson, in his own illustrated travelogue, *Home Town* (1940), claimed that "with the coming of the long depression and the growth of unemployment in the big industrial cities there was a movement back to the towns... There are thousands of farm boys over the country who went away to some industrial center but have now returned."[26]

In response to these new country-dwellers, a number of books appeared, instruction manuals for these reverse migrants. See, for example, M. G. Kains, *Five Acres and Independence* (1935). Subtitled "A Practical Guide to the Selection and Management of the Small Farm," and festooned with epigraphs from Abraham Lincoln and – ironically – Henry Ford, the book's fifty-two chapters provide instruction on everything from farm finance to frost damage, from irrigation methods to the basic agricultural toolkit.

Josephine Winslow Johnson's *Now in November* (1934) is a fictional account of one family's return to the land. In so doing, they hope to re-enter the American past, and recover their emotional and moral equilibrium. The Haldmarnes leave an unnamed city and return to an unnamed countryside when Father loses a good job in a lumber mill and with it any hope of financial security for his wife, Willa, and their three daughters. The mortgaged farm to which the family moves yields little, especially in the killing drought that tortured the Midwest and its people in the 1930s.

November is told by one of the Haldmarne daughters, Marget, in a prose that combines hard-edged representations of daily life with impressionistic images of deprivation and despair: "What use all this in the end? The hope worn on indefinitely... the desire never fulfilled... four o'clock and the ice-grey mornings... There seemed no answer, and the answer lay only in forgetting."[27] Even the family's few moments of happiness are bruised by their poverty. Father is a man made hard by toil and debt; Mother is stolid in her aging patience: "she lived in the lives of others as if she hadn't one of her own" (p. 49); Kerrin, Marget's older sister, likens her father to King Lear but goes mad herself, driven to suicide by disappointment and hate.

[25] Dorothea Lange and Paul Taylor, An *American Exodus: A Record of Human Erosion* (New York: Reynal & Hitchcock, 1939), p. 5.

[26] Sherwood Anderson, *Home Town* (New York: Alliance Book Corporation, 1940), p. 140. *Home Town* has not received much critical attention. For a useful brief commentary, see James Curtis, *Mind's Eye, Mind's Truth: FSA Photography Reconsidered* (Philadelphia, PA: Temple University Press, 1989), pp. 106–107.

[27] Josephine Winslow Johnson, *Now in November* (New York: Simon and Schuster, 1934), p. 38. All but the final ellipses in this quotation are Johnson's.

The novel's central section, "The Long Drouth," provides a day-by-day reckoning of the land's decay into baked and cracking clay – one of the most convincing and indeed hair-raising representations of the Dust Bowl in the literature of the 1930s. The deepening misery is doled out in sad anecdotes. Father reluctantly joins a milk strike, but it fails to raise prices. An aging man living by himself on a nearby farm breaks his hip in a fall, and almost literally shrinks into insensibility. Willa is burned in a fire that ravages the family's few surviving crops, and dies after a couple of months' lingering. A neighboring family, African-Americans named Ramsey, is victimized by a racist exploitation that is piled on top of the hardship they share with the poor whites around them. And each rainless day, as the fields scorch white, brings its added portion of anxiety and fear.[28] In its representation of the ravages of the Dust Bowl, *Now in November* draws much of its iconography and resonance from its use of Biblical images and precedent: the past gives depth and contour to the present.

A quite different version of the early twentieth-century past can be found in the work of Clyde Brion Davis. After dropping out of high school at fourteen, Davis worked at jobs from chimney sweep to electrician, served in France in World War I, and then found work as a journalist in Denver, San Francisco, Buffalo, and Seattle.[29] The first of his novels, *The Anointed*, appeared in 1937, and was quickly followed by *"The Great American Novel–"* the following year. Both books were received quite warmly by reviewers. Along with good notices in the daily press and weekly journals, Davis was singled out as a writer whose work "can be both amusing and heart-wrenching" in John Chamberlain's synoptic essay of Depression-era writing in *America Now* (1938).[30]

The Anointed is a modern picaresque, recounting the adventures of a man named Harry Patterson as he travels from Boston to a Mexican prison during the American invasion of Vera Cruz, open-sea fishing off

---

[28] Written when Johnson was barely twenty-five years old, *Now in November* won the Pulitzer Prize for fiction before sinking from sight. A discussion of the novel, in the context of American patterns of land use, can be found in Dorothee E. Kocks, *Dream a Little: Land and Social Justice in Modern America* (Berkeley: University of California Press, 2000), pp. 114–127. For Kocks, the traditional, patriarchal injustices within the Haldmarne family have as much to do with their travails as economic burdens and the failures of rain.

[29] Thomas Newhouse. "Davis, Clyde Brion"; www.anb.org/articles/16/16-01972.html; *American National Biography Online*, February 2000.

[30] John Chamberlain, "Literature," in Harold E. Stearns. ed., *America Now: An Inquiry into Civilization in the United States by Thirty-Six Americans* (New York: The Literary Guild of America, Inc., 1938), p. 47.

the coast of France, a perilous journey across the Caribbean, and eventually to Rio at carnival time.[31]

Davis's second book, *"The Great American Novel–,"* provides an eccentrically encyclopedic history of America from the 1900s to the early years of the Depression. The book's title is worth a preliminary comment. Three twentieth-century writers have used that wonderfully risky title. William Carlos Williams was the first; his *Great American Novel* (1923), a contribution to a series of new writing commissioned by Ezra Pound, is a fairly amusing parody of James Joyce's *Ulysses*. Fifty years later, Philip Roth's *Great American Novel* (1973), a much funnier travesty, recovers the lost history of baseball's worst team, the Ruppert Mundys of the Patriot League, and their disastrous season of 1943. (They lost 120 of their 154 games, all of which they played on the road, and the entire league was shut down the following year because of alleged communist infiltration.)

Both Williams and Roth, in short, and understandably, built a wall of irony between themselves and the phrase, "great American novel." Davis, who called his second book *"The Great American Novel–,"* proceeded somewhat differently. The book's main character, Homer Zigler, doesn't write the great American novel – he never completes any novel at all – but his failure conveys Davis's belief that the story of the past is where the great work of American fiction might be found.

Told in the first person and organized in a straightforward chronological way, the story opens in 1906, when Homer is fifteen years old, and concludes thirty years later, just after the presidential election of 1936. Homer is a journalist; his job eventually takes him through much of the country. Like *The Anointed*, *"The Great American Novel–"* is picaresque, a form announced in the titles of its five sections: Buffalo, Cleveland, Kansas City, San Francisco, and Denver. Note that the "America" of this novel is to be found in its middling urban places. The largest US cities – New York, Chicago, Detroit, Philadelphia – play no part in Homer's travels or his growth.

Filtered through Homer's newspaper work, the social and political events of those three decades provide the continually visible background to the novel's action. Homer reports on presidential candidates (among them, Bryan, Taft, Theodore Roosevelt, Wilson), popular music (he enjoys "Alexander's Ragtime Band"), prize fights (including Jack Johnson vs. Jim Jeffries), trials (especially the sensational Kansas City case in which

---

[31] *The Anointed* was adapted into a Hollywood film, *The Adventure*, starring Clark Gable (1945). Gable allegedly thought it the worst film he ever made.

Dr. Bennett Hyde was convicted of murdering his patient, Colonel Thomas Swope), labor unrest (the bombing of the Los Angeles *Times*), the sinking of the Titanic, the First World War, movies and movie stars (Homer is a particular fan of Theda Bara), the rise of Mussolini, Lindbergh's flight, the Depression, and much more.

In part, like many of the fictional and non-fictional books of the thirties, *"The Great American Novel–"* provides a historical chronicle, a semi-documentary account of the people and events that occupied and shaped the country in the first third of the twentieth century. The novel interweaves Homer's personal history – an early love affair, an unhappy marriage, and a sustained but imaginary relationship with his first love – with these larger events, and it also provides a diary of his reading, his literary judgments, and his sketches of the great novel he intends to write. It is in these sections that Davis clarifies his book's title. Homer reads voraciously: *Stover at Yale, The Virginian, The Trail of the Lonesome Pine, Winesburg, Ohio, Spoon River, Arrowsmith, Look Homeward, Angel, A Farewell to Arms*, and *Anthony Adverse*, to name just a few of the titles. His judgments are often sound: *Three Soldiers* is "a stark and realistic picture of the war," *An American Tragedy* is "one of the outstanding achievements of the century."[32]

Homer's own literary ambitions, however, are held hostage by grandiose yearnings: "I want my novel to be all-inclusive. I want my novel to be America." And by those declarations, he means: "I want it to hold the high purpose and sufferings of the Pilgrim Fathers. I want it to hold the romance of the Spanish conquistadores and of the French padres who plunged through the terrors of an unknown land for king and church" (p. 64). Later he adds: "Tentatively, I plan to call it 'Restless Dynasty.' And, likewise tentatively, I plan to start it shortly after the War of 1812 in the Lake Champlain region" (p. 86). Finally, in the novel's last chapter, Homer offers a detailed, six-page synopsis of his fictional plans. "I shall," he declares, "write something which, if not the Great American Novel, at least will be the nearest approach to it so far" (p. 302).

Now bearing the working title, "Brutal Dynasty," Homer's book promises to include virtually every romantic and melodramatic cliché: one-dimensional heroes and villains, lots of adolescent adventuring, and an endless sequence of implausible coincidences and revelations. The plot, after retailing the sexual and commercial escapades of three generations of buccaneering, fabulously wealthy, and corrupt Williamses

[32] Clyde Brion Davis, *"The Great American Novel–"* (New York: Farrar & Rinehart, 1938), pp. 255, 273.

(father, son, and grandson all named Jeremiah), will conclude with the last Williams, redeemed by the love of an honest woman, turning over "all his manufacturing plants to the employees to run as co-operatives" (p. 308). He also announces that, with his last million dollars, he is going to buy an island in the South Pacific and form a socialist colony.

Clearly not the stuff of a great, or even a good, American novel. The point that Davis makes, emphatically and indeed laboriously, lies in the contrast between the novel he has written and the novel his main character would write. Though Davis is reserved in the claims he makes for his own book (thus the quotation marks around the title phrase), he stands squarely in the Emersonian-populist American tradition that locates literary significance in the ordinary experiences of ordinary individuals. Homer will never write the great American novel, but a story like his own can provide the needed materials for it.

The most far-reaching attempt ever made to record the past and present of all the nation's states and sections took shape in the 1930s, in the American Guide Series, a New Deal project of unprecedented proportions. Commencing in 1935, the Works Progress Administration (WPA)[33] was among the most ambitious, and controversial, New Deal programs. In its eight years of activity, the WPA spent over $11 billion and employed nearly 9 million men and women. A relatively small percentage of the funds was paid out to artists, but those grants attracted the most notoriety and ultimately galvanized opposition to the entire program.

The arts section of the WPA was divided into four units. The Federal Arts Project gave money to painters, many of whom decorated public buildings with murals, while others taught the rudiments of art in small town schools and libraries. The Federal Music Project subsidized every kind of music, from symphony orchestras to Appalachian banjo players, while collecting archival recordings of music from all over the country. The Federal Theater Project, headed by the brilliant Hallie Flanagan, supported both traditional and innovative productions of Shakespeare, including a landmark, all-black *Macbeth*, as well as the Living Newspaper, which "staged the headlines," by dramatizing current events. The productions, which were often accused (quite justly) of supporting New Deal legislation, included *Triple A Plowed Under* and *One Third of a Nation*.[34]

[33] The title was changed to Works Projects Administration in 1939.
[34] The WPA arts projects have inspired an enormous amount of research. Among many other sources, see Richard D. McKinzie, *The New Deal for Artists* (Princeton, NJ: Princeton University

The fourth section of the WPA arts program, the Federal Writers Project (FWP), which provided small grants to individual writers, sponsored two collective programs, the American Guide Series and a gathering of transcripts of interviews with former slaves.[35] Not all the work was of high quality – much was downright mediocre – but the list of men and women who wrote for the FWP includes a roster of remarkable distinction: Conrad Aiken, Nelson Algren, Saul Bellow, Arna Bontemps, Loren Eiseley, Ralph Ellison, Zora Neale Hurston, Ross Lockridge, Claude McKay, Jerre Mangione, Philip Rahv, Harold Rosenberg, Margaret Walker, Richard Wright, and Anzia Yezierska, to name just a few.[36]

The American Guides comprised over fifty volumes, one for each state and several for individual cities.[37] They were encyclopedic but often wonderfully readable aggregations of geography, culture, politics, and, as we shall see, history. The books comprise 31,000 pages of writing: "at times travel guidance, local-color narrative, regionalist fiction, documentary reportage, tall tale, road map, calendar of events."[38] Taken together, the guides comprised what Alfred Kazin called "an extraordinary contemporary epic."[39]

Since they were written by scores of different men and women, usually residents of the states they reported on, each of the guides has a fairly distinctive and even idiosyncratic quality. At the same time, a shared strength across many of the volumes can be found in the particularity of description. The Connecticut Guide summons the state's "long stone walls, well-stocked woodsheds...great piles of yellow pumpkins...

Press, 1973); Hallie Flanagan, *Arena: the History of the Federal Theatre* (New York: Duell, Sloan & Pearce, 1940); Witham Barry, *The Federal Theatre Project: a Case Study* (Cambridge: Cambridge University Press, 2003); Monty Noam Penkower, *The Federal Writers Project: A Study in Government Patronage of the Arts* (Urbana: University of Illinois Press, 1977).

[35] The Writers Project work on slave narratives is discussed in chapter 6: Black memory.

[36] The oversight committee for all the Federal Writers' Publications also included an impressively diverse list of prominent authors and critics, among them Bruce Bliven, longtime editor of the *New Republic*; Burns Mantle, theater critic and editor of the *Best Plays* series from 1919 through 1947; Henry Seidel Canby, critic and chairman of the Book-of-the-Month Club; Malcolm Cowley; popular artist Rockwell Kent; poet and editor Alfred Kreymborg; poet and teacher Mark Van Doren, and editor and critic Irita Van Doren.

[37] The Guides had several commercial predecessors. Probably the most successful in the twenties and thirties was the "See America First" series, published by the L. C. Page Company, and including such boosterish titles as *Ohio, the Beautiful and Historic* (1931) and *New Mexico, Land of the Delight Makers* (1928).

[38] Petra Schindler-Carter, *Vintage Snapshots: The Fabrication of a Nation in the W.P.A. American Guide Series* (Frankfurt am Main: Peter Lang, 1999), p. 11. This is the most comprehensive survey of the production and content of the guides.

[39] Alfred Kazin, *On Native Grounds: an Interpretation of Modern American Prose Literature* (New York: Reynal & Hitchcock, 1942), p. 393.

[and] stacked hay," but also acknowledges the troubles that beset the unemployed.[40]

The Guides provided a cascade of information which, multiplied across all the volumes in the series, gave unprecedented documentary substance to America's places and people. The facts and statistics are intermingled with a hundred photographs, several dozen prints and drawings, dozens of maps, and passages of novelistic description, fragments in the manner of Dos Passos, that lend texture to the numbers and names. This is from the *New York Panorama*:

in the quieter streets the hawker with the pushcart moves slowly by. *Bababadabada O Gee!* Hawkers of vegetables, plants, fruit. *Badabadabada O Gee!*

In half a million rooming house rooms the call penetrates ill-fitting windows. The boy who came to be a writer is waked in his mid-town room and dresses for his shift on the elevator. In Chelsea the girl who came to be an actress launders her stockings. The boy who was going to Wall Street sprawls on his bed . . .

Shouting screaming kids fill the streets, playing baseball, football, hopscotch, jump-rope, dodging swift-moving trucks and taxis. Down Fifth Avenue marches a May Day parade sixty thousand strong. Solidarity forever, solidarity forever, the portentous tramp, tramp of regimented feet; slogans called, banners flying.[41]

Along with their detailed surveys of the current scene, the guides also offered a primer of American history, since each one incorporated a brief chronicle that proceeded from the founding of each state or territory to the present. Beyond that, as one scholar has observed, all the guides were pervaded with "the presence of the past" (Schindler-Carter, *Vintage Snapshots*, p. 194). The Indiana Guide purports to offer a "study of the past in the light of the future,"[42] and the authors of the Ohio Guide aimed "to connect the present with the past."[43]

When the last of the guides was published, at the end of 1941, Stephen Vincent Benét wrote a long, front-page retrospective review of the whole project for the *New York Herald Tribune* book section. He saluted the series as a cultural landmark, "a broadly conceived and patiently executed cooperative effort in citizenship." After quoting generously from several

---

[40] *Connecticut: A Guide to Its Roads, Lore and People* (Boston: Houghton Publishers, 1939), p. 458.

[41] *New York City Guide: A Comprehensive Guide to the Five Boroughs of the Metropolis: Manhattan, Brooklyn, the Bronx, Queens, and Richmond* (New York: Random House, 1939), p. 50.

[42] Ralph Tirey, "Foreword," *Indiana: A Guide to the Hoosier State* (New York: Oxford University Press, 1941), p. v.

[43] Harlan Hatcher, "The Historical Opportunities Offered Through the Writer's Program," *Ohio Archaeological and Historical Quarterly* (1938); cited in Shindler-Carter, *Vintage Snapshots*, p. 228.

56 *The American 1930s: A Literary History*

of the volumes, Benét suggests that he was especially pleased to read the sections on history: "We think of our nation as having a comparatively brief history – and it is true that sections of our land have a longer history than others. But everywhere there have been men, everywhere the face of the land changes, everywhere men and women have lived."[44]

Taken collectively, in other words, the guides offer an unprecedented compendium of American history, amalgamated out of several dozen local accounts. The history sections, though written independently of each other, share several characteristics. Most of the guides emphasize political and economic history, usually at the expense of social or cultural history. It is typical that every one of the dozen settlers who joined Roger Williams in Rhode Island is named, but not a word is included about Colonial domestic life.[45] And in almost all the guides, pre-contact "Indians" appear in a chapter preceding "history," thus making explicit the assumption that the nation's indigenous peoples are part of its pre-history, not its history.[46] Native Americans re-appear in the "history" sections only as they interact with white settlers and soldiers, usually violently.

For these reasons, as well as the hugely variable scholarly credentials of the guide's writers, the guides provide a limited historical view, one that generally hugs the shore of received opinion. The Southern guides take a collectively benevolent view of slavery, and collectively decry what they term the excesses of Reconstruction and its aftermath. Even a border state such as Kentucky declares: "Such slaves as were brought into the Kentucky country in the early days were usually affectionately attached to the household through long years of service."[47] Invoking the benefits of slavery for African-Americans, the Mississippi Guide submerges contemporary racial reality in the haze of paternal white benevolence: "The Mississippi folk Negro today . . . seems carefree and shrewd and does not bother himself with the problems the white man has to solve."[48]

---

[44] Stephen Vincent Benét, "Patchwork Quilt of These United States," in *New York Herald Tribune Books* (December 28, 1941), pp. 1–2.
[45] *Rhode Island: A Guide to the Smallest State* (Boston: Houghton Mifflin Company, 1937), pp. 33–34.
[46] In a couple of interesting exceptions, the sections on Native Americans in the Louisiana and Texas Guides are called "The First Americans," and "The First Californians" in the California guide. In the Florida Guide, on the other hand, the relevant chapter is actually titled "Archaeology and Indians."
[47] *Kentucky: A Guide to the Bluegrass State* (New York: Harcourt, Brace and Company, 1939), p. 72.
[48] *Mississippi: A Guide to the Magnolia State* (New York: The Viking Press, 1938), p. 30. The Mississippi Guide acknowledges the state's impoverishment, but traces the economic troubles to the Civil War, not the Depression.

Northern and Southern guides differ on the Civil War (invariably called "the War between the States" in the Southern guides), but both regions strive toward a congenial reconciliation. Western guides present the exploration and (white) peopling of the West as a heroic and providential undertaking.

There were exceptions. The Oregon Guide referred to western settlement as "wanton invasions of Indian rights by unprincipled whites."[49] The Alabama Guide includes an uncontested admission that the US Supreme Court twice overturned the convictions of the Scottsboro defendants. The Massachusetts Guide provoked a political donnybrook by expressing sympathy for Sacco and Vanzetti: "Many were convinced that the evidence used against the defendants was circumstantial and inadequate, that their alibis were truthful, and that they were being condemned to the chair more because of their radical views than because of their guilt."[50]

A less scandalous, but in some ways more subversive attitude suffused the famous description of Deerfield, a section subtitled "A Beautiful Ghost." A depopulated survivor of the state's early history, the town is given voice to declare, "the wilderness haunts me, the ghosts of a slain race are in my doorways and clapboards, like a kind of death" (*Massachusetts: A Guide*, p. 223).

Many ghosts walked abroad in the turmoil of the 1930s.

---

[49] *Oregon, The End of the Trail* (Portland, OR: Binfords & Mort, 1940), p. 47.
[50] *Massachusetts: A Guide to Its Places and People* (Boston: Houghton Mifflin Company, 1937), p. 76.

CHAPTER 3

Lost and found: Historical fictions

Historical novels, despite tracing their honorable genealogy back to
Hawthorne, Walter Scott, Tolstoy, and even, arguably, to Shakespeare
and Homer, have long suffered from accusations of triviality. In the early
twentieth century, music fled from the programmatic and the tonal, and
modernist painting subordinated narrative art to formal and increasingly
abstract priorities. Similarly, the triumph of modernist writing, with its
emphases on technique and introspection, has entailed a deep discount
on the value of historical fiction, as first-rate but undervalued writers from
Herbert Gorman to Gore Vidal to E. L. Doctorow can attest. Historical
novels have routinely been lumped with "popular culture," and have been
deemed more interesting to social science than to literary criticism. Thus,
the active academic study of American popular culture (the phrase first
appeared in a book title in 1967) corresponded with the turn toward
sociology in literary study in the last decades of the twentieth century.[1]

Despite recent shifts in scholarly emphasis, it is still a commonplace of
cultural criticism that the historical novels of the 1930s tended toward
escapism and entertainment, thus providing diversions for their middle-
class readers and giving aid and comfort to the status quo. Conjuring up
some famous chapter or other in American history (often the War for
Independence or the Civil War), or reconstructing the European past (the
Crusades, Renaissance Italy, and the England of Robin Hood were
favorite settings), these romances sort out heroes and villains in familiar
ways, subordinate insight and complexity to melodrama, and offer
storylines that follow well-worn grooves leading to conclusions that are
known in advance.[2]

[1] Henry Nash Smith, ed., *Popular Culture and Industrialism, 1865–1890* (Garden City, NY: Anchor
Books, 1967); this was a volume in the series "Documents in American Civilization." Most academic studies of popular culture are catalogued as history, not literary criticism.
[2] "A period of stress and turmoil, leading people to books both for escape and explanation, favored
the revival of historical novels. In a time when to face the present or the future was unpleasant,

There is certainly a good deal of merit in this view, and many of the costume novels of the 1930s successfully provided interludes of escape. Hubert Chambers's *Secret Service Agent 13* (1934), a ripping yarn about Gail Loveless, a spy for the North in the Civil War, Robert Chambers's *Whistling Cat* (1932), the implausibly hair-raising adventures of a Civil War telegrapher, and Harold Sinclair's *American Years* (1938), one of the decade's many fictional tributes to Abraham Lincoln, would qualify primarily as entertainment. So too would Rachel Field's bestseller, *All This, and Heaven Too* (1938), a romantic account of political and sexual intrigue in nineteenth-century France, New York, and New England. Although Field based her larger-than-life heroine on a historical figure, her great-aunt Henriette Desportes, the narrative routinely resorts to the paraphernalia of romance and dime-novel sensation. Clifford Dowdey's *Bugles Blow No More* (1937) re-cycles every cliché of the Lost Cause in painting the Civil War as a struggle in which gallant Confederate heroes must defend their traditions and their womenfolk from the rapacity of dollar-driven Yankee invaders. In the book's final scene, a Confederate soldier returned from Lee's surrender tells his family that he reverently touched the General's stirrup as "the Old Man" rode past.

Imaginative retreat could also take the form of antiquarian immersion. A number of historical novels were motivated by an effort to conserve the nation's vanishing past – rather in the manner of the Index of American Design, discussed in a later chapter. Merle Colby's *All Ye People* (1931), for example, is mainly notable for its encyclopedic inventory of the arts and

looking backward was a comparative pleasure, affording surcease from contemporary problems." James D. Hart, *The Popular Book: A History of America's Literary Taste* (New York: Oxford University Press, 1950), p. 261. That dismissive judgment remains dominant in literary histories, either explicitly or through the exclusion of historical novels from literary historical discussion. See, among other examples, the relevant chapters in the most recent *Cambridge History of American Literature*. Historical novels were the subjects of serious if intermittent academic scrutiny before and during the 1930s. Henry James, in a letter of 1901 to Sarah Orne Jewett, found much to condemn and little to praise: "The 'historic' novel is, for me, condemned . . . to a fatal *cheapness*" (cited in Philip Horne, ed., *Henry James: A Life in Letters* [New York: The Viking Press, 1999]), p. 360. Columbia professor Brander Matthews listed the strengths and (more numerous) weaknesses of the genre in the title article in his collection, *The Historical Novel and Other Essays* (1901). In 1924, the young Herbert Butterfield published *The Historical Novel: An Essay*, which argued for the value of fiction to historical study. Gyorgy Lukács's *The Historical Novel* (1937), written from an idiosyncratic Marxist perspective, put class struggle at the center of the European tradition of historical fiction, beginning with Walter Scott. Critic Bernard DeVoto surveyed American novels of the 1930s in "Fiction and the Everlasting *IF*: Notes on the Contemporary Historical Novel," *Harper's Monthly* (June, 1938), pp. 42–49. Alastair MacDonald Taylor published a more theoretical essay, "The Historical Novel as a Source in History," which compares recent historical novels to earlier examples, in *Sewanee Review* (October, 1938), pp. 458–479.

crafts of America (called "Fredonia") in the early nineteenth century. The novel's main character, a restless man named John Bray, is propelled through a slender westering plot, but his main chore is to report on the tools, grist mills, foods, agricultural practices, local idioms, wagons, canal boats, prayer meetings, and folklore of the plain people. Johnny Appleseed even makes a cameo appearance.

In a concluding "acknowledgment," Colby thanks "the modest makers of almanacs, calendars, yearbooks, registers, chapbooks, songbooks, directories, duty lists, gazetteers, original narratives, historical collections, guidebooks, biographical sketches, journals, road lists, political and utopian pamphlets, currency tables, census enumerations, itineraries, schoolbooks, account-books, statistical catalogues, civil, judicial, ecclesiastical, and military lists, maps, charts, and atlases."[3] Such a single-minded commitment to re-construct every brick and board of a century-old America constitutes a sustained diversion from the present.

But even escapism could have interesting edges in the Depression decade. Consider novels of the frontier, that receding boundary line whose effects Frederick Jackson Turner had famously called "a huge page in the history of society."[4] These tales had a long lineage, but could speak with particular point to the 1930s. In *Jornada* (1935), Robert Duffus sends his main character to the Southwest mainly as a protest against the social and economic confinements of the East. Duffus's wide-open spaces provided a temporary refuge from the crowded cities and – especially relevant in the Depression decade – a chance to make a new start.

More generally, the frontier novels featured self-reliant and virile male characters, capable of overcoming the challenges of outlaws and wilderness with their physical strength and their ingenuity. These were, to be sure, fairly stock figures derived from the earlier Western novel. Nonetheless, taken collectively, these masculine heroes spoke with particular resonance to the widely noted diminishment of American men in the 1930s.[5] Deprived of their traditional role as breadwinner and often left at

[3] Merle Colby, *All Ye People* (New York: The Viking Press, 1931), p. 430.
[4] Frederick Jackson Turner, "The Significance of the Frontier in American History," in *The Frontier in American History* (New York: Holt, Rinehart and Winston, 1962), p. 11.
[5] For a reasonably thorough survey of frontier novels in the first half of the twentieth century, see Nicholas J. Karolides, *The Pioneer in the American Novel, 1900–1950* (Norman: University of Oklahoma Press, 1967). Karolides repeatedly emphasizes the vigorous masculinity of the heroes in these books. An earlier, more impressionistic cultural survey, from the early years of the thirties, can be found in Percy H. Boynton, *The Rediscovery of the Frontier* (Chicago: University of Chicago Press, 1931).

home while their wives worked, unemployed men reported increased rates of depression, anger, and sexual impotence.[6]

Furthermore, beyond its contextual relevance, quite a lot of historical fiction in the thirties eludes conventional wisdom more directly: among other examples, Beatrice Bisno's *Tomorrow's Bread* (1938), proletarian in inclination and set in early twentieth-century Chicago, *Horse Shoe Bottoms* (1935), Thomas Tippett's grim tale of Illinois coalfields, also in the early part of the century, Katherine Brush's *Don't Ever Leave Me* (1935), set in a Pennsylvania mill town, and Arna Bontemps's *Black Thunder* (1936), discussed in a later chapter, which reconstructs a slave rebellion. The decade also produced splendid contrarian historical fictions. *Free Forester* (1935), by Horatio Colony, which is set in eighteenth-century Kentucky, was described in advance publicity as "a combination of James Fenimore Cooper and D. H. Lawrence."[7] Sending up the conventions of frontier fiction, the novel presents a roguish cast of characters defined mainly by their vices: nearly pickled in alcohol and loyal only to instant gratification, they lead lives of easygoing carnality, petty thieving, and nonstop roistering and brawling.

In these and other novels, writers of the 1930s often set out to complicate and even rebut comforting national myths. In doing so, they echoed the country's anxieties by shifting doubt and debate into versions of the past.[8] The decade's historical fiction reached back to Colonial experience, including Puritanism, the Revolutionary and Civil Wars, and the frontier West. American writers also recreated eighteenth- and nineteenth-century European and Latin American history, frequently in ways that illuminate the concerns of the Depression decade.

The American Revolution provided the source for several popular novels, among them *Guns Along the Mohawk* (1936), by Walter D. Edmonds, one of the bestselling books of the mid-thirties. *Guns* follows its mixed cast of fictional and historical characters from 1776 through the end of the war, portraying the difficult choices and intermittent danger that they confront in their encounters with Native Americans, British regular and

---

[6] Louis Adamic devotes an entire section of his travel book, *My America, 1928–1938*, to the psychological and sexual problems of unemployed men in the Depression (New York: Harper & Brothers, 1938), pp. 286ff.

[7] "Book Notes," *New York Times* (May 31, 1935), p. 13.

[8] Historical novels were of course a staple of American literary culture long before the 1930s, and my argument is not that such fictions were peculiar to the Depression decade, but only that they were a major fictional genre, whose recovery amplifies our understanding of literary culture in the thirties.

irregular soldiers, and American politicians. Scrupulously attentive to social detail, the novel is a cornucopia of daily life in upstate New York in the late eighteenth century: every vegetable and food crop raised by the region's plain people, every item of their clothing, their working habits, their houses and furniture. Edmonds's sheer normality elicited praise from at least one influential critic: "Miss Margaret Mitchell, in her recent and now famous opus, attempted to relate history in terms of a pair of freaks," an unkind reference to Scarlett O'Hara and Rhett Butler.[9]

While Edmonds incorporated some of the internal dissent and bickering that afflicted the American side in the war, his lavish recreation of the Mohawk Valley campaigns ultimately served to reinforce received patriotic wisdom. On the other hand, several of the decade's historical novels interrogated the nation's founding myths. Bruce Lancaster's *Guns of Burgoyne* (1939), for example, tells the story of the first major American victory in the Revolution, Horatio Gates's defeat of British General John Burgoyne at Saratoga in 1777. Lancaster's innovation is to establish a group of Hessian soldiers as his central characters and to treat them with great sympathy. The Hessians, a by-word in American lore for mercenary perfidy, emerge from Lancaster's account of them as honorable and courageous men. And "Gentleman Johnny" Burgoyne is rescued from the caricature of bumbling foppery and restored to a measure of humanity.[10]

The most consistently revisionist of the decade's historical novelists was Kenneth Roberts. A veteran of the Siberian campaign at the end of World War I, Roberts had then traveled widely as a foreign correspondent for the *Saturday Evening Post*. He produced a series of influential reports, emphasizing the mediocrity and perhaps even the inherent inferiority of people from Eastern and Central Europe. His Congressional testimony helped win passage for the restrictive McCarren–Walter Act of 1924, which placed tightened quotas on immigration.

In the 1930s, Roberts published half a dozen novels and over two dozen stories and essays – almost all of them in the *Post*. His first novel, *Arundel* (1930), identifies its hero and plot in the subtitle: *A Chronicle of the Province of Maine and of the Secret Expedition led by Benedict Arnold against Quebec*. Shaped by Roberts's Tory preferences, the book portrays Arnold as a heroic figure. The novel's success led to a number of sequels,

---

[9] Ralph Thompson, "Books of the Times," *New York Times* (July 31, 1936), p. 17.
[10] Though it never mentions Lancaster's novel, J. E. Morpurgo's "Richer in Esteem: A Reappraisal of John Burgoyne" is a more recent attempt to rehabilitate the British general. In Joseph Waldmeir, ed., *Essays in Honor of Russel B. Nye* (East Lansing: Michigan State University Press, 1978), pp. 155–167.

including *The Lively Lady* (1931), *Rabble in Arms* (1933), and *Captain Caution* (1934).

The best of these early books is *Rabble in Arms*, a 900-page saga recounting the Northern Campaign of the Revolution's first two years, which concluded with the Battle of Saratoga in October 1777. Told by a young American sailor, Peter Merrill, *Rabble* convincingly reproduces the skirmishes, retreats, forced marches, and set-piece battles of the war. It also captures the experience of those punishing months for ordinary soldiers: long periods of waiting, assailed by hunger, cold, damp, and confusion, intermixed with the occasional terror of brutal fighting, which often leaves them mutilated or dead. Filled with scenes of derring-do and stock characters – the profane but loyal sidekick, the cynical but effective Yankee doctor, even a boy–girl romance and a seductive femme fatale – the novel teems with energy and excitement.

Aside from its irresistibly abundant detail and skillfully managed pace, what lifts the book above the melodramatic average is its subversive political point of view. Amplifying the argument he first made in *Arundel*, Roberts puts *Rabble* at the service of rehabilitating Benedict Arnold. "Nothing," Peter Merrill says in the book's penultimate chapter, "is so valuable to a nation as the truth."[11] And the truth is that Benedict Arnold more or less single-handedly won the Battle of Saratoga, ended the British threat from the north, and thus effectively won the Revolutionary War.

Though the action ends in 1777, Peter Merrill, looking back from some unspecified future, defends Arnold's treason as the sincere choice of a patriot to save the failing struggle for independence. In 1779, negotiating secretly with the British commander, Henry Clinton, Arnold offered both his own services and a plan for taking West Point. The plot failed, and the disgraced Arnold barely escaped with his life. Merrill's judgement of this archetypal treachery: "Of all his brave and patriotic deeds, the one he was surest would, in the end, be most useful to this country, was, I truly believe, the tragic step that branded him forever with the name of traitor" (p. 857). In Merrill's construction, Arnold was attempting to save the Colonies from the French, as a prelude to full American independence. No one except Arnold himself has ever proposed this redemptive motive.

Roberts's near-idolatrous conception of Arnold had little precedent. The general's bravery and brilliance as a military tactician had long been acknowledged. Neither Arnold's dazzling role in the Battle of Saratoga

[11] Kenneth Roberts, *Rabble in Arms: a Chronicle of Arundel and the Burgoyne Invasion* (Garden City, NY: Doubleday, Doran & Co., 1933), p. 856.

nor the historic significance of that episode is much in dispute. Decades before *Rabble in Arms*, historian Charles Burr Todd described Arnold as "ubiquitous and invulnerable" at Saratoga, a general uniquely loved by his troops and envied by his superiors.[12] But Todd's admiration for Arnold's skills on the field is balanced by his recognition of the vanity and recklessness that led to scheming and treason.

Arnold was a frequent biographical subject in the thirties. In just the three years before *Rabble in Arms* was published, a flurry of studies appeared. Both *Benedict Arnold: The Proud Warrior*, by Charles Coleman Sellers (1930), and Oscar Sherwin's *Benedict Arnold: Patriot and Traitor* (1931), offered about the same interpretation: Arnold as a fearless and initially patriotic officer, driven to betray his cause and country by grievances over promotion and salary.[13] Edward Dean Sullivan, on the other hand, took a harder line, from his lip-smacking title on, in *Benedict Arnold: Military Racketeer* (1932): "Benedict Arnold, shorn of his three-cornered hat [and] his five-cornered arguments . . . had literally everything in common with the racketeer as this nation knows him today."[14] The chapters in this rollicking exposé include "Ethan Allen Encounters a Chiseler," " 'General Swagger' Advances," and "Muscling Into Philadelphia."

Although Arnold had always been attractive to historians and biographers, the volume of publications about him increased in the twenties and thirties, perhaps stimulated by some combination of iconoclasm and anxiety about the fragility of the Founders' legacy. In Roberts's case, it seems clear that his interests were more contemporary than antiquarian. Roberts, who worshiped heroic individualism and hated collectivism – he would become an increasingly rumbustious opponent of Franklin Roosevelt through the 1930s – found in Arnold a type of daring and self-reliance, a man unshackled by public opinion, unable to defer to those he thought less fit. And the unfit included every officer and politician on the American side, only Washington and Schuyler excepted.

[12] Charles Burr Todd, *The Real Benedict Arnold* (New York: A. S. Barnes and Company, 1903), p. 161.

[13] Resembling these biographies in his emphases, Frank Hough's novel *Renown* (1938), presents a more mainstream and therefore more critical portrait of Benedict Arnold than Roberts. Hough concedes Arnold's courage and military skill, but emphasizes his egotism and pliable conscience. A more recent biography, *Benedict Arnold: Patriot and Traitor*, by Willard Sterne Randall (1990), absconds with Oscar Sherwin's title but never mentions Sherwin or his book in its source notes or fourteen-page bibliography.

[14] Edward Dean Sullivan, *Benedict Arnold: Military Racketeer* (New York: The Vanguard Press, 1932), p. ix.

Consequently, in *Rabble in Arms* the real threat to American liberty is not the British army but the American Congress: "Arnold despised... pettiness, timidity, inefficiency, futility and hesitation; and it was exactly those traits that were the principal assets of the American Congress in the days when we fought England. Eventually the inefficiency and the cowardice of Congress came to be a more dangerous enemy than England (p. 858)."[15] The enemy, indeed, is democracy itself, which inevitably yields "the dreadful and criminal follies always perpetrated by legislators whose positions depend on the votes of the masses" (p. 860).

In 1937, Roberts published his most durable book, *Northwest Passage*, in which the intrepid Major Robert Rogers leads a band of rangers (guerrilla fighters), first on the British side in the French and Indian war, then in the search for the legendary passage of the title.[16] As he did in the Arundel novels, though with a hero less well known than Benedict Arnold, Roberts wants to rehabilitate his main character. The historical Rogers seems to have been a braggart, a counterfeiter, an embezzler, an alcoholic, and – in George Washington's judgment – a Tory spy during the Revolution. Roberts includes some of the warts in his portrait of Rogers, in particular his weakness for alcohol and his sexual rapacity, but he insists that the major was a gifted and honest soldier, a charismatic leader, and a generally reliable man. As Mark Twain wrote, in a passage quoted by Roberts, even Satan deserves to have someone tell his side of the story.

Langdon Towne, a young man who bolts from Harvard College and its bad food in 1759 to fight against the French, is the novel's first-person narrator, telling the story from the vantage point of the late 1770s, in the midst of the Revolution. His youthful response to Rogers is star struck: "Rogers, it seemed to me, could go beyond the limits of human endurance; and then, without rest, buoyantly hurl himself against the fiercest opposition of Nature or man, or both."[17] Eventually, Towne's enthusiasm will cool, as he watches Rogers deteriorate from the simple certitudes of

[15] If his opinion wasn't sufficiently clear, Roberts added a few epithets to a later edition of the novel: the men of Congress were "dwarf-brained creatures, shallow, bigoted, opinionated, contrary, unreasonable, hidebound, time-serving: strong only in their unyielding ignorance: in their determined avoidance of intellectual integrity" (1947).
[16] *The Saturday Review of Literature* conducted a poll of critics and reviewers in April 1938, in which the majority named *Northwest Passage* as the best novel of 1937. Shortly thereafter, the Pulitzer Prize went to John P. Marquand's *The Late George Apley*. In 1939, the first section of *Northwest Passage* was quite successfully adapted as a film, directed by King Vidor and starring Spencer Tracy.
[17] Kenneth Roberts, *Northwest Passage* (Garden City, NY: Doubleday and Company, 1937), p. 175.

battle to the slippery ambiguities of political intrigue, but he insists to the end that an indestructible grandeur survives Rogers's decline.

Encounters with Native Americans take up much of the book's military and pioneering action. Dozens of tribes and clans are described in differentiating detail, and Towne's attitude is characteristically respectful. Pontiac, in particular, is presented as a strategist and diplomat of exceptional skill: "wiser than most white statesmen, and vastly more honest" (p. 520). Towne's disgust at the shabby ways in which English authorities treat the Native Americans provokes his heavy-handed irony: "I don't wish to argue with the churchmen who hold all Indians to be savages, but it has seemed to me that Indians who haven't been wrecked by rum and white man's tricks have a better grasp of the ten commandments, and practice them with greater regularity, than any churchmen I know" (p. 670).

Roberts's most systematic revision of America's founding mythology is recorded in his remarkable *Oliver Wiswell* (1940). For over 800 crowded pages, the novel offers a full-scale contrarian account of the Revolutionary War from the Loyalist point of view. In *Oliver Wiswell*, honor and courage belong almost exclusively to the Tory Americans, while the self-styled patriots are presented as incompetent, untrustworthy rebels, a ragtag collection of opportunists who stumble from one defeat to another, plundering and terrorizing innocent civilians, breaking every treaty they sign, and eventually securing an undeserved victory exclusively through the combination of bad British strategy, French intervention, and sheer chance.[18]

The title character is a young New Englander, driven from his home by a rebel mob, who spends the entire war working as a courier and spy on the Loyalist side. His adventures take him to Halifax, London, New York, Paris, and Virginia. He is a witness to the Loyalist evacuation of Boston, Parliamentary debates in England, diplomatic maneuvers in France, the battles of Long Island, and the war's final campaigns in the South. Everything he sees provides further evidence of the illegitimacy of the rebel cause.[19]

---

[18] The writer Alan Jay Nock shared Roberts's views. Of the American Tories, he says in his diary entry for September 16, 1933: "Our nation started by crowding out most of its best material, and it has consistently done so ever since; it has been the steadfast implacable enemy of intelligence, culture, high-mindedness." Nock, *A Journal of These Days, June 1932–December 1933* (New York: William Morrow & Company, 1934), p. 249.

[19] Along with several other of the historical novels discussed in this chapter, *Oliver Wiswell* refutes the claim that historical fiction in the 1930s served one of only two functions: escape, or affirmation of traditional mainstream values. Malcolm Cowley, looking back in one of his many influential essays, dogmatically but wrongly asserts that the "historical romancers [of the 1930s] were turning

The novel dismantles every pious chapter in America's founding mythology, and almost all of the Revolution's leading figures. Thomas Jefferson, George Washington, and other Southerners prate of liberty while owning slaves. "In the south," according to Oliver's friend Tom Buell, "when a man says 'Give me liberty or give me death,' he's usually got from two or three to fifty or so black people belonging to him . . . it's freedom for just a picked circle."[20] Rebel soldiers are more likely to flee than fight. Washington is probably the best of the rebel lot, but that merely makes him "an eagle among crows" (p. 362). His inferior generalship leads him to a series of defeats, and he does not hesitate to send Loyalist and British officers to certain death in notorious prison camps.

Roberts elaborates his most sustained assault on the integrity of the rebellion in his recreation of the Convention Army. Following the British defeat at Saratoga in 1777, the opposing generals Gates and Burgoyne signed the Saratoga Convention, which guaranteed safe passage to Europe for the British and allied soldiers captured in the battle. Instead, Congress unilaterally revoked the promise, consigning the 6,000 men to a series of prison camps for the duration of the war. Hundreds died of disease, malnutrition, and violent treatment. The episode, which had little visibility in American history books, was for Roberts a summary parable of rebel depravity.

The rebel Americans didn't win the war; the British generals lost it. Oliver's contempt for the Revolutionaries is matched by his disdain for Britain's political and military leadership. On almost every occasion, General Howe turns battlefield victories into stalemates by refusing to pursue the Americans aggressively. "Too late," should be the British motto, in Oliver's discouraged view. Predictably perhaps, the most astute general on either side is Benedict Arnold, presented once again as an honorable man who was insulted and betrayed by the rebel Congress and who then did "his utmost, singlehanded . . . to save America from self-ruin and French domination" (p. 577). And of all the troops on both sides, the most disciplined, humane, and effective are the Hessians.

As history, *Oliver Wiswell* makes strong claims. Aside from the fictional characters, every checkable fact is accurate; underlying the partisan narrative is a base of meticulous research in primary and secondary sources.

---

toward the past, not simply because it was picturesque but also to find heroes whose example would assure us about the future." Cowley, "The 1930s Were an Age of Faith," *New York Times Book Review* (December 13, 1964), p. 14.

[20] Kenneth Roberts, *Oliver Wiswell* (New York: Doubleday, Doran & Company, 1940), p. 107.

In short, it is not facts but ideology that separates Roberts's rendition of the War for Independence from the dominant version. Uniquely among American novels of its period, *Oliver Wiswell* turns the story of the Revolution upside down. For readers on the brink of yet another war on behalf of America's putative ideals, the novel provided a counter-narrative to the nation's founding myths.

Benedict Arnold, Robert Rogers, and Revolutionary Tories: a sequence of history's losers. Perhaps one reason for the extraordinary success of Roberts's novels in the 1930s was the resonance between the fates of his characters and the personal threats that hovered over Depression America. Revision served the purpose of challenging piety, while unmerited failure mirrored the anxieties of many readers.

The indignities George Washington suffered at the hands of Kenneth Roberts had been anticipated by a certain amount of debunking in the twenties. In the thirties, however, Washington regained and mostly retained his iconic status. The bicentennial of his birth, in 1932, gave rise to nationwide celebrations. Washington is treated with respect verging on reverence in James Truswell Adams's *The Epic of America* (1933). An especially heroic Washington is the main figure in Maxwell Anderson's *Valley Forge* (1934), a verse drama set in the terrible winter of 1777. Arthur Hobson Quinn, in *The Soul of America* (1932), assured his readers that "the futile attempts to make literary capital out of a few minor peccadilloes in Washington's career deserve the oblivion into which they will pass."[21]

Perhaps more significantly, Washington is presented in unambiguously heroic terms in David Saville Muzzey's *American History*, published in 1911 and still the leading school text through the 1930s, and indeed beyond. The consensus was literally carved in stone. Beginning in 1927, and continuing throughout the thirties, Gutzon Borglum jackhammered four presidential faces into the granite of Mount Rushmore in South Dakota. It is clear from the topography of the site that Washington has been given pride of place, followed by Lincoln, Jefferson, and Theodore Roosevelt.[22]

---

[21] Arthur Hobson Quinn, *The Soul of America* (Philadelphia: University of Pennsylvania Press, 1932), p. 27.

[22] Roosevelt's generally high standing is demonstrated by his inclusion among the four presidential likenesses carved on Mount Rushmore – the most extravagant gesture of filiopiety in the nation's history – begun in the 1920s and completed in the 1930s. At the same time, most Americans would have agreed that Roosevelt was a figure of decidedly less significance than his predecessors. See, for example, Gamaliel Bradford's chapter, "The Fury of the Living Roosevelt," in *The Quick and the Dead* (Boston: Houghton Mifflin Company, 1931), pp. 3–39. Henry Pringle offered a more

If Roberts's more disenchanted view was a minority report, it found an echo in the fiction of Katherine Mayo. In the interwar years, Mayo had become a figure of international notoriety because of her sensational attack on Indian culture and Hinduism, *Mother India* (1927). A polemic aimed primarily at the practice of child marriage, the book "created a sensation on three continents"; Mayo was attacked and defended in newspapers, foreign offices, and legislatures around the world. More than fifty books and pamphlets were published in response, and the controversy about the value of Mayo's observations and opinions roils to this day.[23]

Mayo's earlier career had included a remarkable if disjointed sequence of experiences: articles in the New York *Post* in the 1890s on Colonial American subjects; eight years in Dutch Guiana, as companion to her engineer father, during which she wrote essays, for such magazines as *Scribner's* and *Atlantic Monthly*, on Dutch Guianan life and on entomology; several years as research assistant to Oswald Garrison Villard as he prepared his life of John Brown (published in 1910); travel to the Philippines, Panama, and Europe. Between 1917 and 1922, she wrote three books on the Pennsylvania State Police, whose general tone is indicated by the title of the third, *Mounted Justice*.

Most of Mayo's books were reportorial. However, in the late thirties she published a novel that inquired provocatively into George Washington's reputation for integrity. *General Washington's Dilemma* (1938) recreates an actual though long-forgotten incident, in which Washington cynically authorized the hanging of an innocent British soldier in retaliation for the lynching of a Revolutionary privateer. Unlike Kenneth Roberts, in *Oliver Wiswell*, Mayo apportions brutality and incompetence rather evenly on both the Loyalist and Revolutionary side: "in the final reckoning little remains to choose, whether in numbers or in horrors, between the savageries . . . of the two American elements in the field."[24]

Nonetheless, in the climactic events in the novel, Mayo presents a morally bewildered Washington, motivated by reasons of state to allow the execution of a man chosen by lot from a group of British officers, in violation of all existing rules of war. In retaliation for the murder of a Revolutionary captain, Jack (Joshua) Huddy, Washington demands that

methodical dissent in *Theodore Roosevelt, a Biography*, which won the Pulitzer Prize in 1931. Pringle traced Roosevelt's accomplishments mainly to his impulsiveness and his appetite for power.

[23] Mrinalini Sinha, "Introduction" to Katherine Mayo, *Mother India* (Ann Arbor: University of Michigan Press, 2000), p. 2.

[24] Katherine Mayo, *General Washington's Dilemma* (New York: Harcourt, Brace and Company, 1938), p. 50.

an officer of equivalent rank be turned over for execution – not because of that man's involvement in the murder, but merely for the sake of a lethal reciprocity. Mayo lists, by name, the thirteen British officers who were brought together for the grisly lottery: "One of those thirteen, as all thirteen knew, was doomed to imminent death in cold blood" (p. 123). Washington's crime was exacerbated by the fact that all thirteen of the officers were specifically protected by treaty and convention from mis-treatment. In the end, the British officer, a nineteen-year-old captain named Charles Asgill, is saved from the gallows, not by any change of heart on Washington's part, but through the intervention of his French allies.

Its long narrative based on a good deal of archival research, with twenty-four pages of footnotes and photostats of relevant correspondence, *General Washington's Dilemma* is, in effect, a non-fiction novel. Though the genre had not yet been named in the 1930s, the mixture of docu-mentary and fiction was a relatively common technique in the decade. Dos Passos's *U.S.A.* trilogy, Steinbeck's *The Grapes of Wrath*, Maxwell Anderson's verse drama *Winterset*, and James Agee and Walker Evans's *Let Us Now Praise Famous Men* are some of the more familiar examples.

The accuracy of Mayo's account is not at issue here, of course, but her version of the story is not incompatible with the briefer discussions in more scholarly treatments of Washington's career.[25] Her novel also demonstrates, once again, the variety of ideological opinion that marked the return to the past in the Depression decade. That complexity is stifled by a homogenizing generalization such as this of David Lowenthal's: "during the 1930s Americans viewed Founding Fathers with renewed respect, shoring up battered self-esteem by identifying with a successful past."[26] As we have seen repeatedly: sometimes they did and sometimes they didn't.

The literary response to George Washington in the 1930s found an echo in painting. Along with a gallery of reverent portraits, which were produced and reproduced, often on the covers of popular magazines such as *The Saturday Evening Post* and *Collier's*, there were far more interesting responses.[27] Grant Wood greeted the Washington bicentennial with the

[25] See, for one authoritative example, James Thomas Flexner, *George Washington in the American Revolution* (Boston: Little, Brown and Company, 1968), pp. 479–482.
[26] David Lowenthal, *The Past is a Foreign Country* (New York: Cambridge University Press, 1985), p. 41.
[27] In 1935, A. Felix du Pont, and several other of Philadelphia's great and good, published *The American Historical Scene* (Philadelphia: University of Pennsylvania Press), an illustrated tribute to the artist Stanley Arthurs. A conventionally heroic portrait of Washington, standing on a hilltop with America's sunny landscape rolling out behind him, serves as the book's frontispiece.

Illustration 5. Grant Wood, "Daughters of Revolution"

mischievously funny painting "Daughters of Revolution" (1932), in which three elderly and quite frightening ladies (presumably members of the DAR) huddle in front of a copy of Leutze's "Washington Crossing the Delaware," and peer out at the viewer, porcelain teacups in hand. Washington is not the target of the satire. Rather, the juxtaposition of the familiar, heroic image with the dimity gentlewomen who claim to be his contemporary torchbearers comically enacts the nation's decline.[28]

Wood's painting of 1939, "Parson Weems' Fable," offers a more complex inquiry into Washington's legacy. The "fable" Wood refers to is, of course, the tale of six-year-old George Washington cutting down a cherry tree and then confessing the deed to his father. The story, widely known to be a fabrication, was first included in the fifth edition of Mason Locke Weems's *Life* (1806). Significantly, the moral that Weems intended by the edifying anecdote had less to do with young George's honesty than with his father's success as a parent. An enlightened father, Washington senior had never beaten his son, and George's confession proved the value of this liberal system of childrearing. When the young Washington confesses, his father answers (in Weems's invented dialogue): "Glad am I, George, that you killed my tree; for you have repaid me for it a

---

[28] Social historian Dixon Wecter might have read the painting as more critical of Washington. Wecter makes fun of Washington's aristocratic pretensions in his once-popular survey, *The Saga of American Society: A Record of Social Aspiration, 1607–1937* (New York: Charles Scribner's Sons, 1937), pp. 68–73.

Illustration 6. Grant Wood, "Parson Weems' Fable"

thousandfold. Such an act of heroism in my son is worth more than a thousand trees."[29]

Wood's painting offers an elaborate travesty of America's most familiar myth. The parson himself, slyly grinning, pulls back a curtain to reveal the scene within. The composition is derived from eighteenth- and nineteenth-century portraits. The most important predecessor painting is Charles Willson Peale's "Artist in His Museum" (1822), in which Peale holds back a curtain and discloses the collections of art and natural history that filled his Philadelphia galleries. But the curtain also functions as a theatrical prop, framing the enclosed tableau in declarations of artifice. The moment of Washingtonian truth is farcically rendered, in particular because the adult head of Gilbert Stuart's "Athenaeum" portrait surmounts young George's body.[30]

---

[29] Mason L. Weems, *The Life of Washington*, ed. Marcus Cunliffe (Cambridge, MA: The Belknap Press of Harvard University Press, 1962), p. 11.
[30] Among the more useful discussions of the sources and composition of "Parson Weems' Fable" are those in Wanda M. Corn, *Grant Wood: The Regionalist Vision* (New Haven, CT: Yale University

This is all good fun, but it also raises serious questions about the validity of American filiopietism. The picture's irony is not directed either toward Weems or Washington but toward the self-deluding taste of a republic that prefers fairy tales to truth. (The anonymous, laboring slaves in the background of the painting reinforce the point.) Wood turns the revered Athenaeum image into a comic mask, and in doing so ridicules the patriarchal myth. He renders Washington, impossibly, as older than his father, portrays him indeed as already the "Father of His Country," the role with which the Athenaeum portrait was universally associated. By confronting Washington's father with a son who has become the "Father," Wood reverses father–son relations and comically questions the paternity of the Father's father. (Wood himself claimed that the painting was intended "to reawaken interest in the cherry tree story" as a way of preserving our patriotic mythology. So much for artistic intentions: the painting obviously tells a more ironic story.[31])

Isabel Bishop produced another unsettling image of Washington, indeed one of the most enigmatic history paintings of the thirties, in her "Dante and Virgil in Union Square" (1932). Bishop typically found her subjects in small urban sketches, usually of young women. "Dante and Virgil" is a big painting, four feet across by two feet high; the two title characters, draped in cloaks and seen from the back, face a crowd of well-dressed men and women, almost all of whom ignore the two poets. Although Union Square, a regular scene of political activism, allegedly belonged "to the working people of New York," there are no working people in sight: white collars and fur collars are much in evidence.[32]

Despite the title, and despite Bishop's claim that she was inspired by reading a translation of *The Divine Comedy*, the most conspicuous image in the painting is Henry Kirke Brown's famous equestrian statue of George Washington, which has been located in Union Square since its installation in 1865. Washington, whose likeness occupies the center of Bishop's picture, and whose massive figure dominates all the others, is the undeniable focus of the scene. Surely this is another contribution to the Washington bicentennial birthday. Two histories converge in the scene: the literary and religious traditions represented by Dante and Virgil, and

Press, 1983), pp. 120–123, and James M. Dennis, *Grant Wood: A Study in American Art and Culture* (Columbia: University of Missouri Press, 1987), pp. 112–114.
[31] Cited in Cecile Whiting, *Antifascism in American Art* (New Haven, CT: Yale University Press, 1989), p. 100.
[32] *New York City Guide: A Comprehensive Guide to the Five Boroughs of the Metropolis* (New York: Random House, 1939), p. 198.

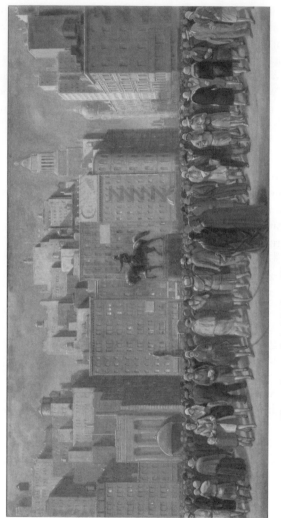

Illustration 7. Isabel Bishop, "Dante and Virgil in Union Square"

America's heroic past, embodied in the larger-than-life Washington. Indeed, it might be said that American history subsumes European myth, as Washington's benevolently outstretched arm suggests.

Esther Forbes was descended from an old New England family; her father was a judge, her mother was an authority on Colonial artifacts and documents. Forbes combined a deep interest in the past of her region with an exceptional and independent historical imagination. Along with her training in history (she studied with several prominent Americanists at the University of Wisconsin), Forbes also had the practical experience of working from 1920 to 1926 as an editor at Houghton Mifflin. Her accomplishments there included the acquisition of Rafael Sabatini's immensely popular historical novel, *Captain Blood* (1922). This would prove to be her own most successful genre.[33]

Forbes, along with her reconstructions of early New England and the Revolution, also wrote interestingly about Native Americans. Until relatively recently, Native Americans were either written out of the nation's history, or consigned to a small handful of predictable and stereotypical roles.[34] Through the 1930s and beyond, Western historiography was still dominated by the influential views of Frederick Jackson Turner, who conceived of the frontier as a more or less empty space in which white settlers defined themselves. Native Americans barely existed for Turner, and the challenge of the frontier was defined almost exclusively in topographical and geographical terms. Popular culture made more room for Native Americans, but typically represented them in one of two opposed but equivalently simplified ways. In most cases, Native Americans were the enemies of white settlers or soldiers, often with an emphasis on Native American cruelty and inhumanity. This was almost invariably the Hollywood Native American. Less often, Native Americans

---

[33] Just before the period we are exploring, Forbes published *A Mirror for Witches* (1928), which reconstructs a small New England town, Cowan Corner, in the early 1670s. The village is a moral world turned upside down, in which an innocent girl is condemned as a witch, generosity is mocked as weakness, and Christian charity dissolves in the acid of paranoia. In 1944, Forbes won the Newberry Medal for *Johnny Tremain*, a children's book whose teenaged title character evolves from apprentice to a Boston silversmith into a patriotic hero in the Revolutionary War. Herbert Gorman, most of whose historical novels were set in Europe, published a pioneering story of American witchcraft, *The Place Called Dagon*, in 1927. In that same year, he also published the biography, *Hawthorne: A Study in Solitude*.

[34] See Steven Conn, *History's Shadow: Native Americans and Historical Consciousness in the Nineteenth Century* (Chicago: University of Chicago Press, 2004).

were portrayed as victimized and vanishing, creatures of the pre-civilized landscape, perhaps noble, but primitive and doomed.[35]

Forbes's fourth novel, *Paradise* (1937), presented an exception to these practices. In some measure, the book's more enlightened attitude toward its Native American characters reflects the somewhat improved political climate Native Americans encountered in the thirties. Native American rights made a significant advance in the decade, with the repeal of the Dawes Act. Passed into law in 1887, the Dawes General Allotment Act had converted all Native American tribal lands to individual ownership, with a view toward encouraging Native Americans to assimilate into mainstream culture. In fact, the law eroded tribal life and ultimately reduced Native American holdings by millions of acres. The policy was reversed by the Indian Reorganization Act (1934), which allowed the return of land to tribal ownership.[36] John Collier, Commissioner of Indian Affairs in the Roosevelt administration, identified land ownership as one of his major aims: "to help the Indians to keep and consolidate what lands they have now and to provide more and better lands upon which they may effectively carry on their lives."[37]

Paradise expresses some of that spirit of reconciliation. The novel follows two generations of the Parre family across forty years of seventeenth-century Massachusetts history. The story opens in 1639, when Jude Parre leads a small band of settlers out from Boston to found a new community called Canaan. "Paradise" is the name that Parre gives to his own house, the largest in the settlement. The choice may be a self-flattering pun on his own name, or a hopeful prophecy, but initially the building is little more than a leaking shack with tarpaper windows.

The fortunes of the Parre family, Jude and his sons and daughters, along with their wives and husbands, are embedded in a richly furnished and thickly peopled account of the politics, economic development, theological debates, and daily life of the Bay Colony. Throughout the

---

[35] Frank Linderman published several sympathetic renderings of Native American culture in the 1930s, among them *American: the Life Story of a Great Indian, Plenty-coups, Chief of the Crows* (1930), and *Red Mother* (1932). Reconciliation between whites and Native Americans sometimes entailed the decision of white protagonists to become adopted members of Native American tribes. See, for example, Stewart Edward White, *The Long Rifle* (1930).

[36] See Delos Sacket Otis, ed., *The Dawes Act and the Allotment of Indian Lands* (Norman: University of Oklahoma Press, 1973).

[37] John Collier, "A New Deal for the Indian," in the *Annual Report of the Secretary of the Interior for the Fiscal Year Ended June 30, 1938*, re-printed in *The Annals of America, Volume 15, 1929–1939: The Great Depression* (Chicago: Encyclopaedia Brittanica, Inc., 1968), p. 524. Collier, a fervent admirer of Native American cultures, served as Commissioner of Indian Affairs through the whole of Franklin Roosevelt's presidency.

novel, Forbes demonstrates a mastery of detail and a strong gift for narrative pace. As the setting alternates between Boston, Canaan, and several Native American encampments, each is patiently constructed and abundantly realized. Each is the site of the objects and activities that define the societies of town, country, and wilderness: clothing and food, tents and houses, weapons and prayers, implements of farming, fishing, and hunting.

In the early days of Canaan's settlement, whites and Native Americans live in peaceful and generally respectful proximity. Trade is mutually beneficial, promises are kept, and contracts are fulfilled on both sides. Forbes symbolizes the initial success of co-existence in the relationship between two of her main characters, Fenton Parre, Jude's elder son, and Totonic, the sachem of the neighboring Nipmuc tribe. Both Fenton and Totonic have been nursed as babies by the same Native American woman; the two men refer to each other as "milk brothers," and they feel a strong, fraternal bond.

Relentless white expansion across Native American lands makes continued peace impossible. The novel's several plots move inexorably toward the catastrophe of King Philip's War in 1676.[38] This was the major military conflict between whites and Native Americans in the seventeenth century. Taking casualties as a proportion of the population, it was probably the bloodiest war – on both sides – in all of American history. It also entailed – on both sides – acts of extraordinary cruelty, along with remarkable instances of restraint.

Forbes's depiction of the war is vivid and historically well informed; among other things, she notes the large number of Native Americans that fought on the colonists' side. Those alliances, along with superior military technology, made the outcome inevitable. The Native Americans eventually suffered a defeat from which they never recovered. When Fenton Parre reluctantly executes the captured Totonic, the severed bond between the races is given symbolic finality. In the novel's last pages, Fenton has joined the concluding stages of the war, in the Maine woods, an assignment from which he is convinced he will not return alive.

Paradise is guided by a more ambitious intention than triumphalism or escapism. In the novel, Esther Forbes broods over the tragedy that overtook two groups of people, profoundly different but equivalently

[38] I use the familiar terminology. There is much debate about the proper way to refer to this series of events: "Metacom's Rebellion" (using Philip's Wampanoag name), and "Puritan Conquest" are among the proposed alternatives.

human. In so doing, she restored the Native American to the center of attention in understanding early American history.[39] Forbes's rigorously balanced portrayal of Native Americans not only improves on the mainstream stereotyping of Western novels and films; it also avoids the contrary tendency: the ostensible idealization of Native Americans as a way of legitimating European expansion in the New World. In particular, the Native American women Sacagawea and Pocahontas were used in this way.

Star of the West (1935), by Ethel Hueston, is a fictional reconstruction of the Lewis and Clark expedition. In her foreword, Hueston claims that she has "merely novelized the Original Journals" of the venture, and she appends several dozen source notes to the text.[40] In fact, she has borrowed much of her story from the rumors, tall tales, and legends that have barnacled the expedition since the early nineteenth century. In consequence, *Star of the West*, with its worshipful portrait of the white explorers, also exalts the role of Sacagawea. Never described in the *Journals*, Hueston's Sacagawea combines beauty, high intelligence, and courage with an eager capacity for romantic entanglement. Sacagawea emerges from *Star of the West* (and other nineteenth- and early twentieth-century novels) as a feisty harlequin heroine rather than a figure out of history. When she is sold to the French trader, Charbonneau, and forced to enter his tent: "her slender shoulders were not bowed, and her brave head was proudly lifted" (p. 35). When she first meets the white explorers, she feels a "childish curiosity" and her "eyes glowed with pleasure" (p. 94).

What can be deduced from the *Journals* suggests a woman of considerable ingenuity and resilience, who knew some of the tribal languages Lewis and Clark encountered, and gathered edible wild plants as food. Going far beyond her alleged primary sources, Hueston re-cycles the century of fable-making that propelled Sacagawea into a role she almost

---

[39] Another nuanced account of Native Americans can be found in the work of Walter D. Edmonds. The plot of Edmonds's story, "Delia Borst," which was published in the *Saturday Evening Post* in 1937, resembles a conventional captivity narrative. In 1778, a young white woman is taken off as the squaw of an Native American sachem following a bloody raid on her frontier home. During the months of her captivity, Delia is increasingly touched by the humanity and generosity of her captors. In the end, the Native Americans are doomed by white encroachment. Another sympathetic account of Native American history can be found in Stanley Vestal's biography, *Sitting Bull* (1932). In Vestal's interpretation, Sitting Bull and his people were admirable figures brought to ruination by the greed and opportunism of white speculators. Vestal numbers Sitting Bull among "the Makers of the Nation."

[40] Ethel Hueston, *Star of the West: The Romance of the Lewis and Clark Expedition* (Indianapolis, IN: Bobbs-Merrill Company, 1935), p. 7. Yet another fictionalized version of Sacagawea's story is told in Julia Davis's *No Other White Men* (1937).

certainly never filled: as the interpreter and wise counselor who makes the expedition's success possible.[41] This is the enduring if imaginary figure of whom it has been said, "there are more monuments, memorials, rivers, lakes, and mountain areas named for her than for any other American woman."[42] As several recent scholars have argued, the sort of Sacagawea Hueston creates, through her enthusiastic cooperation with Lewis and Clark, confers a degree of moral legitimacy on the white conquest of the Native American West.[43]

Pocahontas has served a rather similar function. For nearly four centuries, one version or another of this Native American woman has been a fixture of the Anglo-American imagination.[44] At the center of every retelling is the dramatic scene in which Pocahontas rescued John Smith from execution by putting herself between the white man and his Indian executioner. Assumed as true for generations, the authenticity of the account has been debated since the nineteenth century. In the mid-thirties, Virginian Branch Cabell declared that the story was "pure balderdash," but "very excellent balderdash," since it spoke to a young nation's mythologizing needs.[45]

As Cabell's remark suggests, the literal accuracy of the Pocahontas story is of less interest than its enduring appeal: here was a narrative flexible enough to bear a dozen different if sometimes conflicting interpretations and uses. Christian preachers could point to Pocahontas as a model of charity and self-sacrifice, Christ-like though heathen, and thus a rebuke to believers who exhibited lesser virtue. (Pocahontas's later conversion to Christianity also made a satisfying conclusion to the parable.) Apologists for European expansion could point to Pocahontas as a visionary who instinctively understood the need for cooperation between native peoples

[41] An ostensibly non-fiction version of the Sacagawea story, which repeated the exaggerated claims for her leadership, appeared just two years before *Star of the West*. See Grace Raymond Hebard, *Sacajawea: Guide of the Lewis and Clark Expedition* (Glendale, CA: Arthur H. Clark Co., 1933). Hebard's addition to the legend was the almost certainly fictitious notion that Sacagewea lived to be 100 years old.

[42] Sally McBeth, "Sacagawea," in *American National Biography* www.anb.org/articles/20/20–00891.html

[43] For a pair of revisionist inquiries into Sacagawea's part in the expedition, see Donna Kessler, *The Making of Sacagawea, A Euro-American Legend* (Tuscaloosa: University of Alabama Press, 1996), and Gary Moulton, ed., *The Journals of the Lewis & Clark Expedition* (Lincoln: University of Nebraska Press, 2003).

[44] The best account of the development of the Pocahontas story is Robert S. Tilton, *Pocahontas: The Evolution of an American Narrative* (New York: Cambridge University Press, 1994). Tilton traces the legends through the nineteenth century, adding only a postscript on the twentieth.

[45] Branch Cabell, *Ladies and Gentlemen: A Parcel of Reconsiderations* (New York: Robert M. McBride & Company, 1934), p. 203.

and invaders. Antebellum Southerners could find in Pocahontas a source
of regional pride – Princess Pocahontas – and thus an alternative to the
national narrative that placed New England at the center of legitimacy.

Pocahontas was ubiquitous in the 1930s, as a few examples chosen more
or less at random from across the decade will demonstrate. Pocahontas
was the only woman included in *The Virginia Plutarch* (1930), Philip
Alexander Bruce's two-volume history of Virginia. She appeared as "The
Little Wanton" in Mount Holyoke's spring festival in 1930. Pocahontas's
rescue of John Smith was re-enacted on a float presented by the Improved
Order of Red Men at the 1930 Rose Bowl parade. Three years later, the
Degree of Pocahontas, the Ladies' Auxiliary of the Improved Order of
Red Men, marched in Franklin Roosevelt's first inaugural parade in 1933.

Pocahontas was included in a revue called "Bathing Beauties of History" at the 1934 Beaux Arts Ball in Atlantic Beach, New Jersey. In that
same year, the American Children's Theater showed a short play called
"Pocahontas" in repertory with several other one-act historical dramas.
The movie "Ruggles of Red Gap" (1935) opens with a funny exchange
between Ruggles and the Earl of Burnstead, whose meaning (and joke)
depends on the viewer's knowledge of Pocahontas. A horse named
Pocahontas is a model of determination in the children's book *Sleepy Tom*
(1939), by Dwight Akers. In the Metropolitan Museum's 1939 exhibit
"Pictorial History of America," the first item was a portrait of Pocahontas. In that same year, a new Pocahontas doll was featured in the
Christmas ads for several department stores, and a tableau of the famous
rescue was included in the Wax Museum that opened at Broadway and
50th Street.

Grant Wood announced plans for a painting of Pocahontas to follow
his tongue-in-cheek canvas, "Parson Weems' Fable," discussed above.
Paul Cadmus produced "Pocahontas Saving the Life of Captain John
Smith" (1938), a WPA commission that found a home in a Richmond,
Virginia, post office. Elizabeth Madox Roberts included Pocahontas,
along with Washington, Nelly Bly, and Moby Dick, in "Conversations
Beside a Stream," one of the poems in *Song in the Meadow* (1940).
Pocahontas was a feature of the New York World's Fair. Lincoln
Kirstein's American Ballet Caravan performed "Pocahontas," with music
by Elliott Carter; and thousands of spectators watched the Pocahontas
Day Parade at the Fair on September 21, 1940.

The most significant literary representation of Pocahontas in the 1930s
can be found in the second section of Hart Crane's ruined epic, *The
Bridge* (1930). The five sub-divisions of "Powhatan's Daughter" examine

America's history, with an emphasis on Native American contributions to the nation's heritage. In a letter to Otto Kahn, Crane explained that "Powhatan's daughter, or Pocahontas, is the mythological nature-symbol chosen to represent the physical body of the continent, or the soil . . . The five sub-sections of Part II are mainly concerned with a gradual exploration of this 'body' whose first possessor was the Indian."[46]

Significantly, Crane uses as epigraph for the section a famous, titillating remark of William Strachey, who had spent time in Jamestown but had never actually seen the young woman he described. "[A] well featured, but wanton yong girle," Strachey wrote, "Powhatan's daughter, sometymes resorting to our fort, of the age then of eleven or twelve yeares, get the boyes forth with her into the markett place, and make them wheele, falling on their hands, turning up their heeles upwards, whome she would followe and wheele so herself, naked as she was . . ."[47] Though Crane's Pocahontas will ultimately transcend Strachey's exhibitionist little girl, the prominence of his citation in the poem inevitably smudges Crane's mythmaking.

Crane described "Powhatan's Daughter" as the "basic center and antecedent of all motion . . . power in repose."[48] The poem celebrates the Native American woman's beauty and strength, the magical powers of her dancing, her symbolic identification with timeless truth and with the river of life. Crane's Pocahontas differs from most of the others in America's cultural history. Nonetheless, the Native American woman disappears under layers of imputed meanings that ignore her humanity. "Powhatan's Daughter" represents an act of visionary appropriation in which the Native American woman provides the literal ground on which the poetic imagination is based.

Were Indians part of America's history or were they a part of the nation's prehistory, fixed in ahistorical myth?[49] Fictional representations of Native Americans in the 1930s should be framed within the context of contemporary anthropological ideas. The white effort to come to terms with the nation's indigenous peoples can be traced back to first contact.

[46] Hart Crane, letter to Otto Kahn, in Brom Weber, ed., *The Letters of Hart Crane, 1899–1932* (New York: Hermitage House, 1952), p. 305.

[47] Crane took the Strachey quote from a tertiary source, Kay Boyle's review in *transition* of William Carlos Williams's *In the American Grain*.

[48] Hart Crane, letter to Waldo Frank (August 3, 1926), in Langdon Hammer and Brom Weber, eds., *O My Land, My Friends: The Selected Letters of Hart Crane* (New York: Four Walls Eight Windows, 1997), p. 267.

[49] See the exclusion of Native Americans from most of the historical sections of the American Guide books, discussed above.

While it would be reductive to assert that any distinctive set of interpretations emerged in the thirties, in the summary estimate of one
scholar, the years between the world wars saw a "fundamental shift in the
scientific and scholarly understanding of the Indian through acceptance
of the concept of culture and the ideal of cultural pluralism."[50] A survey
of the decade's ethnography and social anthropology (as it was then
called) indicates that the relativizing views of Franz Boas shaped most
professional analyses. Indeed, without succumbing to the counter-
stereotype of the "noble savage," the comparisons between white and
Native American culture often concluded that Native American practices
and beliefs might be superior.

Clark Wissler's *Indians of the United States* (1941) was probably the
most authoritative summary text of the period. Wissler, who had taken
his PhD in psychology at Columbia and had collaborated with Boas, was
the Dean of the Scientific Staff at the American Museum of Natural
History. *Indians of the United States* recapitulated the fieldwork and
analyses that he and other Boasians had been pursuing for over two
decades.[51] The book is taken up mainly with detailed accounts of tribes,
tribal families, and language groups. The concluding chapters, however,
address more general questions, including the increasingly perilous conditions under which Native Americans lived. Wissler impatiently dismantles such clichés as those that viewed the Native Americans as
"children of nature." Likewise, the point of a chapter called "The Mystery
of the Indian Mind" is that the so-called mystery has its source in the
inability and unwillingness of the white man to see: "He made a mystery
of the Indian because he was less observing."[52]

George Santayana was seventy-two years old when he published his first
(and only) novel, *The Last Puritan: A Memoir in the Form of a Novel*.
After half a century of prolific metaphysical and aesthetic writing, an
internationally distinguished philosopher had authored a work of fiction;
that circumstance accounts for much of the considerable publicity
attending the book's appearance.[53]

---

[50] Robert K. Berkhofer, Jr., *The White Man's Indian: Images of the American Indian from Columbus to the Present* (New York: Vintage Books, 1979), p. 176.

[51] In 1917, Wissler had written one of the first general books on Native Americans, *The American Indian: An Introduction to the Anthropology of the New World*.

[52] Clark Wissler, *Indians of the United States: Four Centuries of Their History and Culture* (Garden City, NY: Doubleday, Doran & Company, Inc., 1941), pp. 270, 279.

[53] Santayana's first book of philosophy, *The Sense of Beauty*, had appeared in 1896, his earliest essays a decade before that.

Deference to Santayana's perceived virtuosity explains at least a portion of the response *The Last Puritan* evoked upon its publication in January 1936. The book was widely reviewed, often in a leading position. Most of the reviews were favorable, and several were downright reverential. The popular press joined the more serious quarterlies in welcoming what the Boston *Transcript* called "a brilliant picture of New England life." Writing in the *New Republic*, Conrad Aiken announced that the "whole book is a delight," while Henry Hazlitt wrote in the *Nation* that the "merits of the book make up for everything, and sweep all its faults before them."

The comparisons that reviewers proposed between Santayana and such writers as Proust, Joyce, Henry James, and Pater (whose *Marius the Epicurean* was indeed one of Santayana's sources) suggest something of the esteem that was immediately bestowed upon the novel. Along with its good notices, *The Last Puritan* also earned a large commercial success. The book was in fact a bestseller. Santayana's picture adorned the cover of *Time* magazine's February 3, 1936 issue – a notoriety that few writers have enjoyed – and his novel was chosen as a main selection of the Book-of-the-Month Club.[54]

Santayana's easygoing technique, along with his indifference to both modernist experiment and to proletarian realism, helped to define the special and separate status of his book. In an admiring review in *Books*, Ellen Glasgow distinguished the novel from what she termed "the flourishing cults in recent American letters." Implicitly defending her own fictional choices as well as Santayana's, Glasgow wrote that *The Last Puritan* would appeal "to all those who prefer to think while they read." On the other hand, the novel would affront readers she labeled disapprovingly as "the sentimental conservative, the new barbarian, or the earnest believer in social regeneration through literary violence."[55] (She undoubtedly expected her readers to think of Faulkner in that last phrase.)

For a good many readers, the novel's relationship to American culture was mostly antiquarian. Such readers valued the book as an evocative backward glance, an expansive act of fictive reminiscence with little pertinence to the issues and personalities dominating the American scene in the mid-1930s. Instead, *The Last Puritan* offered a demystified and

[54] Santayana's memoir, *Persons and Places* (1944), was also a Book-of-the-Month Club main selection; Edmund Wilson called it one of the few first-rate autobiographies produced on either side of the Atlantic.
[55] Ellen Glasgow's review appeared in *Books* (February 2, 1936), p. 1.

disillusioned recollection of a vanished and rather picturesque social and intellectual world, the Brahmin society of Harvard and Cambridge, Massachusetts in the years around the turn of the twentieth century, and the cloistered eccentricity of prewar Oxford. As a "study of a certain strain of New Englandism," Christopher Morley wrote, "as a sentimental-ironic dissection of a North American tradition . . . it is superb."[56] Several of the novel's first readers noted a likeness between *The Last Puritan* and Henry Adams's *Education*. The comparison is apt. Like Adams, Santayana's Oliver Alden is the descendant of generations of New England worthies (he can trace his American forbears back to John and Priscilla Alden); like Adams, too, Oliver Alden sees himself as belated: a relic of an earlier age, shrunken and irrelevant to his times.[57]

Born just before the turn of the century, Oliver is the only child of a loveless marriage. His father, Peter, resigned from Harvard after accidentally killing a night watchman during a prank that misfired in the college chapel. Within a few years of Oliver's birth, Peter has effectively abandoned him, spending most of his time sailing around the world on an endless search for relief for his boredom. Eventually, he will commit suicide more or less out of exhaustion. Oliver's mother, Harriet Bumstead, desiccated product of another old New England family, treats him with loveless rigor, replacing maternal affection with relentless criticism. The boy feels effectively orphaned. He transforms his loneliness into a search for purpose and perfection. With more reluctance than enthusiasm, he engages himself in football at Williams College, travels around the world with his father, undertakes the study of philosophy at Harvard with Santayana and Royce, and eventually goes to war. In each case, he can find no remedy for his profound dissatisfaction.

Oliver embodies what Santayana, in his most famous essay, had derisively called "the genteel tradition." In an opinion that he first publicized in a lecture at Berkeley in 1911, Santayana traced America's failure of imagination to the legacies of Calvinism and Transcendentalism. Santayana saw the American character divided between the domain of aggressive enterprise and will, on the one hand, and a separate realm of

---

[56] Christopher Morley, "Book-of-the-Month Club News," *Book of the Month Club* (January, 1936), p. 1.

[57] A few years earlier, James Truslow Adams had published the first biography of Henry Adams (no relation). Following Henry's lead in *The Education of Henry Adams*, James Truslow comments on the resemblance between his subject and the first Henry Adams, a seventeenth-century Puritan. James Truslow Adams, *Henry Adams* (New York: Albert & Charles Boni, Inc., 1933), p. 60. In several places, James Truslow Adams also salutes Henry Adams as prophetic of the economic and political confusion of the 1930s (pp. 181, 193, 203).

art and culture. The former "roars on as though leaping down a sort of Niagara Rapids"; the latter is "slightly becalmed, floating gently in the backwater."[58] The cleavage between sentiment and action, in Santayana's view, was disabling, and Oliver Alden's futility therefore dramatizes a more general national dilemma. Even Oliver's death gives ironic emphasis to his irrelevance. Having enlisted in the United States Army and survived the Western Front during World War I, he is killed in a car crash several days after the Armistice.

The Last Puritan is a long, slow-moving, densely allusive, discursive and often digressive book. The prose is stylish though sometimes self-indulgent in its leisurely parentheses. Philosophical discussion alternates with extended narrative set pieces, and characters are described and re-described at considerable length. While Santayana intends Oliver's story as a tragedy, the narrator's tone is quite supple, as he tries to embed that sad story in a thick texture of comedy and satire. The first Alden we meet, Oliver's uncle Nathaniel, emerges as a splendid caricature of New England rectitude, a man who believes that "one's property... formed the chief and fundamental part of one's moral personality."[59] Nathaniel has strong opinions about the protocol governing funerals, about the impropriety of using public transportation, about the unsuitability of friendships across class lines.

Santayana lived for almost forty years in the United States. However, by the time he published *The Last Puritan*, he had been removed from America for over two decades, and harbored no regrets about returning to Europe. In 1940, he asserted: "If I had been free to choose, I should not have lived there, or been educated there, or taught philosophy there or anywhere else."[60] In a sense, the novel was more revenge than reminiscence, and its success in America may be further evidence of the parlous state in which the figure of the Puritan continued to languish through the 1930s.[61]

---

[58] George Santayana, "The Genteel Tradition in American Philosophy," in Douglas L. Wilson, ed., *The Genteel Tradition: Nine Essays by George Santayana* (Lincoln: University of Nebraska Press, 1998), p. 40.

[59] George Santayana, *The Last Puritan: A Memoir in the Form of a Novel* (New York: Charles Scribner, 1936), p. 35.

[60] George Santayana, "Apologia Pro Menta Sua," in *The Philosophy of George Santayana*, ed. by Paul Arthur Schilpp (Chicago: Northeastern University, 1940), p. 601. Cited in Dan Miller, "'Harvard, We Have a Problem': Santayana and the New University," *Essays in History* http://etext.virginia.edu/journals/EH/Eh38/Miller.html

[61] One of Puritanism's influential defenders was the Harvard historian, Samuel Eliot Morison, notably in his book, *Builders of the Bay Colony* (1930), written in part as a response to James Truslow Adams's *The Founding of New England* (1921). In his 1931 essay, "Those Misunderstood

Frances Winwar's *Gallows Hill* (1937) provides another portrait of Puritan excess, in this case by resurrecting the Salem witch trials. A grim-visaged Cotton Mather broods over the novel's action, burdening the populace with warnings about the Devil's work in New England, and the novel's climax includes the execution of Bridget Bishop and several other accused witches. Winwar superimposes a romantic plot on her historical materials, which allows Bishop's daughter, Mary, to find both safety and an erotic satisfaction that belies the pinched codes of the clerical regime.

Writers of all sorts continued the attack on Puritanism through the 1930s. In the American Guide to Connecticut, an anonymous historian commits a small epigram followed by a small joke to describe the settling of New Haven: "Although the Colony was founded to promote the peculiarly Puritan combination of piety and commercialism, its commercial enterprises did not thrive, and its piety was over-zealous and repressive. Its shipping activity was short-lived, and was featured by the loss at sea of 'The Wonder-working Providence' with several leading citizens on board."[62]

John P. Marquand's *The Late George Apley* (1937), one of the fine, neglected books of the 1930s, also offers a wonderfully satiric social history of New England. A 1915 Harvard graduate, Marquand served as an artillery officer in the last year of World War I, surviving some of its bloodiest battles. Upon his return to civilian life, Marquand found a job as a journalist in New York, but soon shifted to advertising, which paid a good deal more money. In 1921, he published his first story, called "The Right That Failed," in the *Saturday Evening Post*. He quickly became one of the most successful writers in America. In a career of nearly four decades, he published upwards of 150 stories, most of them in the *Post*, others in such large-circulation magazines as *Collier's*, *Woman's Home Companion*, and *Cosmopolitan*. He wrote a handful of forgettable novels in the twenties and thirties; the best of them was probably *Haven's End* (1933), told through a series of flashbacks, which surveys the decline of an old New England family. (He also invented the Japanese detective, Mr. Moto.)

Puritans," Morison blamed the Victorian nineteenth century for creating a joyless Puritan culture that could serve as foil to nineteenth-century enlightenment.
[62] *Connecticut: A Guide to Its Roads, Lore, and People* (Boston: Houghton Mifflin Company, 1938), p. 28. The reference is to Edward Johnson's history, *The Wonder-Working Providence of Sion's Saviour, a History of New England* (1654).

It isn't clear that Marquand consented to the distinction between popular and serious literature, but he worked unusually hard on *Apley* and earned the multiple satisfaction of large sales, respectful reviews in all the major newspapers, and the Pulitzer Prize. The book comprises one of the most adroitly crafted historical satires in American fiction. An epistolary biography assembled just a couple of years after George Apley's death in his late sixties, the text consists mainly of letters between the title character and his friends and family, with interpolated commentary by a writer and Harvard classmate named William Willig. George Apley is an enormously wealthy and patrician member of Boston's social elite, the son and heir to generations of custom and tradition. His life is devoted to the maintenance of that heritage, against all the forces of modernity and change – from Freud to socialism to Irish politicians – that threaten what he invariably calls "the better sort."

In the course of its 400 pages, the novel reveals both Apley and Willig as reactionaries, philistines, and snobs. Apley's is the sort of family in which every new acquaintance is evaluated according to lineage, and all instincts are smothered in deference to respectability. Through Apley's letters and Willig's supportive editorial comments Marquand captures the complacency of an American aristocracy, comfortable in the knowledge that its affluence proves God's good judgment.

Apley is a man who carries Boston with him on his travels. He looks at the Colosseum and wishes it "was situated in a more open space as is our Harvard Stadium."[63] When he sees the fountains at the Villa of Frascati he worries that he has forgotten to turn off the plumbing at his estate back in Massachusetts (p. 385). The forest at Fontainebleau recalls Uncle Horatio's beech woods, and the "courtyard where Napoleon took farewell of the Old Guard" reminds him "of the space in back of the State House" (p. 111).

All of Apley's choices are guided by the burden of inherited obligation. He has made a collection of Chinese bronzes, despite the fact that he knows nothing about them and doesn't like them. As he tells his son, John, in one of his letters: "I have made this collection out of duty rather than out of predilection, from the conviction that everyone in a certain

[63] John P. Marquand, *The Late George Apley: A Novel in the Form of a Memoir* (New York: Time Incorporated, 1963 [1937]), p. 384. Several reviews compared *Apley* to Santayana's *Last Puritan*. Santayana's subtitle, "A Memoir in the Form of a Novel," anticipated Marquand's. Santayana read *Apley*, and found it "too external, too verbal . . . Mr. Marquand's hero seems to me not so much Bostonian as provincial." Cited in Millicent Bell, *Marquand: An American Life* (Boston: Little, Brown and Company, 1979), p. 252.

position owes it to the community to collect something" (p. 182). Having perceived that the Art Museum was "short of" Chinese bronzes, Apley decided that it was his unappealing job to assist.

Apley assumes that his status will follow him to the grave. When he learns that a distant cousin, Aunt Hattie, has been buried in the section of the family plot he intends for himself, George insists that she be exhumed and re-buried. The broad comedy of the sequence typifies Marquand's attitude throughout the book: Apley represents a dying breed, more amusing than threatening, and soon to be interred in its own obsolescence.

While it effectively dismantles its title character, the novel also acknowledges the co-existence of Apley's undeniable virtues. He is more than the sum of his blinkered prejudices and back-looking loyalties. If his convictions are outmoded, he demonstrates considerable courage in defending them, along with a warped but genuine integrity. Above all, George Apley displays a poignant self-awareness that grows more acute as he ages, an insight into his own irrelevance. In the final paragraph of a memorial he wrote for his father – a paragraph he did not read in public – George proposes that "most of us have obeyed the older generation so implicitly that now they are gone there is nothing left for us but to continue in the pattern they have laid down for us . . . It may be, like the Chinese, that we are finally ending in a definite and static state of ancestor worship" (p. 168).

In the first of Apley's words that are quoted in the book, he says of himself: "I am the sort of man I am, because environment prevented my being anything else" (p. 1). The comment is elaborated in one of Apley's last letters, to his son John: "I have always been faced from childhood by the obligation of convention, and all of these conventions have been made by others, formed from the fabric of the past. In some way these have stepped in between me and life" (p. 389). In his son's view, George Apley "was a frustrated man [who] had been trying all his life to get through the meshes of a net, a net which he could never break, and in a sense it was a net of his own contriving" (p. 265).

In short, Marquand's purposes in *The Late George Apley* reach beyond his mordant assessment of the old New England aristocracy. Apley makes a fine comic target, but he also embodies a larger issue: the power of the past and the limits that environment and received imperatives place on individual effort.

Writing in an altogether different register, Henry Roth also produced one of the decade's indispensable fictional social histories, reproducing the immigrant experience in turn-of-the-century Brooklyn. *Call It Sleep*

(1934) provides an unforgettable portrait of urban pathologies that take shape as a past that haunts the present. The novel itemizes in meticulous detail the hunger and fear that attend poverty. No writer more faithfully transcribed the cruelty with which the hapless denizens of the urban jungle prey on each other. Roth's point of view throughout the book is that of a child. And to David Schearl, who grows from six years old to eight in the course of the story, the realities of poverty are not problems in political economics but mysterious wonders in an untrustworthy world.

His father seethes with an irremediable anger, creating an atmosphere of domestic terror for both David and his beloved mother, Genya. David is introduced to sex by a neighbor girl, who gropes him in a cellar and urges him to put his "petzel" into her "knish." The scene oozes with a revulsion born of Roth's most shameful secret: the incest in which he engaged with his own younger sister when both were in their teens.[64]

The outside world proves as threatening and dangerous as his father. Fleeing from a gang of older boys, for example, David stumbles blindly into an urban wasteland:

David climbed up the junk heap and threaded his way cautiously over the savage iron moraine . . . Before him the soft, impartial April sunlight spilt over a hill of shattered stoves, splintered wheels, cracked drain pipes, potsherds, marine engines split along cruel and jagged edges. Eagerly, he looked beyond – on the suddenly alien, empty street and the glittering cartracks, branching off at the end.[65]

This litter may be the excrement of capitalism, but protest is irrelevant to Roth's use of it. Rather, the vacant lots and their garbage, along with the cellars and streets of Brownsville and the Lower East Side, are the arena in which young David grows up, and grows into knowledge. David learns much of fear and pity, but he has glimpses of beauty, too.

Call It Sleep, which deployed the personal past with idiosyncratic but exceptional power, received an encouraging critical welcome when it was published in 1934. In the *New York Times*, John Chamberlain said that Roth "has done for the East Side what James T. Farrell is doing for the Chicago Irish."[66] The book went through a respectable first and second printing, and then dropped from sight along with its author. In fact, despite its immersion in the lives of ghetto immigrants, the book is not "proletarian," at least not in the narrow and usual sense. *Call It Sleep* is

---

[64] Steven G. Kellman, *Redemption: The Life of Henry Roth* (New York: W. W. Norton & Company, 2005), pp. 67–69.
[65] Henry Roth, *Call It Sleep* (New York: Avon Books, 1964 [1934]), p. 251.
[66] John Chamberlain, "Books of the Times," *New York Times* (February 18, 1935), p. 13.

indifferent to party ideology, and that was surely part of the reason for its obscurity. The novel's recovery, in the 1960s, brought the restoration of a major document in the Depression decade's imagination of the past.

Nathanael West, perhaps the least explicitly historical of the major writers of the 1930s, repeatedly manipulated the national and mythic past as part of his campaign to dramatize the dislocations of Depression America. The maimed dreamers who people West's peculiar half-worlds are the creatures of their own nightmares. Their deformities and the surreal plots they act out seem more proportionate than patient realism to the anxieties and alarms of their times. Riots, crucifixion, dismemberment: in West's fictions, the open road so cherished by generations of American writers ended in a dark cul-de-sac. West's preoccupation with violence did not have obvious sources in his own life. The son of relatively prosperous immigrant parents, he attended Tufts and Brown, conniving toward a degree by receiving credit for courses he did not take. It was after college that West changed his name from Nathan Weinstein, spent six months in Paris, and found a job as assistant manager of a New York City hotel.

West's four novels appeared between 1931 and his death in an automobile accident in 1940. All of them make use of the past, in particular the mythic past, and all detect in the past the seeds of contemporary anxiety and defeat. His first book, a fifty-page novella called *The Dream Life of Balso Snell* (1931), parodies the classics, along with an assortment of other cultural material; his next, *Miss Lonelyhearts* (1933), depends on a sustained ironic parallel between the title character and Christ; *A Cool Million* (1934), dismantles the central nineteenth-century American myth of success; and *The Day of the Locust* (1939), deploys the illusions of Hollywood history for apocalyptic purposes.

Conceived as a satire, *Balso Snell* proves to be a back-looking hodge-podge of puns, bad jokes, studiously surreal episodes, and miscellaneous cultural allusions (Rimbaud, Picasso, Blake, Juvenal, Boswell, Lucretius, among dozens of others). Balso is a would-be poet who finds himself in the presence of the wooden horse outside the walls of ancient Troy. There is only one way of entering: through the posterior opening of the alimentary canal. "O Anus Mirabilis!" shouts Balso exultantly, offering a true prediction of the bad-boy high-jinks that will persist throughout the book.[67]

---

[67] Nathanael West, *The Dream Life of Balso Snell* (New York: Farrar, Straus and Giroux, 2006 [1931], p. 3. The book was originally published by the small press, Contact Editions, on the recommendation of advisory editor William Carlos Williams.

Balso's journey through the horse's intestines brings him into contact with an assortment of fantastical creatures. Maloney the Areopagite, naked except for a derby hat, is trying to crucify himself with thumb tacks. Maloney tells the story of Saint Puce, a "great martyred member of the vermin family" (p. 10), a flea who lived his life in Christ's armpit. John Gilson has taken the name Raskolnikov, and leaves a journal confessing a gruesome and pointless murder. Janey Davenport, a hunchback who would be seven feet tall if she could stand up, carries an illegitimate child in her hump and commits suicide out of loneliness.

Throughout the novel, West's target is tradition itself; the past yields material fit only for sneering and often ribald comedy. *Balso Snell* reads like the field report of a lunatic archaeologist, the record of an excavator intent on discovering the cultural past only to dismantle it. History is bunk and the history of art is a mournful sequence of false starts and dead ends, as one poet or painter after another tries unsuccessfully to impose some sort of order on the untamable disorder of the world.

West's next novel, *Miss Lonelyhearts*, is a much better book and makes a quite different use of the past. The story's eponymous hero is an otherwise-unnamed newspaper reporter who takes on the advice column, initially as a joke. On a typical day, he receives more than thirty letters, "all of them alike, stamped from the dough of suffering with a heart-shaped cookie knife."[68] What begins as a joke leads to tragedy. Submerged continuously in the suffering and heartache of the men and women who turn to him in despair, Miss Lonelyhearts finds himself engaged sympathetically, ultimately to the point of obsession, with his diseased, impoverished, and grotesque correspondents. Trying to heal these physically and spiritually wasted lives with love, Miss Lonelyhearts only brings on his own murder, shot in the novel's closing paragraphs by a crippled man he wants to save.

Where *Balso Snell* piled one historical reference on top of another, heterogeneously mixing the classics and the Bible and art, *Miss Lonelyhearts* elaborates a single link between past and present: Miss Lonelyhearts and Christ. Through a tormented and ultimately crazy embrace of his emotionally and physically crippled clients, Miss Lonelyhearts eventually believes himself transformed into the crucified Christ. Dostoyevsky looms over the book; West shares his predecessor's fascination with characters who combine the identities of saint and psychopath.

---

[68] Nathanael West, *Miss Lonelyhearts* (New York: New Directions, 1950 [1933]), p. 1.

Once again, West's use of the past is subversive: all traditions, no matter how encrusted with piety, are collections of empty promises. Echoing Henry Adams's famously disenchanted view of history, Miss Lonelyhearts broods that "[m]an has a tropism for order," but the "physical world has a tropism for disorder" (pp. 30–31).[69] Shrike, the supremely cynical editor, proposes, "God alone is our escape. The church is our only hope, the First Church of Christ Dentist, where He is worshipped as Preventer of Decay" (p. 35). The humor is sophomoric, but the corrosive message lies near the disillusioned heart of the novel.

West's third novel, *A Cool Million*, discloses much of its plot in the subtitle: *The Dismantling of Lemuel Pitkin* (1934). The book, dedicated to West's brother-in-law, S. J. Perelman, begins with an epigraph of sorts, identified as an unlikely "old saying": "John D. Rockefeller would give a cool million to have a stomach like yours."[70] The plot, if that is the correct word, is little more than a picaresque armature on which West wraps a sequence of atrocious episodes. Young Lemuel is forced to seek his fortune when his mother's house is threatened with villainous foreclosure. In the course of the book, the innocent (and frankly rather dim-witted) Lemuel is repeatedly robbed, beaten, and unjustly imprisoned. He loses all his teeth, one eye, a leg, and his scalp – the dismantling of the subtitle – and is finally assassinated.[71] His legend survives in the lore of the National Revolutionary Party, a fascist organization with which he was associated by inadvertence.

A Cool Million is usually read as a parody of the Horatio Alger tales.[72] Aside from the general correspondence, there is even a scene in which

[69] "[O]ne had learned from Socrates to distrust, above all other traps, the trap of logic – the mirror of the mind." Ernest Samuels, ed., *The Education of Henry Adams*, (Boston: Houghton Mifflin, 1974), p. 429.
[70] Nathanael West, *A Cool Million, or The Dismantling of Lemuel Pitkin* (New York: Farrar, Straus and Giroux, 2006 [1934]), p. 65.
[71] Stories of dismemberment, or conversely of persons made out of non-human materials, have a long history in American literature, going back at least to Edgar Allan Poe's "The Man That Was Used Up" (1839). Perhaps the several crises of the 1930s provided an especially fertile ground for such tales. In addition to West's *A Cool Million* and Dalton Trumbo's *Johnny Got His Gun* (1939), another example from the decade can be found in Charles G. Finney's cult classic, *The Circus of Dr. Lao* (New York: The Viking Press, 1935). Along with the strange creatures in the circus – a sphinx, a mermaid, a medusa who turns spectators to stone – the novel includes in its cast of characters an apparently ordinary American named Frank Tull. "A man of artificial parts was Lawyer Frank Tull." Aside from false teeth, a hearing aid, a wig, a truss, and glasses, Tull has a silver plate in his skull, a false leg made of metal and fiber, a platinum wire in place of the humerus in his left arm, one collapsed lung, and a steel brace to support his broken neck (pp. 75–76). Tull is Finney's ham-handed satiric emblem of the divorce of modern Americans from nature.
[72] Insofar as the documentation is useful, Jay Martin reported that West had read many of the Alger stories before he was ten years old. In *Nathanael West: The Art of His Life* (New York: Farrar, Straus and Giroux, 1970), p. 24.

young Lem saves a young woman and her rich father from a runaway horse – an episode right out of *Tattered Tom* and *Ragged Dick* – but in this case, Lem's reward is a beating and the loss of his eye: the father is hard of hearing and assumes that Lem was responsible for the accident. Voltaire's *Candide* also hovers over the book; no matter how bad his situation, Lem refuses "to be discouraged or grow bitter and become a carping critic of things as they are" (p. xx).

The bread lines and unemployment offices of the Depression are quite visible throughout the book, and the triumph of fascism expresses a widely shared anxiety – in some cases, a hope – of the period. At the same time, the novel is removed from ideology through its commitment to absurdity. West's manic concentration on Lemuel's weird adventures turns the story into a carnival of brutality. As in his two earlier novels, the lurid exhibitionism has a serious point: Lemuel's dismantling serves as emblem for the disintegration of America's mythic past, its assurances that virtue and effort are linked to prosperity.

The Day of the Locust, which completes West's tetralogy of disillusionment, incorporates a memorable sequence of images specifically intended to embody America's bankrupt past. The novel's central character is Todd Hackett, a Yale graduate and fledgling artist whose models include Goya, Daumier, Guardi, Desiderio: "painters of Decay and Mystery."[73] Todd has come to the West coast to find his subject matter: the glassy-eyed people who come to California from all over the country to die. The book's action leads to a twinned apocalypse, when a riot provoked by a movie premiere re-enacts Todd's prophetic painting, "The Burning of Los Angeles."

History has shrunk to the ersatz scenery and props that form the settings for Hollywood movies. As he walks across the back lot of a production studio, Todd moves from an ocean liner made of painted canvas, past a forty-foot papier-mâché sphinx, and pauses for a cigarette on the porch of the Last Chance saloon. From there he crosses a Romanesque courtyard, a Greek temple dedicated to Eros, the skeleton of a Zeppelin, the wooden horse of Troy, a Dutch windmill, and a Mayan temple. The climax of his journey, and of the book's symbolic diminishment of the past is a weedy, ten-acre field:

In the center of the field was a gigantic pile of sets, flats and props. While [Todd] watched, a ten-ton truck added another load to it. This was the final dumping

[73] Nathanael West, *The Day of the Locust* (New York: New Directions, 1962 [1933]), p. 132.

ground. He thought of Janvier's "Sargasso Sea." Just as that imaginary body of water was a history of civilization in the form of a marine junkyard, the studio lot was one in the form of a dream dump. A Sargasso of the imagination! (p. 132)

Playwrights made substantial contributions to the collective search for the past in the 1930s. The repressions of New England Puritanism also pervade Eugene O'Neill's *Mourning Becomes Electra*, which opened in New York in October 1931. O'Neill was already established as America's leading playwright – his first full-length play, *Beyond the Horizon* (1920), had earned the first of the three Pulitzer Prizes he received in his lifetime. (A fourth Pulitzer, for *Long Day's Journey Into Night* [completed 1941, first produced 1956], was posthumous.)

In *Mourning*, he was reaching for a new tragic amplitude; the play's three parts occupy six hours of stage time. Based on Aeschylus's *Oresteia* trilogy, *Mourning* takes place at the time of the Civil War. General Ezra Mannon plays the part of Agamemnon, who returns from battle to an unfaithful wife, Christine, who, like Clytemnestra, murders him so that she can marry her lover, Adam Brant, whose character is based on Aegisthus. In turn, Ezra's children, Lavinia and Orin (Electra and Orestes) murder Adam. Like their ancient predecessors, Christine and Orin commit suicide.[74]

Mourning is, as one of its best readers reminds us, "a history play."[75] In addition, O'Neill appropriated both the classic and American past as vehicles to explore his own family history. The fall of the House of Atreus and the catastrophically divided house of the American Civil War are pressed into service to commemorate the tragic story of the O'Neills. Lavinia, the sole survivor and the playwright's surrogate, declares at the end: "I'm not going the way Mother and Orin went. That's escaping punishment. And there's no one left to punish me. I'm the last Mannon. I've got to punish myself! Living alone here with the dead is a worse act of justice than death or prison . . . I'll live alone with the dead, and keep their secrets."[76] When his brother Jamie died in 1923, following the deaths of both his mother and father, Eugene had declared, "I'm the last of the O'Neills."[77] Like Lavinia, he spent the rest of his life remembering and grieving, turning

---

[74] Robert Turney's *Daughters of Atreus* (1936), which had a brief run on Broadway, also re-cycled Greek mythology, compressing almost the entire Agamemnon–Electra saga into a single play. Most critics found the three acts high-minded and dull.

[75] "The mixure of ancient and modern, Aeschylus and Freud, has tended to obscure [the important fact] that it is a history play, and an excellent one." Travis Bogard, *Contour in Time: The Plays of Eugene O'Neill* (New York: Oxford University Press, 1972), p. 342.

[76] Eugene O'Neill, *Mourning Becomes Electra* (New York: Horace Liveright, Inc., 1931), p. 256.

[77] See Arthur and Barbara Gelb, *O'Neill* (New York: Harper & Row, 1973 [1962]), pp. 721–724.

the pain of his losses into the finest plays America had yet produced: *Long Day*, and *The Iceman Cometh* (1939). O'Neill's self-lacerating immersion in the past was rooted in his complex personal needs rather than the political and social history of the 1930s. Nevertheless, his plays enriched the conversation between past and present that marked the decade.

O'Neill's epic exploration of the American and mythic past was only one of a large number of important historical dramas that reached the stage in the thirties, including T. S. Eliot's *Murder in the Cathedral* (1935), which dramatizes the assassination of Thomas à Becket in Canterbury Cathedral in 1170. Maxwell Anderson, one of the most versatile and prolific playwrights of the decade, wrote several plays that took British and American history for their settings. Anderson's first play, a verse drama called *White Desert* (1923) that tried to recreate the harsh winters of North Dakota that he had known as a child, was a failure. A year later, he teamed with Laurence Stallings on *What Price Glory?*, a bitter, darkly funny, and enormously successful indictment of the folly of war.

In the thirties, Anderson returned to verse and produced a remarkable series of plays. He wrote, among other work, two plays on Tudor England, *Elizabeth the Queen* (1930), and *Mary of Scotland* (1933), *Night Over Taos* (1932), a revisionist account of America's nineteenth-century conflict with Spain in the Southwest, *Both Your Houses* (1933), in prose, an exposé of American political corruption which won the Pulitzer Prize, and *Winterset* (1935), discussed elsewhere, a remarkably effective piece of poetic politics, loosely but unmistakably based on the case of Sacco and Vanzetti. Anderson's biographer, in a partisan but defensible judgment, concludes that "[j]ust as the 1920s in the American theater had belonged to Eugene O'Neill, so the 1930s belonged to Maxwell Anderson."[78]

Elizabeth and *Mary* both had considerable critical and commercial success.[79] There is no point in pressing for relevance or parallelism to explain the plays' popularity. Audiences were attracted, as they still are, by the sheer entertainment value of world historical figures arrayed in gorgeous period costumes and addressing each other in an updated and quite serviceable blank verse. Summarizing the consensus, Brenda Murphy calls *Elizabeth* "the first successful drama of the modern American theatre to be written in verse."[80] Featuring an exceptional performance by Lynn

---

[78] Alfred S. Shivers, *The Life of Maxwell Anderson* (New York: Stein and Day, 1983), p. xviii.
[79] Anderson wrote *Anne of the Thousand Days* (1948) as the third part of a Tudor trilogy.
[80] Brenda Murphy, "Plays and Playwrights: 1915–1945," in Don B. Wilmeth and Christopher Bigsby, eds., *The Cambridge History of American Theatre, Volume Two: 1870–1945* (New York: Cambridge University Press, 1999), p. 331.

Fontanne in the title role, *Elizabeth* played to full houses for its entire season. The play concentrates exclusively on the doomed love between Elizabeth and Essex, which creates numerous opportunities for splendid speeches on the competing demands of love and duty. In Anderson's version of her, the queen is uncommonly brave, wiser than her advisors, and quick enough to out-debate them, both in English and Latin. (*Elizabeth* is surely one of the few popular plays that includes a witty argument in Latin.)

The most prolific source of historical plays in the 1930s, perhaps surprisingly, was the Federal Theatre Project (FTP). Throughout the four years of its short life, from its founding in 1935 to its elimination in 1939, the FTP was a target of right-wing politicians and journalists, intent on ferreting out the project's allegedly subversive inclinations, including its commitment to hiring racial minorities as actors and playwrights. Martin Dies, the Texas Congressman who chaired the House Un-American Activities Committee, fulminated that "racial equality forms a vital part of the Communistic teachings and practices."[81]

It is certainly the case that some of the FTP's most famous productions declared their solidarity with the voices of dissent: *One Third of a Nation* (1937), *Triple-A Plowed Under* (1936), *It Can't Happen Here* (1936), based on Sinclair Lewis's novel of 1934, Marc Blitzstein's *The Cradle Will Rock* (1937), and much of the work of the Negro Theatre unit. However, co-existing with these offenses to patriotic piety, the FTP also commissioned a long series of plays in what FTP director Hallie Flanagan called "our American historical series."[82] The list included *The Ballad of Davy Crockett* (1938), by Hoffman Hayes, Frank Wells's *John Henry* (1937), and Paul Green's re-creation of the doomed Roanoke Island settlement, *The Lost Colony* (1937).

The Asian and European past also attracted American writers in the 1930s, most notably Pearl Buck, Hervey Allen, and Herbert Gorman. Buck's *The Good Earth* (1931), one of the bestselling novels of the decade, dramatizes rural life in China in the early years of the twentieth century: it provided a lesson in Chinese history for readers who knew little or nothing of that country. The popularity of the novel requires some comment. *The Good Earth* was the first American novel set in Asia to become a bestseller. Indeed, twenty publishers had rejected Buck's first

[81] Cited in Ronald Ross, "The Role of Blacks in the Federal Theatre, 1935–1939," *Journal of Negro History* (January, 1974), p. 43.
[82] Hallie Flanagan, "Introduction," *Federal Theatre Plays* (New York: Random House, 1938), p. x.

book in large part because the market for Chinese material was believed to be non-existent.[83] Within that framework, the outsized success of Pearl Buck's *The Good Earth* was particularly noteworthy. Hers was the first attempt to represent Chinese characters neither as idealized paragons of humanity nor as dangerous agents of the yellow peril, but simply as human beings, responding to their choices and troubles in recognizably human ways. Though her literary techniques were generally conventional, and even old-fashioned, her subject matter and the stance she took toward her material were close to revolutionary.

In some measure, the book succeeded because of its narrative pace, the excitement of its plot, and the verisimilitude of its setting. In addition, though it was set in the past and in Asia, Buck's novel bore a resemblance to contemporary American experience. Underneath its alien details, the novel is a story of the land, a familiar American genre. And the formula that depicts the struggles of farmers on their soil had a particular appeal to Americans in the Depression decade.

The Good Earth also intervened, inadvertently but effectively, in the domestic politics of the 1930s. By a coincidence of timing, the publication of the novel coincided with Japan's invasion of Chinese Manchuria. Though Americans had evinced little interest in any Asian country heretofore, turmoil in the region would become an increasingly unavoidable subject through the thirties.[84] Buck's portraits of China's common people did much to prepare isolationist Americans for their wartime alliance with the Chinese. Through the 1930s and 1940s, she would exert more influence over Western opinions about Asia than any other American.[85]

Before he wrote his stories of World War I, Hervey Allen had become, with the publication of *Anthony Adverse* (1933), one of the bestselling novelists of the first half of the twentieth century.[86] In 1,200 pages, with a

[83] An exception could be made for travesties and thrillers such as Sax Rohmer's Fu Manchu books, and the (Japanese) Mr. Moto series of John P. Marquand.
[84] Another sign of rising interest in China was the 1933 award of the prestigious Newberry Medal in children's literature to *Young Fu of the Upper Yangtze* by Elizabeth Lewis (Philadelphia: J. C. Winston, 1932).
[85] In the late 1950s, Harold Isaacs published *Scratches on Our Mind*, a pioneering survey of American attitudes toward the people of Asia. Isaacs asked a cross-section of Americans where their images and ideas came from, and discovered that "no single book about China has had a greater impact than . . . *The Good Earth*" (New York: The John Day Company, 1958), p. 155. Buck's only competitor was Henry R. Luce, founder and publisher of *Time* magazine, whose parents had also been Presbyterian missionaries in China.
[86] While sales figures are notoriously unreliable, literary historians have concluded that only *Gone With the Wind* outsold *Anthony Adverse* in the thirties, and that total sales of Allen's book make it one of the bestselling novels of the first several decades of the century. Stuart Knee, in his

plot that spans five decades and half a dozen countries on three continents, *Anthony Adverse* combines history, melodrama, exotic settings, romance, intrigue, scenes of unusually explicit sex, warfare and duels, a species of rhapsodic poetry, mysticism, and indefatigable narrative ingenuity. There were dissenters (the *Nation*'s review comprised an extended sneer), but the critical response was consistently enthusiastic, including frequent suggestions that Allen had produced the long-sought Great American Novel.[87]

Anthony is divided into three large volumes, each of which consists of three books. The novel moves at a stately, indeed a glacial, pace: three pages to describe a ship's rigging and furnishings, a page on New England cemeteries, another two or three for every meal, a page on the many kinds of sewing stitches, and so on. Every description is extended, and then extended further. For Allen, more is more. A hundred and more characters enter and exit. The pages are crowded with the sights and sounds and smells of impoverished hovels and great houses, festivals and religious processions, ice-covered mountains and tropical jungles, carriages and naval vessels. Throughout, there is a cascade of technical information that confers the glamor of fact on each fictional scene: the names of forty tropical flowers, the mathematics of navigation, the language of voodoo, the techniques of bullfighting, the architecture of a prison.

Commencing in 1775, the novel's first volume describes the title character's illegitimate birth, the son of a British officer and the wife of a Spanish nobleman, and his childhood as an orphan in an Italian convent. Slowly, the novel follows Anthony from youth through early manhood. He spends ten years in Livorno as a merchant's apprentice and eventual heir: in one of the novel's many improbable contrivances, the merchant, a Scot named John Bonnyfeather, turns out to be Anthony's grandfather.[88] When Napoleon approaches the city – "a tyrant who comes proclaiming liberty," in Bonnyfeather's opinion – the merchant closes his trading house and sends Anthony to Cuba on his first commercial expedition.[89]

---

biography *Hervey Allen (1889–1949): A Literary Historian in America* (Lewiston, NY: The Edwin Mellen Press, 1988), also documents the intensive and even revolutionary marketing campaign that supported the novel. The book was adapted as a Warner Brothers film (1936), directed by Mervyn LeRoy and starring Frederic March, Claude Rains, and Olivia de Havilland. The movie was nominated for four Academy Awards. Jack Warner, who bought the rights, reportedly said that he hadn't read the book, and added: "I can't even lift it."

[87] The *New York Times* declared that *Anthony Adverse*, which was "America's most original contribution to the great tradition of the picaresque novel," might well "become the best-loved book of our time." Peter Monroe Jack, "A Titanic Novel of Adventure," *New York Times Book Review* (June 25, 1933), p. 1.

[88] An earlier version of John Bonnyfeather appears in Allen's *Israfel*.

[89] Hervey Allen, *Anthony Adverse* (New York: Farrar and Rinehart, Inc., 1933), p. 297.

Anthony's sojourn in Cuba takes up the first half of Volume Two. Growing in skill and confidence, he masters the intricacies of international finance, soon becoming the most able businessman on the island. At the same time, his scruples gradually decay, a transformation that is sealed by his decision to become a slave trader, the most lucrative career available in the late eighteenth century. In the subsequent chapters of this second volume, the most chillingly sensational in the novel, Anthony takes up residence in Africa, personally managing the capture, imprisonment, and sale of thousands of black men, women, and children over the next several years. These pages lay out in harrowing detail the steps through which new slaves are stolen, brought to barracoons, stripped, examined, appraised, and chained. Anthony feeds them well, but only to improve their chances of survival on the slave ships, which in turn increases his profits. And the profits, as laid out in a historically accurate two-page ledger statement, are tremendous.

Anthony's moral adversary throughout this portion of the book is a saintly Catholic missionary, Brother François, who loathes slavery, risks his life continuously to aid the slaves, and warns Anthony that the trade will cost him his soul. The opposition between the two men is the allegorical fulcrum on which the contest over values is tested. François also threatens the authority of the local witch doctor, who ultimately retaliates by having the missionary crucified on a jungle hilltop.

François's death marks a turning point for Anthony, who gives up the trade (though not the money it has brought) and returns to Europe. The third volume of the novel traces his moral reclamation, which takes place in tiny increments over the book's last 500 pages. Initially, Anthony agrees to immerse himself in the financing of the Napoleonic wars; his business partners include the rising banker, Nathan Rothschild. When these various schemes grow into the "largest commercial operation of modern times" (p. 922), Anthony moves to New Orleans to supervise the shipment of silver from Mexico to bankers in Paris and Amsterdam. Motivated as much by the risks and adventure as by greed, Anthony piles up an immense fortune, builds a plantation – staffed by several hundred slaves – and retires to a kind of peace. When a fire consumes his house, killing his wife and child, he sees an act of divine retribution, and from that point on embraces asceticism and self-sacrifice.

The unprecedented success *Anthony Adverse* enjoyed had several sources. To begin with, Allen incorporates just about every cliché of the ripping yarn: impossible coincidences, hairbreadth escapes, exotic settings, passages of overheated romance. In the course of his travels,

Anthony barely escapes from an African crocodile by climbing a tree; he is attacked by a one-eyed pirate who actually throws a knife that pins Anthony's sleeve to a wall; he is pursued for over two decades by a theatrically malignant villain, Don Luis da Vitata (the cuckolded husband of Anthony's mother, who has murdered Anthony's father in revenge); he wins a lethal stagecoach duel high in the Alps; and much, much more. The intermixture of major historical figures – Napoleon, Rothschild, the Spanish Prince of the Peace, the first American Governor of Louisiana – lends a veneer of authenticity to the proceedings.[90]

Beyond the color and non-stop action, the novel also offered its Depression-era readers the pleasure of vicarious financial success. Indeed, though Anthony takes several lovers and is twice married, the romance of money lies at the center of the story. At a time of crisis, when effort had become decoupled from prosperity and financial ruin had become a commonplace, Anthony ratified assumptions about the power of individualism. He is an orphan who grew up in poverty: "If he did not know who he was he must go out and become somebody" (p. 300).

At the same time, Anthony's eventual growth out of materialism allowed readers to experience both the excitement of accumulation and the moral reassurance of renunciation. Specifically, Anthony becomes an increasingly spiritual person, and his evolution spoke to the deeply felt religious aspirations that have always defined the identities of Americans. Throughout the novel, Anthony carries a small Madonna, the only legacy of his unknown mother. Sometimes forgotten, occasionally damaged, the statuette stands as a symbol of the spiritual alternative Anthony seeks. Allen himself described the novel as an "accessible allegory," intended as a "protest against the futility of materialistic civilization."[91]

Anthony Adverse proved to be Allen's single major success. Attracted to the Civil War by his desire to find a "big" subject, something on the epic scale of *Anthony Adverse*, Allen published *Action at Aquila* (1938). The book

[90] Allen's research into social and political history was impressive, and he defended his scholarship in several publications, most extensively in an essay in the *Saturday Review of Literature* (January 13, 1934), in which he itemized several dozen primary and secondary sources and referred to scores of others. "For the Spanish section alone," Allen wrote, in connection with a relatively small portion of the novel, "I read fifty or sixty books dealing with Charles V" (p. 409). Nonetheless, he routinely invented fictitious versions of historical events in the service of his narrative. He re-arranged the dates of several Napoleonic battles, for example; and the scheme in which he involves Nathan Rothschild has no basis in fact. See Niall Ferguson's magisterial two-volume history, *The House of Rothschild* (New York: The Viking Press, 1998).

[91] From a letter of Hervey Allen to John Farrar, cited in Stuart E. Knee, *Hervey Allen, 1889–1949: A Literary Historian in America* (Lewiston, NY: The Edwin Mellen Press, 1988), p. 241.

recycles a good many conventional gestures and events from Civil War romances, including the marriage of the Yankee officer, Colonel Nathaniel Franklin, and the Southern belle. In a kind of coda, set in 1898, the elderly and dying colonel watches troops marching off to yet another war. Thinking back on his father's soldiering in the Mexican War, his own fighting in the Civil War, and the new campaign against the Spanish, Allen shifts from patriotism to a meditation on the futility of war. Standing on the steps of Philadelphia's Union League, Franklin takes the salute of the men marching off to battle – men who were "glad they had been called out. It was an adventure. They were tired of their jobs. They were the center of attention." The colonel "leaned on his crutch, sick in mind, body, and soul."[92]

Allen's absorption in the religious dimension of human experience found a counterpart in another of the bestselling historical novels of the 1930s, Willa Cather's *Shadows on the Rock* (1931). Shaken by her father's recent death, Cather found in seventeenth-century Quebec an opportunity to explore both father–daughter relations and the centrality of faith. The novel recounts a year in the life of a devout Catholic girl, twelve-year-old Cecile Auclair, and her father, an apothecary in the service of the French crown. Although it has been "one of Cather's least discussed novels," *Shadows* exhibits many of her characteristic themes and strengths.[93] The descriptions of the harsh Canadian landscape, the evocation of domestic life, and the illumination of the power that custom and tradition exert even over the lives of the very young are among Cather's accomplishments in the novel. In one of her own comments on the book, Cather referred to early Quebec as a place where one found "the curious endurance of a kind of culture, narrow but definite."[94] Aware of its narrowness, she was nonetheless attracted to that culture because it illustrated the strength of the past, and provided the framework within which individuals might find a nurturing solidarity.

The prolific Herbert Gorman, whose war novel, *Suzy*, was discussed earlier, had a particular interest in French culture and history. He published a biography of Alexandre Dumas, *père* (1929), and an introduction to Cami's *The Son of the Three Musketeers* (1930).[95] Jonathan Bishop (1933)

[92] Hervey Allen, *Action at Aquila* (New York: Farrar & Rinehart, 1938), p. 359.
[93] Ann Romines, "After the Christmas Tree: Willa Cather and Domestic Ritual," *American Literature* (March, 1988), p. 62.
[94] Cited in *ibid.*, p. 71.
[95] The bulk of Mark Longaker's study, *Contemporary Biography* (Philadelphia: University of Pennsylvania Press, 1934), deals with British writing. In the final chapter, a survey of American writers, Longaker devotes several pages (pp. 226–232) to Herbert Gorman's biographies.

tells the story of the Franco-Prussian War of 1870 and the Communard Rising of 1871 through the eyes of the title character, a young American living in Paris. Jonathan is professedly apolitical, but his sympathies lie with the French in their battle with Prussia, and with the established order during the Rising. The novel is an eloquent defense of established orders, American as well as European, a counter-statement to the revolutionary texts of the 1930s that preached the need for fundamental and even violent change.

Through a carefully plotted irony, Jonathan is impressed into service by the Communards when he is captured with only the identity papers of a young Frenchman, killed in the Battle of Sedan, whom he had befriended and whose papers he has carried as a mark of respect. His involuntary service, and his intimate contact with the revolutionaries, confers authority on his skeptical evaluation. "I have lost my faith in demagogues and prophets of Utopia," he remarks at one point.[96] Gorman skillfully evokes the furious destruction that the Communards inflict on the people and buildings of Paris. Jonathan reflects on these vivid scenes of riot and murder, and repudiates any millennial scheme that justifies destruction by appeal to an imaginary better world: "[t]his impossible idea of saving the world, this childish dream of the future, this restless concern about the equality of man . . . this *sentimentalization* of the proletariat, all these messianic urges left him cold and unresponsive" (p. 305).

As in all Gorman's fiction, the governing principle at work in *Jonathan Bishop* is loyalty to the past and its traditions: "Man was afraid of his history and sought to flee from it, to bury it . . . to forget it, and yet it was by that history that Man lived and knew himself" (p. 371). Though the Commune is ultimately crushed, the novel's final tone is far more bitter than celebratory: violence has been met with greater violence, continuing a resistless cycle of blood. Toward the end of the novel, Jonathan arrives at a stasis of despair: "the gods had withdrawn themselves forever from . . . this meaningless savagery, this mutual destruction of puny anatomies, this malignant and widespread cancer called Man" (p. 406).

In the book's final episode, Jonathan, attempting to escape from his captivity, is mistaken for a Communard and killed. Because he is still carrying the Frenchman's papers, even the identity of his corpse is mistaken. Jonathan Bishop has simply disappeared into the reigning chaos. His inadvertent and utterly pointless death, and the accidental name

---

[96] Herbert Gorman, *Jonathan Bishop: A Novel* (New York: Farrar & Rinehart, 1933), p. 298.

under which he is buried, comprise a grimly appropriate emblem for a world emptied of significance.

The Mountain and the Plain (1936) is a lavish and sprawling, 700-page historical romance set in the first few years of the French Revolution. Probably Gorman's most important novel, at least one reviewer calling it a masterpiece, *The Mountain and the Plain* is encyclopedic in its command of details.[97] Gorman dedicated the book to G. Lenotre, the pen name of Louis Gosselin, a major historian of the Revolution, whose work provided the novel's principal scholarly foundation.[98] One of the book's considerable strengths lies in Gorman's virtuoso reconstruction of the sights and sounds of late-eighteenth-century France: a panorama that encompasses every variety of food and drink, all manner of clothing, every class and trade. *The Mountain and the Plain* interweaves historical facts with a fictional adventure plot.[99] A large cast of invented characters share the pages with skillfully rendered portraits of the Revolution's leading figures: Mirabeau, Danton, Marat, Robespierre, Louis XVI, and many others. Reconstructing the years from 1789 to 1794, the novel follows events from the fall of the Bastille through the failures of the constitutional monarchy, the Terror, and the execution of Robespierre. Napoleon makes a brief cameo appearance late in the book, but only as an able, still obscure soldier.

The novel's main character is a young American merchant named David Livingstone, who more or less stands as surrogate for the reader: a curious, open-minded outsider for whom the momentous events of the time comprise an education in political reality. David is initially sympathetic to the aspirations of the Revolution, seeing in them a kinship to the establishment of a republic in his own country. A fire-breathing Tom Paine instructs David in the gross injustices that have defined the Old

---

[97] Olga Owens, "Echoes from the French Revolution," *Boston Evening Transcript* (August 15, 1936), p. 1. Critic Albert Guerard, Sr., compared Gorman's novel favorably with *Anthony Adverse*. "Gorman Surveys the French Revolution," *New York Herald Tribune Books* (August 16, 1936), p. 3.

[98] Not well known today among historians of the Revolution, Lenotre was the author of over thirty books, many of them translated into English. Those translations, and his election to the French Academy just before his death, testify to his considerable prominence. A comparison with standard sources of the 1930s confirms that Gorman worked hard to get his facts straight. See, for example, Leo Gershoy, *The French Revolution, 1789–1799* (New York: Holt, Rinehart and Winston, 1932), and Crane Brinton, *A Decade of Revolution, 1789–1799* (New York: Harper & Brothers, 1934). Brinton summarily described the French Revolution as "fatally mad" (p. 13).

[99] The novel's title is taken from the metaphorical shorthand of the Revolution's politics. The deputies to the National Convention of 1792 divided themselves into the Jacobins on the Left, who occupied high seats called the Mountain, the Girondins on the Right, and the majority of delegates occupying the Center, or the Plain.

Regime and have reduced the mass of its citizenry to poverty and rage. The Revolution's most eloquent foreign ally, Paine tells David that anywhere in the countryside he will see "the dried-out bodies hanging in chains from the King's gibbets – eternal warnings to whoso might protest against this iniquitous state of affairs... [and] a whole people trodden into the mud like starving pigs rooting for acorns while an exempted class, brave in laces and furbelows, drives over them in painted coaches."[100]

The evils of the old order are manifest and undeniable; reform is long overdue. The novel emphasizes the weaknesses of the monarchy in its cruelly funny portrayal of the king. Louis is a slow-witted, self-indulgent, weak-willed, overweight, unattractive emblem of his own corrupt rule. His most distinguishing features are his moist hands and his hanging underlip; his consistent failures of insight and nerve inadvertently collaborate with his enemies, and ensure his undoing. Gorman accords Louis a single moment of dignity, when he goes to the scaffold. Otherwise he is an apt representative of a flyblown system.

In short, the Revolutionaries initially have justice on their side. However, even Paine eventually concludes that the realities of the Revolution, with its relentless decline into the barbarism of the Terror, are worse than what it has replaced. As a punishment for his growing insight and moderation, Paine himself, who had been lionized by the National Assembly, is condemned to a year in prison, and escapes execution by a hair. If his death sentence had been carried out, he would have joined 20,000 other men and women who went to the guillotine, most of them after hasty show trials that condemned their victims with or without proof.

In addition to its historical judgments, *The Mountain and the Plain* offers a conservative intervention into the politics of contemporary America. Gorman began writing *The Mountain* in January 1935 – less than two years after the inauguration of Franklin Roosevelt, at a time when the US economic and political crisis continued to deepen. Indicators such as unemployment and the stock markets had responded only feebly to the palliatives of the New Deal. A number of radical alternatives, from both right and left, seemed to be gaining momentum.

The Mountain and the Plain proclaims an uncompromising warning against revolution. Conditions in late-eighteenth-century France were incalculably more grievous for common people than those in Depression America, and a violent uprising was more understandable. Even in France, however, revolutionary upheavals led to a bloody interlude of

---

[100] Herbert Gorman, *The Mountain and the Plain* (New York: Farrar & Rinehart, 1936), p. 81.

inflamed ideologies and mob rule. In Gorman's view, even a bad status quo is preferable to "the growling waves of anarchy" and "politico-religious hysteria" into which violent revolutions inevitably collapse (pp. 264, 310).[101]

The 1930s were marked by an upsurge of interest in all things Mexican. The Museum of Modern Art staged two major exhibitions of Mexican art, and Macy's joined in with heavily advertised sales of Mexican crafts and clothing. The Mexican muralists Diego Rivera, Jose Orozco, and David Siqueiros exerted a widespread influence on North American artists; Katherine Anne Porter made her reputation with "Flowering Judas" (1930) and other stories of Mexico. Composers were also influenced by Mexican music. Aaron Copland completed the suite *El Salon Mexico* in 1936.[102] The prolific economist Stuart Chase published *Mexico: A Study of Two Americas* in 1931, whose central thesis was a warning against the influence of machinery. North America had created a machine-made society, which offered material advantages, but had paid heavily in the insults inflicted on both landscape and resources. Mexicans, on the contrary, lived in less affluent circumstances, but were sustained and even ennobled by living "an organic life."[103]

In 1932, Archibald MacLeish turned to Mexican history for the subject of *Conquistador*, a long narrative poem that takes the Spanish conquest of Mexico as its subject. MacLeish freely adapted the story from Bernal Diaz del Castillo's *True History of the Conquest of New Spain*. The poem is written in a flexible terza rima that replaces end rhymes with shifting patterns of related vowel sounds. The verse form recalls Dante, from whose *Inferno* the poem's epigraph is taken; in addition, MacLeish

---

[101] During the Depression years, the biographer and short story writer Meade Minnigerode was also attracted to the French Revolution. Along with a non-fiction survey of French experience in the 1790s, *The Magnificent Comedy* (1931), Minnigerode published two biographies, *The Son of Marie Antoinette* (1934) and *Marie Antoinette's Henchman: the Career of Jean, Baron de Batz in the French Revolution* (1936). Unlike Gorman, who insisted on the contemporary political relevance of his historical fiction, Minnigerode used the events of the Revolution exclusively for their romantic possibilities. Rapiers are keen, bodices are ripped, escapes are hairbreadth, and glamor breathes over all.

[102] More generally, by "the midthirties, Latin rhythms had insinuated their way into Tin Pan Alley and Hollywood." George Gershwin wrote his "Cuban Overture" in 1932, and Vincent Youmans included a samba and a tango in his music for the film, *Flying Down to Rio* (1933). See Wilfrid Sheed, *The House That George Built: With a Little Help from Irving, Cole, and Crew of About Fifty* (New York: Random House, 2007), p. 66.

[103] Stuart Chase, *Mexico: A Study of Two Americas* (New York: Macmillan, 1931), p. 205. The book is illustrated with several dozen line drawings by Diego Rivera.

employs an abundant alliteration, homage to Anglo-Saxon prosody and another declaration of the poem's epic intentions.[104]

In the preface, Diaz, a soldier who had served under Cortez, identifies himself as an old man, one of the few survivors of the invasion. He represents the common soldiers, the men who suffered and died and have been written out of history by the aristocrats and priests who have authored the official chronicles. Diaz complains about the "school-taught" professors, writing in "pompous Latin," who know none of the facts and merely celebrate "the big names."[105] In a notebook entry, MacLeish commented that Diaz "is against the heroes... He knows. He is trying to give the lowdown."[106] Glory has gone to the leaders while the soldiers ended up as food for tigers and serpents. In Dias, MacLeish found a prototype of the "forgotten man" so often invoked by the politicians of the thirties.

The body of the poem comprises fifteen short books, in which Diaz re-creates the deprivations and dangers the Spaniards faced on the long expedition through the Central American mountains, the bloody battles they fought against the native people, and their eventual victory over Montezuma. The Spanish soldiers become weary with their efficient slaughter: "Our hands were lame with the sword when the thing was done" (p. 79). The "place smelled... of hunger and / Sick men's nights and of death" (p. 102). Along with their experiences, Diaz conveys the shifting emotions that he and his fellow soldiers felt, their anxiety, curiosity, and fear, and ultimately their unrepentant satisfaction in the victory they have won for King and Cross:

> And we laid them a Christian siege with the sun and the vultures:
> And they kept us ninety and three days till they died of it:
> And the whole action was well conceived and conducted... (p. 113)

Though MacLeish himself did not encourage allegorical interpretations of the poem, for many readers the Spanish triumph over the Aztecs becomes an emblem of the complex fate of white European engagement in the New World. History teaches a lesson in the rapacity of conquest, a subject that would become increasingly relevant as the thirties slouched toward global war.

---

[104] "'O frati,' dissi, 'che per cento milia / Perigli siete giunti all'occidente'"; the lines, from Canto XXVI, can be translated: "'Brothers,' I said, 'who through a hundred thousand / Dangers have reached the west...'"
[105] Archibald MacLeish, *Conquistador* (Boston: Houghton Mifflin Company, 1932), pp. 9–10.
[106] Cited in Scott Donaldson, in collaboration with R. H. Winnick, *Archibald MacLeish: An American Life* (Boston: Houghton Mifflin Company, 1992), p. 216.

CHAPTER 4

Backward glances: Biography and autobiography

According to scholar Mark Longaker, writing in 1934:

Biography has become one of our most popular literary forms . . . Men who read little else read Lives . . . [I]f the torrent of Lives continues to fall upon us, a Commissioner of Biography should be appointed in Washington, who, with a large staff of assistants, would issue permits only to those who have more than a nimble pen, and who have a subject which has not been treated more than ten times during the year. Heavy fees would accompany the granting of a license to write about Washington, Lincoln, Napoleon or any of Queen Victoria's prime ministers.[1]

The humor is labored, but Longaker's point is well taken. The Depression decade was an immensely productive biographical and auto-biographical period. Looking over the decade, Alfred Kazin concluded: "Never were so many biographies written."[2] For a single reference point: most of the twenty volumes of the *Dictionary of American Biography*, dedicated to the impossible task of recording those who had made "a significant contribution" to the nation's history, appeared in the 1930s. Political biographies were in particular vogue. Aside from biographies of William James and Harvard President Charles W. Eliot, and along with studies of Benjamin Franklin and Andrew Jackson, discussed below, the decade's Pulitzer Prize-winning books included lives of Theodore Roosevelt (1932), Grover Cleveland (1933), Robert E. Lee (1935), and Hamilton Fish (1937).

Not surprisingly, a cluster of Founding Fathers and early Presidents provided subjects for several large and conspicuously successful bio-graphies that appeared across the thirties. These early statesmen had always been subject to much biographical writing: the first more or less scholarly

---

[1] Mark Longaker, *Contemporary Biography* (Philadelphia: University of Pennsylvania Press, 1934), pp. 3–4.
[2] Alfred Kazin, "What Have the 30's Done to Our Literature," *New York Herald Tribune Books* (December 31, 1939), p. 1.

biography published in the USA was Jared Sparks's twelve-volume *Life of George Washington* (1834–1837). By 1930, several hundred books and pamphlets had been published on Washington's life. The 200th anniversary of the first President's birth, which was marked in early 1932, provoked an especially vigorous outpouring of attention.

Congress established a George Washington Bicentennial Commission; quite a few states also set up committees. Collectively, they were responsible for such projects as a compendium of "Pageants and plays depicting the life of George Washington and his time," intended for use by "educational, patriotic, religious, social, civic, fraternal, and dramatic organizations" (a pamphlet published by the Government Printing Office in 1931), and "Sermons on George Washington," a compendium of thirty-four sermons, specially prepared by ministers of various denominations in different sections of the United States (1932). Books appeared describing Washington's views on education, naval strategy, cartography, religious liberty, "the Negro," and the West. August Thomas provided a four-act play, *Colonel George of Mount Vernon* (1931). The American Society of Landscape Architects published *Colonial Gardens: the Landscape Architecture of George Washington's Time* (1932). John C. Fitzgerald edited the multi-volume *Writings of Washington* (the first of several volumes appeared in 1932), the most complete and accurate transcription of Washington texts to date.

Benjamin Franklin had long been a favorite subject for historians and biographers: he was the most down-to-earth of the Founders, the man in the leather apron who had earned his money with his hands and brain. In the "Preface" to his enormous biography of Franklin (1938), Carl Van Doren wearily points at the "many volumes [that] have been written on many periods and phases of [Franklin's] career, and countless special studies." In the previous twenty years, says Van Doren, "a Franklin science" has grown up.[3]

Even before his death, Franklin had achieved symbolic status as the representative American man – an identification he continues to enjoy.[4] His own best publicist, Franklin himself had set the terms of that

[3] Carl Van Doren, *Benjamin Franklin* (New York: The Viking Press, 1938), pp. v, viii.
[4] The Franklin industry continues apace, energized recently by the 2006 tercentenary of his birth. As the titles of several of the most popular new biographies indicate, the symbolic link between Franklin and the American character remains robust. See, for just a few examples: H. W. Brands, *The First American: the Life and Times of Benjamin Franklin* (2000); Walter Isaacson, *Benjamin Franklin: an American Life* (2003); Gordon S. Wood, *The Americanization of Benjamin Franklin* (2004), and Joyce E. Chaplin, *The First Scientific American: Benjamin Franklin and the Pursuit of Genius* (2006).

connection in his own writing. In the *Autobiography*, and in many other writings, he carefully portrayed himself as a plain-speaking, honest, industrious, and generous man. Above all, he seems eminently accessible and approachable: less formidable than the other Founders, less distant, and – very important – gifted with a wonderful sense of humor. Through his life and writing, Franklin helped to invent the gestures and vocabulary that have defined the American character, these qualities – for better and worse – that would come to be associated with the inhabitants of the new American nation: hard work, thrift, pragmatism, and an unshakeable belief that merit, rather than a privileged birth, should lead to advancement. He was, in short, just the sort of person many of his readers would like to be. Especially in the Depression, a crisis that challenged many of the assumptions in which Franklin's legend was anchored, readers demonstrated a considerable appetite for the re-affirmation of those traditional ideas.

Van Doren enlists himself without reservation on Franklin's side. His biography is a sustained tribute to its subject's wisdom, generosity, and uncommon common sense. Of his intellectual curiosity: Franklin was "the most insatiable and acquisitive" mind in America (p. 11); he was "more curious than ordinary men and followed up what they only looked at" and was "magnificent in outlook" (pp. 181–182). Of his physical stamina: Franklin "had as happy a constitution as any in the world" (p. 281); he was "an ageless man with ageless energy" (p. 435). He was modest and was "not ambitious" (pp. 172–173). That last remark is manifestly wrong-headed, but the others are plausible – Franklin was an extraordinary man, D. H. Lawrence's derision notwithstanding.[5]

In other words, Van Doren's partisanship is defensible, but it also reflects his method. This portrait is constructed out of long quotations taken verbatim from Franklin's published and unpublished writing, the letters, essays, and journalism, as well as the *Autobiography*. Van Doren's reliance on Franklin's prose conferred a signal advantage: only Lincoln among American statesmen wrote as well.

Lincoln was also the subject of a huge and landmark biography in the thirties. Near the end of the decade, Alfred Kazin spoke of the nation's "passionate addiction to Lincoln" ("What Have the 30's Done," p. 1). Carl Sandburg had published a two-volume life of Lincoln, *The Prairie*

---

[5] In Lawrence's opinion, Franklin was a "dry, moral, utilitarian little democrat," and a "virtuous... automaton." He added, somewhat redundantly: "I do not like him." *Studies in Classic American Literature* (New York: Thomas Seltzer, 1923), pp. 31, 23, 20.

Years, in 1926. Just over ten years later, he completed the biography with four volumes under the collective title, *The War Years* (1939). The book won the Pulitzer Prize and, despite its 2,500 pages, sold well and steadily for many years. For many readers, Sandburg's *Lincoln* became the definitive portrait.

Sandburg was already a celebrated poet by the time his biography appeared. Prominent among the writers who created the "Chicago Renaissance" in the early years of the century, Sandburg was celebrated as Whitman's heir by those who admired his work, and derided as a sentimental windbag by those who didn't. He considered himself a populist in his verse and a socialist in his politics. He canvassed for Eugene V. Debs in the 1908 presidential campaign, and worked with Jack London on the *International Socialist Review*. In the 1930s, his views would move center-ward: he put his considerable reputation at Franklin Roosevelt's service in all of his campaigns.

Sandburg's first successful book, *Chicago Poems* – "hog butcher for the world . . . city of the big shoulders," and so on – had appeared in 1916. He published his most popular book of poetry, *The People, Yes*, in 1936. A sequence of over a hundred versified anecdotes, political lectures, tall tales, and moralizing fables, *The People* is punctuated with invocations to "the family of man"[6] and portentous tributes to the plain people whom Sandburg revered:

> In the people is the eternal child,
> the wandering gypsy, the pioneer homeseeker,
> the singer of home sweet home . . .
> Who else speaks for the Family of Man?
> They are in tune and step
> with constellations of universal law . . .
>
> Man is a long time coming.
> Man will yet win.
> Brother may yet line up with brother . . .[7]

Sandburg's life of Lincoln appeared in the midst of a nearly manic season of biographical interest in the sixteenth President. Historian Merrill Peterson has described "[t]he unprecedented abundance of books about Lincoln" that were published "in the years between 1926 and 1933

---

[6] Two decades later, Sandburg wrote the Prologue for *The Family of Man* (1955), the catalogue for his brother-in-law Edward Steichen's exhibition of 500 photographs from nearly seventy countries.
[7] Carl Sandburg, *The People, Yes* (New York: Harcourt, Brace and Company, 1936), p. 129.

[which] included not only a number of biographies but historical fiction, juvenilia, poetry, special studies such as Lloyd Lewis's *Myths After Lincoln*...and a spate of books on Mary Todd Lincoln."[8] Lives of Lincoln continued to appear through the rest of the decade: illustrated books, books for children, even a 500-page book purporting to expose Edwin Stanton's role in the assassination.[9] A very few of the writers dissented from the received hagiographical wisdom. In *Lincoln the Man* (1931), perhaps the most notable example, Edgar Lee Masters blamed Lincoln for destroying the democracy that Jefferson had helped to invent, and for being an ignorant lout into the bargain.

For Carl Sandburg, on the contrary, no one had better epitomized the virtues of democracy and the common man than Lincoln. Indeed, the facts of Lincoln's life become in Sandburg's account of them the symbols of America's distinctive qualities. At the same time, those "facts" are everywhere hostage to Sandburg's mythmaking inclinations. Feeling a bond of likeness with his subject that reached beyond loyalty, Sandburg never hesitates to invent what is needful to embellish and elaborate his heroic vision of Lincoln. A rhapsodic rhetoric, sometimes soaring and sometimes congealing into treacle, attends every step of Lincoln's journey. Chosen almost literally at random, here is a sketch of young Abe: "in the spring of 1831, Abraham Lincoln, 22 years old, floated down the Sangamon River [in a canoe], going to a new home, laughter and youth in his bones, in his heart a few pennies of dreams, in his head a rag bag of thoughts he could never expect to sell."[10] Who could resist such a man?

A few years later, Lincoln has begun to assume the sacerdotal role Sandburg wants him to play. A wall of mysterious difference separates him from his fellows. Sandburg quotes with approval the impression that Whitman gave of the paradox of Lincoln's elusive accessibility: "his look, though abstracted, happen'd to be directed steadily in my eye...None of the artists have caught the deep, the subtle and indirect expression of this man's face. They have only caught the surface. There is something else

[8] Merrill D. Peterson, *Lincoln in American Memory* (New York: Oxford University Press, 1994), p. 285. Sandburg himself produced one of the books about Lincoln's wife, *Mary Lincoln: Wife and Widow* (1932). In the same year, Dale Carnegie published a slender saint's life called *Lincoln the Unknown*. A few years later, Carnegie distilled what he thought he had learned from Lincoln and other successful men into one of the bestselling books of the twentieth century, *How to Win Friends and Influence People* (1936).
[9] Otto Eisenschiml, *Why Was Lincoln Murdered?* (Boston: Little, Brown, and Company, 1937).
[10] Carl Sandburg, *Abraham Lincoln: The Prairie Years*, Vol. 1 (New York: Harcourt, Brace and Company, 1926), p. 132.

there."[11] Though he was adept at mingling and persuading, he was also a seeker, a man whose humor concealed a melancholy gravity that bespoke intimacy with the limits of mortality. On the eve of his election, Sandburg prophesies that Lincoln would "be one of God's miracles, he would be one of the storm-stars lighting the history of the world" (*War Years*, vol. II, p. 357).

Above all, Lincoln merges with America itself: "America had at last a President who was All-American. He embodied his country . . . The inventive Yankee, the Western frontiersman and pioneer, the Kentuckian of laughter and dreams, had found blend in one man who was the national head." Lincoln embodies the nation, and he carries all of it "in his breast." It is a proposition that Sandburg documents rhetorically, itemizing the regions of the country in a catalogue that recalls his poetic chants: "Cape Cod, the Shenandoah, the Mississippi, the Gulf, the Rocky Mountains, the Sacramento, the Great Plains, the Great Lakes, their dialects and shibboleths. He must be instinct with the regions of corn, textile mills, cotton, tobacco, gold, coal, zinc, iron. He would be written as a Father of his people . . ." Ordinary citizens began to understand that "Lincoln might be leading them toward something greater than they could have believed might come true" (*War Years*, vol. II, p. 332).

Not surprisingly, Sandburg treats Lincoln's assassination as tantamount to deicide. The chapter in which he tells the story is called "Blood on the Moon," and it has a quotation from the Book of Revelation for its epigraph: "And I looked, and behold a pale horse: and his name that sat on him was Death" (*War Years*, vol. IV, p. 272). In the course of the exposition, proper names are subsumed in allegory: John Wilkes Booth becomes The Outsider and The Stranger, Lincoln is transformed first into the Human Target and then the Friend of Man.

Professional historians, stung equally by Sandburg's slippery devices and his phenomenal success, found much to criticize.[12] But academic commentary paled beside Edmund Wilson's ferocious attacks. After condemning Sandburg's sentimentality and slapdash scholarship, Wilson memorably concluded that "[t]he cruelest thing that has happened to Lincoln since he was shot by Booth has been to fall into the hands of Carl Sandburg."[13]

---

[11] Carl Sandburg, *Abraham Lincoln: The War Years*, vol. II (New York: Harcourt, Brace and Company, 1939), p. 276.

[12] For a balanced estimate of Sandburg's strengths and weaknesses, see Jim Cullen, *The Civil War in Popular Culture: A Reusable Past* (Washington, DC: Smithsonian Institution Press, 1995), pp. 31–49.

[13] Edmund Wilson, *Patriotic Gore: Studies in the Literature of the American Civil War* (New York: Oxford University Press, 1962), p. 115.

Some years later, Gore Vidal acidulously labeled Sandburg "a biographer of awesome badness."[14]

Robert Sherwood's *Abe Lincoln in Illinois* (1938) was also inspired by a lifetime of reverence for its subject, but it was catalyzed by Sandburg's *Prairie Years*. By the time he wrote *Abe Lincoln*, Sherwood had a long and successful theatrical career behind him: a dozen Broadway productions, including *Reunion in Vienna* (1931), *Idiot's Delight* (1935), and *The Petrified Forest* (1936), which won the Pulitzer Prize for Drama. He was also an active screenwriter, eventually producing over twenty credited scripts. *Abe Lincoln* comprises a series of twelve episodes, connected by chronology and by Lincoln's emerging personality.

Sherwood's portrait of the President is worshipful; in a comment quoted by one of his biographers, he referred to Lincoln's "fundamental, unshakeable nobility," and said that "in his living words are the answers – or the only conceivable answers – to all the questions that distract the world today."[15] *Abe Lincoln* was written with Raymond Massey in mind, and his masterful performance contributed to the play's commercial and critical success, which included the Pulitzer Prize for Drama. In 1940, the play was turned into a superb movie, with Massey once again taking the leading role and Ruth Gordon creating an unforgettable portrait of Mary Todd.[16] The success of both play and film, as several critics noted, had something to do with its propitious timing: once again the nation stood on the brink of an unwanted but inevitable war, with the future in the balance. Lincoln's strength and purpose provided a model of reassurance for a nervous population.

The 1930s included a number of other theatrical tributes to the sixteenth President, including a short-lived play about John Wilkes Booth, *The Man Who Killed Lincoln*, dramatized by Elmer Harris from a book by Philip Van Doren Stern, in the 1939–1940 season. E. P. Conkle's *Prologue to Glory* (1938), a production of the Federal Theatre Project, dramatized Lincoln's early years, in New Salem.[17]

---

[14] Gore Vidal, "A Note on Abraham Lincoln," in *The Second American Revolution and Other Essays* (New York: Random House, 1982), p. 273.

[15] John Mason Brown, *The Worlds of Robert Sherwood: Mirror to His Times, 1896–1939* (New York: Harper & Row, 1962), p. 370.

[16] Just a few months earlier, John Ford directed Henry Fonda in *Young Mr. Lincoln*, a frothy and somewhat confused confection of comic episodes punctuated by portents of greatness and tragedy. The concluding dissolve, to Daniel Chester French's statue at the Lincoln Memorial, tries unconvincingly to establish a final tone of solemnity.

[17] The many Hollywood tributes to Lincoln addressed every dimension of his story. To give one example, John Ford's *Prisoner of Shark Island* (1936) offered a quasi-factual account of Dr. Samuel Mudd's imprisonment for the "crime" of setting John Wilkes Booth's broken leg.

Allan Nevins and Marquis James shared a remarkable distinction: each published two biographies in the 1930s, both of which won Pulitzer Prizes. Nevins was honored for his books on Grover Cleveland, one of only two Democratic Presidents between Lincoln and Franklin Roosevelt, and Hamilton Fish, who had served as Secretary of State in the administration of Ulysses Grant. In both books, Nevins attempted to renovate the reputations of political figures whom he thought had been neglected or undervalued. The subtitle of the Cleveland biography correctly indicates its tone: *A Study in Courage*. And the Fish book, subtitled *The Inner History of the Grant Administration*, depends principally on Fish's own diaries and letters, consequently elevating Fish at the expense of the other members of Grant's ill-equipped and in some cases corrupt cabinet. Neither Cleveland nor Fish was a "common man," to invoke a phrase much used in the 1930s, but their elevation by Nevins served as a kind of analogy for that equalizing tendency.

Marquis James's *The Raven* (1931) was a glamorized portrait of Texas soldier and governor, Sam Houston. The two volumes of James's life of Andrew Jackson, *The Border Captain* (1933) and *Portrait of a President* (1937), were re-packaged in a combined one-volume edition, *The Life of Andrew Jackson*, which received the Pulitzer in 1938. James had grown up in the Oklahoma Territory, where he absorbed tales of frontier heroism supplemented by intermittent formal education. He became a journalist, and worked on papers in Chicago, Kansas City, St. Louis, and New Orleans. Two years on the *New York Tribune* were followed by service in World War I, after which James wrote for the *New Yorker* until the mid-twenties.[18]

The relentlessly celebratory tone of *Andrew Jackson* grew out of James's enthusiasms, but also corresponded to the political temper of the 1930s. To put it summarily: Jackson is presented as the first "people's president," a plain-speaking man who used the power of his office to fight against the banking interests on behalf of the nation's working men and women. James was not alone in insisting on the relevance of Jackson's precedent to the Depression decade. Not long before his death, Arthur M. Schlesinger, Jr., looked back at his own influential studies of Jackson in precisely those terms:

The Age of Jackson was written more than sixty years ago in another America, and reflected FDR's struggles to democratize American capitalism. I was an ardent young New Dealer, and I sought precedents in American history for the

---

[18] The biographical details are taken from Richard A. Reiman, "Marquis James"; www.anb.org/articles/14/14-00315.html; *American National Biography Online*, February 2000.

problems that faced FDR. In advancing my interpretation, I was conditioned by the passions of my era. Conservatives in the angry Thirties used to fulminate against the New Deal as "un-American." I wanted to show that far from importing foreign ideas, FDR was acting in a robust American spirit and tradition. Jackson's war against Nicholas Biddle and the Second Bank of the United States thus provided a thoroughly American precedent for the battles that FDR waged against the "economic royalists" of his (and my) day.[19]

Marquis James was neither a professional historian nor an "ardent New Dealer." His rendition of Jackson is nonetheless based on a similar desire to justify popular sovereignty and executive action in the struggle between haves and have-nots. Indeed, James in several places uses the anachronistic and politically loaded term "proletarian" to describe the ordinary Americans ground down by big money, thus underscoring the parallels.

But James is more interested in memorializing Jackson's personal qualities than in mapping the intricate economic debates of the 1830s.[20] In James's star-struck rendition of him, Jackson is a man of inexorable will, "a man of fire and tenderness, of strong and sincere, if sometimes rash, emotions," a "superior being, a chieftain and a gentleman," the most Popular of all our Presidents, and "the savior of the Union."[21] The hero-worship found a responsive audience: a long and reverential review in the *New York Times* calls the book "an accurate and properly proportioned portrait of Andrew Jackson," which illustrates "the observation of Carlyle that a well-written life is almost as rare as a well-spent one."[22]

James spent several months living in a cabin in the Great Smoky Mountains in order to experience something of the frontier that Jackson had known. He also claimed that he consulted 40,000 documents in preparing *Jackson*, and the thousand pages of the life bear the stamp of that research. But the learning is fully absorbed in narrative of a high

---

[19] Arthur M. Schlesinger, Jr., "History and National Stupidity," *New York Review of Books* (April 27, 2006), p. 14.

[20] Samuel Hopkins Adams created a colorful and swashbuckling Jackson in his novel, *The Gorgeous Hussy* (1934), which moves from frontier to White House, placing Jackson's protégée, the lively Peggy Eaton, at the center of the story. Adams co-wrote the screenplay for the MGM film version of his novel (1936), which received two Academy Award nominations. The once-scandalous Peggy Eaton was also the subject of a biography in the thirties, Queena Pollack's *Peggy Eaton, Democracy's Mistress* (1931).

[21] Marquis James, *The Life of Andrew Jackson* (Indianapolis, IN: The Bobbs-Merrill Company, 1938), pp. 227, 330, 507, 625, 637.

[22] Hugh Russell Fraser, "Marquis James's Portrait of Andrew Jackson," The *New York Times* (October 3, 1937), p. 30. Fraser was President of the Andrew Jackson Society of Tennessee; this acknowledged but still slightly scandalous conflict of interest suggests that the editors of the *Times* were committed to a positive partisan review.

order: propelled by an energy that reflects and implicitly authenticates Jackson's own restlessness, and filled with closely observed scenes of action. James lingers over the arguments, duels, battles, and riots in which Jackson found himself, always emphasizing his hero's courage under fire.

The terms of the encounter between Jackson and the bankers are typically moral and almost allegorical: the banks have engaged in "an orgy of speculation"; they created "an artificial prosperity" based on "shady devices" that "squeeze" the common people who are victimized by the system (*Andrew Jackson*, pp. 565, 718, 632, 650). Jackson mobilized public opinion against Nicholas Biddle, President of the Second Bank of the United States, and the nation's leading financier. After many months of increasingly acrimonious campaigning against Biddle, Jackson effectively abolished the Bank by vetoing re-charter legislation passed by both houses of Congress in 1832. Though James provides many of the economic details of the struggle, his real interest lies in documenting Jackson's stamina, political skill, and rhetorical ingenuity.[23] *Andrew Jackson* is a story of winning and losing, and Jackson is the paramount winner; indeed, in James's opinion, he is one of the most eminent figures in the nation's history.

The principal losers in the book are Native Americans and African-Americans. An Indian-fighter from his early days, Jackson led the campaigns that crushed the Creek nation in 1812. Even the admiring Marquis James admits that Jackson routinely broke treaties that supposedly restrained white incursions into Indian Territory, and he includes a summary of Jackson's first presidential message to Congress, in which he proposed the lethal Indian Removals Act. While Jackson occasionally expressed sympathy for the suffering that Native Americans endured at the hands of whites, his own role was overwhelmingly destructive.

On the other hand, Jackson expressed neither sympathy nor respect for African-Americans. Nor does his biographer. Describing a famous race between horses owned by Jackson and a Captain Joseph Erwin, James sets the scene: "One pen was filled with horses . . . another with negroes, chuckling and nudging one another in expansive enjoyment" (p. 111). Jackson was a slaveholder – "an ideal slave-owner" according to James (p. 349) – with an abiding contempt for abolitionists, and he tended to

---

[23] Walter D. Edmonds had a more skeptical view of Jackson's populism and his reliance on the spoils system. In a story called "Young Mr. Ames Goes Down the River," Edmonds's narrator describes young Ames as "a Jackson man, passing out the Federal money. You passed a law and filled your pockets and those of your friends." Reprinted in *Post Stories of 1938* (Boston: Little, Brown and Company, 1939), p. 206.

think of black people and animals in more or less similar terms. From the White House, he wrote inquiring letters to his foreman at the Hermitage: "How fared the negroes, the stock of blooded horses, the work horses and mules . . . What of births and deaths – negro babies, colts and calves?" (p. 544).

James's own views of slavery echo the pro-slavery arguments popular in the 1830s and still current – as we will see again in the case of *Gone with the Wind* and kindred works of fiction and non-fiction – a hundred years later: "In retrospect it seems fairly clear that nowhere in the contemporary world did the negro find tutelage in the arts of civilization on the whole so beneficial to him as in the American slavery states." Whether consciously or not, James paraphrased such antebellum advocates of slavery as George Fitzhugh in *Cannibals All!* (1857), arguing that "serfs" in New England mill towns fared worse than slaves.

Except for the nearly instinctive connection between the words "Webster" and "dictionary," Noah Webster was no more a household name in the 1930s than he is today. (A recent survey of historical knowledge suggests that most of the respondents confused Noah Webster and Daniel.) Nonetheless, two full-length biographies of Noah Webster were published in the thirties, both in 1936: *Noah Webster: Pioneer of Learning*, by Ervin Shoemaker, and *Noah Webster: Schoolmaster to America*, by Harry Warfel. These were the first lives of Webster in over fifty years, and there would not be another for several decades thereafter.[24]

Concede the assumption that the turmoil of the Depression decade stimulated intense reflection on the origins and meaning of the nation's identity, and interest in Webster's life and work follows with speculative but attractive logic. To put it summarily, Webster was the linguistic nationalist of the early Republic.[25] He spent his long life challenging the new nation to develop its own language, distinctively American, in support of American ideas, American book publishing, American commerce, American culture. A young soldier in the Revolution, Webster was among the most voluble patriots of a volubly patriotic era, and he was

---

[24] Horace Scudder's *Noah Webster* was published in 1881. Finding it insufficiently admiring, Webster's great-granddaughter, Mrs. E. E. F. Skeel, published the uniformly adulatory *Notes on the Life of Noah Webster* (1912), a collection of sketches and primary sources, including Webster's diary.

[25] "Perhaps the greatest of the forces that gave impetus to Webster's many activities was his patriotic fervor, his chauvinistic support of the spread-eagle doctrine." Ervin C. Shoemaker, *Noah Webster: Pioneer of Learning* (New York: Columbia University Press, 1936), p. 303.

convinced that language was the key to full independence and national maturity. Indeed, since American history was not much taught in the nineteenth century (textbooks came into wide use only in the 1890s), Webster and William Holmes McGuffey stood at the nation-making center of education.[26]

Warfel's *Schoolmaster* is the more comprehensive and durable of the two lives. Noah Webster emerges from these pages as a man both of his time and of the present. Warfel emphasizes in particular Webster's early acquaintance with Benjamin Franklin, and his intellectual descent from Franklin as a useful polymath: aside from his works on language, Webster wrote on philosophy, meteorology, statistics, copyright law, and agriculture, and played a major role in the founding of Amherst College. He mastered over a dozen languages to enable his research on the history of language. His attempts to map the course of the yellow fever epidemic of 1793 led to the important contributions he made to the nascent science of epidemiology.[27]

Trained as a lawyer, Webster soon turned from the practice of law to the theory and practice of education. His *American Spelling Book* (1783) was the country's first, and he summarized his intentions in the famous preface: "To diffuse an uniformity and purity of language in America, to destroy the provincial prejudices that originate in the trifling differences of dialect and produce reciprocal ridicule, to promote the interest of literature and the harmony of the United States." In short, if variations in spelling (and pronunciation) could be eradicated, so too could sectional differences: "Customs, habits, and language, as well as government should be national. America should have her own distinct from all the world."[28]

Despite opposition from conservative teachers, politicians and clergymen, the *Spelling Book* was immensely popular: one estimate places total sales at over 20 million. According to Warfel: "No other book, the Bible excepted, played so unifying a part in American culture..."[29] In rapid

[26] Frances Fitzgerald, *America Revised: History Schoolbooks in the Twentieth Century* (New York: Little, Brown, 1979), p. 50.

[27] C.-E. A. Winslow, a professor of public health at Yale, acknowledged that William Thompson Sedgwick deserved to be called "the father of epidemiology in the U.S.," but insisted that Webster should be considered "the great uncle." In "The Epidemiology of Noah Webster," *Transactions of the Connecticut Academy of Arts and Sciences* (January, 1934), p. 23.

[28] Noah Webster, *Dissertations on the English Language* (Boston: Isaiah Thomas and Company, 1789), p. 179.

[29] Harry R. Warfel, *Noah Webster: Schoolmaster to America* (New York: The Macmillan Company, 1936), p. 77.

succession, Webster published his *American Grammar* (1784) and his *American Reader* (1785). Among them, these books represented a call for cultural independence that predated Emerson's more famous statements in "The American Scholar" (1837) and the "Divinity School Address" (1838). To advance the nationalist cause, Webster's *Reader* replaced biographies of religious leaders and biblical figures, standard in readers before his, with sketches of Revolutionary heroes and other patriotic figures.

Webster's most ambitious project, one on which he spent nearly three decades, was his *Dictionary of the English Language*, which appeared in two large volumes in 1828. In this vast project, with its pugnacious corrections of Samuel Johnson and its insistence that the American language assured America's place among the community of nations, Webster brought his efforts to a close. It was the climax of his efforts to use words "to make sure the people of the United States remained as separate as possible from the rest of the world," as one scholar has phrased it.[30]

Webster's hostility to European, and especially to English, influence, his celebration of the nation's cultural achievement, and his reliance on "the people" as his standard of lexical judgement may have renewed interest in Webster's ideas in the thirties decade, when Americans were discovering the virtues of the common man and woman, and were reacting with increasing antagonism to entanglement with foreign powers. While some writers and activists on the Left sought models abroad, particularly in the Soviet Union, the great majority of Americans continued to rely on America's past for guidance.

Indeed, at one point Warfel summarizes Webster's achievements in phrases that make the old lexicographer sound more than a little like a New Deal reformer: "In addition to fostering Americanism in language, education, manners, and politics, he proposed unemployment insurance, city planning, cleansing of city streets, improvement of penal laws, investigation of diseases, collection of statistics, forest conservation, organization of charity societies . . . he wrote a history of commerce and the first pages toward a history of epidemics" (*Schoolmaster*, p. 225). By a small but fine coincidence, it was also in the 1930s that Webster finally won his battle over pronunciation. According to a recent scholar of American English: "A history of the attitudes and practices of the

---

[30] Jill Lepore, *A is for American: Letters and Other Characters in the Newly United States* (New York: Alfred A. Knopf, 2002), p. 60.

National Council of Teachers of English (in America) tells us that British received pronunciation was still the standard up to about 1930; [and] that an alternative colloquialism became positively approved in the period 1930–35 . . ."[31]

John James Audubon was another great figure of the early nineteenth century who devoted his life to the creation of a distinctively American identity. In Audubon's case, the vocabulary was painterly, and the subject was birds. His masterpiece, *Birds of America*, published in four large "elephant folios" over the course of eleven years, from 1827 to 1838, virtually created an entire branch of American art. The hundreds of pictures he produced, despite the controversy they have consistently aroused on both scientific and aesthetic grounds, also served to enhance national pride. The appearance of his work coincided with the founding, in 1826, of the National Academy of Design in New York. Managed by artists themselves, the Academy asserted the value of American art and its independence from Europe.

Not surprisingly, Constance Rourke, who devoted her entire career to the search for an American "usable past," found Audubon a congenial subject. Rourke, whose first published article celebrated vaudeville,[32] energetically defended the proposition that America should not be depreciated as a cultural backwater. Instead, she described the characteristic productions of American writers and artists in terms that linked mythmaking and pragmatism. Influenced by cultural anthropology, she argued that the job of the critic was "discovering and diffusing the materials of the American tradition."[33]

Rather than capitulating to the snobbery that separated high art from popular expression, Rourke insisted on continuity. The subtitle of her most important book, *American Humor* (1931), was *A Study of the*

---

[31] David Simpson, *The Politics of American English, 1776–1850* (New York: Oxford University Press, 1986), p. 13.

[32] Constance Mayfield Rourke, "Vaudeville," *The New Republic* (August 27, 1919), pp. 115–116.

[33] Constance Rourke, *American Humor: A Study of the National Character* (New York: Harcourt, Brace and Company, 1931), p. 236. "The idea of tradition itself . . . becomes increasingly important in the period [of the 1930s]." Warren I. Susman, *Culture as History: The Transformation of American Society in the Twentieth Century* (New York: Pantheon Books, 1984), p. 176. One scholar went further, assigning a "profoundly conservative" influence to the Depression. Alfred Haworth Jones, "The Search for a Usable American Past in the New Deal Era," *American Quarterly* (December, 1971), p. 717. Leveling notions of culture reached the higher levels of the Roosevelt administration. Defending the grants doled out to artists and writers by the Works Projects Administration, WPA director Harry Hopkins said, "I use the word culture as including everything from basketball to a violin performance." Harry Lloyd Hopkins, *Spending to Save: the Complete Story of Relief* (New York: W.W. Norton & Company, 1936), p. 175.

National Character. In this path-breaking attempt to define America through its mythic characters, Rourke landed on the figures of the Yankee peddler, the backwoodsman, and the blackface minstrel. What they had in common was masquerade, improvisation, and a rhetoric that leapt over mountains and rivers: a talent for "upsetting many stabilities" (p. 266). Her opening sentences, a sketch of a Yankee peddler's visit to a village, and the hilarious consequences that follow, were once famous:

> Toward evening of a midsummer day at the latter end of the eighteenth century a traveler was seen descending a steep red road into a fertile Carolina valley. He carried a staff and walked with a wide, fast, sprawling gait, his tall shadow cutting across the lengthening shadows of the trees. His head was crouched, his back long; a heavy pack lay across his shoulders.
>
> A close view of his figure brought consternation to the men and women lounging at the tavern or near the sheds that clustered around the planter's gate. "I'll be shot if it ain't a Yankee!" cried one. The yard was suddenly vacant. Doors banged and windows were shut. The peddler moved relentlessly nearer, reached a doorway, and laid his pack on the half hatch. The inhabitants had barred their doors and double-locked their money-tills in vain. With scarcely a halt the peddler made his way into their houses and silver leapt into his pockets. When his pack was unrolled, calicoes, glittering knives, razors, scissors, clocks, cotton caps, shoes, and notions made a holiday at a fair. His razors were bright as the morning star, cut quick as thought, and had been made by the light of a diamond in a cave in Andalusia. (pp. 15–16)

In the words of one student of her work: "More than anybody else, Constance Rourke tried to provide a coherent theory not only for folk painting and sculpture but also for the whole range of American vernacular expression."[34] Despite the pioneering significance of her work, and the admiration of writers such as the young Ralph Ellison, she was barely noticed by the academic establishment. As one scholar points out, "none of her books was ever reviewed in the *American Historical Review*."[35] Her preference for fictionalized vignettes, such as the one quoted above, was one defensible reason for the exclusion; snobbish suspicion of her subject matter was another; her gender was surely a third.[36]

---

[34] Charles C. Alexander, *Here the Country Lies: Nationalism and the Arts in Twentieth-Century America* (Bloomington: Indiana University Press, 1980), p. 213.

[35] Joan Shelley Rubin, *Constance Rourke and American Culture* (Chapel Hill: University of North Carolina Press, 1980), p. 169.

[36] Studies of American humor had appeared in the nineteenth century, among them *American Humorists* (1882) by H. R. Haweis. It was in the 1920s and 1930s, however, that the subject began to emerge as a major field; Rourke's book is just one example. Thomas L. Masson published *Our American Humorists* in 1931. Martha Bruere and Mary Ritter Beard's *Laughing Their Way*, a study

Her 1936 biography of Audubon exemplifies her views. In Rourke's rendering of him, Audubon is kin to the pioneers and explorers whose exploits pushed back the frontier, and who was at the same time an artist of considerable sophistication. A man who lived easily and self-sufficiently in the wilderness, Audubon transformed the material of America's forests and rivers into works of substantial artistic accomplishment. His vision was founded on the evidence of his eyes, rather than fancy: "romanticism played almost no part in his work."[37] As Rourke evokes him, Audubon most closely resembles Whitman in the epic scale and democratic energy of his work (*Audubon*, p. 285). Whitman's example lies behind Rourke's prose as well, in particular her frequent long catalogues of the birds and animals that Audubon encountered in his traveling:

he was dazzled by the myriads in the great flocks of spring and autumn and by the rich variety he found everywhere, unknown warblers in the deeper forests, snowy egrets, whooping cranes, whole heronries – of blue herons, the great blue and the smaller blue, the black crowned night heron – and the brilliant, gay wood ducks whose flight was sudden, strong, and high. He listened to the hollow yank, yank, yank of the ivory-billed woodpecker in the deep woods and saw this magnificent bird again and again, showy, with white curving lines down his back, a fine spread of wings, a red and black crest. He heard the American bittern with its odd voice like the workings of an old-fashioned wooden pump . . . (p. 55)

Resembling the folk art of Pennsylvania Dutch and Native American, Audubon's images validate the integrity of those traditions. Specifically, Rourke repeatedly emphasizes Aububon's powers of design as the key to his artistic achievement: "Design marches through all of Audubon's work; in study after study his instinctive preoccupation is clear" (p. 293). That same criterion recurs in Rourke's judgments of other artists. For example, in her next book, *Charles Sheeler: Artist in the American Tradition* (1938), she located Sheeler's significance in the similarities between his forms and those of rural and frontier crafts.[38]

Rourke's *Audubon* lent support to the nationalist cultural aspirations of the Depression decade. There were other points of connection as well. Audubon began in poverty and obscurity – he apparently did not know who his parents were – and achieved fame and eventual prosperity. His

of American women's humor, appeared in 1937. In that same year, Walter Blair, who would become the nation's leading scholar of the subject, published his first book, *Native American Humor*.

[37] Constance Rourke, *Audubon* (New York: Harcourt, Brace and Company, 1936), p. 307.

[38] Along with her studies of Audubon and Charles Sheeler, Rourke also wrote a biography of frontiersman Davy Crockett (1934).

self-authorship and success found a responsive audience in the 1930s. In addition, Rourke uses Audubon's life to dramatize an environmental warning: the "unspoiled country" that Audubon loved, with "its curious sights, its wealth of small mysteries, the pleasures for the five senses which it offered," is rapidly disappearing a century later (p. 64). Rourke acknowledges that Audubon usually killed the birds he painted, and she traces modern violations of nature to Audubon and his contemporaries: "hunters were brutal; white men were careless of life in all ways on the frontier." James Fenimore Cooper had explored the struggle between wilderness and the encroachments of civilization, in a series of novels that were contemporary with Audubon's travels. Echoing one of Cooper's most famous passages, Rourke writes at one point: "When great flocks of wild pigeons darkened the sky they were shot for the excitement of shooting" (p. 97).

But the killing of Audubon's time was merely a foretaste of the wholesale destruction that would follow, including the industrialized slaughter of animals, the deforestation of large portions of the country, and the widespread pollution of rivers and streams. For the men and women of the Depression decade, the Dust Bowl would become the symbol of an insulted environment. Human brutality to the animal kingdom emerged as a prominent theme in historical fiction. The title of MacKinlay Kantor's novel, *The Noise of Their Wings* (1938), to give a single example, derives from the extermination of the passenger pigeon in the nineteenth century.

Tracing its roots to the conservation efforts of Gifford Pinchot and Theodore Roosevelt, an environmental movement organized itself in the 1930s. The Civilian Conservation Corps (CCC), one of the agencies of the New Deal, deployed thousands of young men in a quasi-military campaign to re-forest denuded land, repair erosion, and build roads in national parks. An estimated 3 billion trees were planted. Among the policy architects of the period, the most important was Stuart Chase, an economist and pioneer in regional planning, who published *Rich Land, Poor Land* (1936), an environmental history of America. Specifically, Chase told a story of 300 years of accelerating waste, with the Dust Bowl the most spectacular but only the most recent example of centuries of misuse. A section called "In the Year 2000" forecasts an apocalyptic outcome.[39]

---

[39] Stuart Chase, *Rich Land, Poor Land: A Study of Waste in the Natural Resources of America* (New York: Whittlesey House, 1936), p. 48.

Illustration 8. From the *Index of American Design*

Somewhat ironically, Audubon himself has become the symbol of conservation efforts. The Audubon Society, founded in 1896, has grown into one of the largest environmental organizations in the United States.

Rourke had the opportunity to extend her cultural analyses more broadly when she became editor of the *Index of American Design* in 1936, the year that *Audubon* was published. The *Index* comprises a repository of nearly 18,000 images of American decorative objects gathered between 1935 and 1942. Sponsored initially by the Federal Arts Project, the *Index* represented another attempt to secure the material legacy of the American past. The project's mission suited Rourke down to the ground.

Aspiring to "record and thereby constitute an idea and history of authentic American material culture," the *Index* documented the hand-made past in drawings and watercolors.[40] (Photography was forbidden, on the claim that it could only reproduce surfaces, not the texture and inherent quality of objects.[41]) In doing so, it extended the earlier work that had produced the reconstruction of Colonial Williamsburg, the furniture collections of Henry Francis du Pont at Winterthur, and the unrivalled collection of American objects that Henry Chapman Mercer put on display in suburban Philadelphia.[42]

The literary biographies of the 1930s encompassed both established and emergent opinion. To be sure, such a broad claim about literary history is not quite demonstrable, but Carl Van Doren and Harry Hayden Clark provide useful reference points. Van Doren, a senior editor of the *Dictionary of American Biography*, co-founder of The Literary Guild, and popular Columbia lecturer, was one of the more conspicuous arbiters of taste throughout the interwar years. *The American Novel, 1789–1939* (1940) was his summary statement on 150 years of American fiction. The book rather closely tracks the essays he had written some years earlier for the *Cambridge History of American Literature*. In *The American Novel*, there are separate chapters on nine writers: James Fenimore Cooper, Nathaniel

[40] Jonathan Harris, *Federal Art and National Culture: The Politics of Identity in New Deal America* (New York: Cambridge University Press, 1995), p. 85.

[41] A. Joan Saab, *For the Millions: American Art and Culture Between the Wars* (Philadelphia: University of Pennsylvania Press, 2004), p. 77.

[42] In the first three decades of the twentieth century, Mercer gathered upwards of 50,000 objects of "ordinary American use." These tools, toys, kitchen appliances, articles of clothing, and myriad other artifacts are displayed in the grandly bizarre concrete gothic castle he designed for them in Doylestown, PA. For the most perceptive analysis of Mercer and the importance of his collection, see Steven Conn, "Henry Chapman Mercer and the Search for American History," *Pennsylvania Magazine of History & Biography* (July, 1992), pp. 323–355.

Hawthorne, Herman Melville, William Dean Howells, Mark Twain, Henry James, Theodore Dreiser, Willa Cather, and Sinclair Lewis. In addition three writers are treated in individual sub-sections: Edith Wharton, James Branch Cabell, and Thomas Wolfe.[43]

Assuming that these dozen novelists comprise Van Doren's canon, most of his choices remain viable seven decades later: Hawthorne, Melville, Twain, James, Dreiser, Cather, and Wharton continue as central to an understanding of the dimensions of American fiction through the 1930s. Faulkner would replace Cabell in most modern lists, while F. Scott Fitzgerald and Ernest Hemingway would probably be added. Sinclair Lewis, whose reputation has only recently begun to recover from several decades of disparagement, deserves his inclusion. All in all, a defensible sorting for its time.[44]

Harry Hayden Clark's *Major American Poets* (1936) offers one version of the poetic canon as seen from the vantage point of the academic mid-thirties. Clark, a professor of English at the University of Wisconsin, claimed that his volume included "the ten generally recognized major American poets."[45] The list includes William Cullen Bryant, John Greenleaf Whittier, Ralph Waldo Emerson, Edgar Allan Poe, Henry Wadsworth Longfellow, James Russell Lowell, Oliver Wendell Holmes, Emily Dickinson, Sidney Lanier, and Walt Whitman. Seventy years later, six of these ten poets, Bryant, Whittier, Longfellow, Lowell, Holmes, and Lanier, would appear in no similar gathering. Emerson and Poe have

---

[43] Van Doren published critical biographies of Cabell and Lewis, in 1925 and 1933 respectively. Predictably, there were numerous calls for a "new" American literature, to meet the new demands of a "new" age, but they co-existed with stout defenses of tradition and the status quo. In a belligerent article called "American Loyalties," in the inaugural volume of *The American Scholar* (January, 1932), for example, classical scholar Paul Shorey aligned himself with received American values (as he called them) against the claims of Europeans and modernists.

[44] Arthur Hobson Quinn's *American Fiction: An Historical and Critical Survey* (New York: D. Appleton-Century Company, 1936), at nearly 800 pages, provides a much more detailed survey of short stories and novels up through the First World War than Van Doren's *American Novel*. Along with the writers Van Doren emphasizes, Quinn includes chapter-length studies of Charles Brockden Brown, Edgar Allan Poe, Bret Harte, Weir Mitchell, Joel Chandler Harris, Francis Marion Crawford, James Lane Allen, Lafcadio Hearn, Anne Douglas Sedgwick, and Booth Tarkington.

    Reader's Guide to Prose Fiction (New York: D. Appleton-Century Company, 1940), edited by Elbert Lenrow, head of the English Department at New York's Fieldston School, is a quite different sort of book. Sponsored by the Commission on Secondary School Curriculum, Lenrow's volume arrays 1,500 novels, in English and translation, under three large thematic headings: "The Individual's Need for Entertainment and 'Escape,'" "The Individual and His Personal Environment," and "The Individual and His Social Environment." Those headings are in turn subdivided into more than a hundred individual topics, from "Woman's Changing Status" and "Negro Problems" to "Radicals and Radicalism" and "Frontier Life."

[45] Harry Hayden Clark, *Major American Poets* (New York: American Book Company, 1936), p. v.

endured, their poetic reputations bobbing up and down. From Clark's selection, only Whitman and Dickinson remain as incontestably poets of the first rank, and in both cases Clark's presentation of them is denatured and domesticated. Nothing of Whitman's sexuality is discussed or discussable, and Dickinson emerges as a fey little spinster who thought "beauty and truth and goodness are one" (p. 897).

Several of the decade's biographies ratified the established hierarchy. Nathaniel Hawthorne, Henry James, Washington Irving, Henry Wadsworth Longfellow, and John Greenleaf Whittier were each the subject of a single biography, while three books each addressed the life and work of James Fenimore Cooper and Edgar Allan Poe.[46] These were predictable choices, as the opinions of Van Doren, Clark, and other critics suggest.

Emily Dickinson was the subject of five full-length biographies in the 1930s. The twenties and thirties were the decades of Dickinson's emergence as an incontestably major writer. A season of interest had attended the publication of two volumes of her poems in the 1890s, but she slipped back into the category of "minor poetess" in the years before and after the First World War.[47] The publication in 1924 of what was called *The Complete Poems* (in good faith, though many items were still missing) provoked a renewed and lively interest. "The growing fame of Emily Dickinson," said one critic in 1930, "is one of the most remarkable events in literary history."[48]

In that same year, three biographies appeared: *Emily Dickinson, Friend and Neighbor*, by MacGregor Jenkins; *Emily Dickinson: the Human Background of Her Poetry*, by Josephine Pollitt; and Genevieve Taggard's

[46] Edward Mather, *Nathaniel Hawthorne, a Modest Man* (New York: Thomas Y. Crowell Company, 1940); Cornelia Pulsifer Kelley, *The Early Development of Henry James* (Urbana: University of Illinois Press, 1930); Stanley T. Williams, *The Life of Washington Irving* (New York: Oxford University Press, 1935); Hildegarde Hawthorne, *Poet of Craigie House: the Story of Henry Wadsworth Longfellow* (New York: D. Appleton-Century, 1936); Albert Mordell, *Quaker Militant: John Greenleaf Whittier* (Boston: Houghton Mifflin, 1933); Henry Walcott Boynton, *James Fenimore Cooper* (New York: The Century Company, 1931); Robert E. Spiller, *Fenimore Cooper: Critic of His Times* (New York: Russell & Russell, 1931); Dorothy Waples, *The Whig Myth of James Fenimore Cooper* (New Haven, CT: Yale University Press, 1938); Hervey Allen, *Israfel: The Life and Times of Edgar Allan Poe* (New York: Farrar & Rinehart, 1934); Una Pope-Hennessy, *Edgar Allan Poe, 1809–1849: A Critical Biography* (London: Macmillan, 1934); Edward Shanks, *Edgar Allan Poe* (New York: The Macmillan Company, 1937).

[47] The shifting response to Dickinson's poetry was first documented in Caesar R. Blake and Carlton F. Wells, eds., *The Recognition of Emily Dickinson: Selected Criticism since 1890* (Ann Arbor: University of Michigan Press, 1964).

[48] Harry Hansen, cited in Alfred Leete Hampson, "Foreword," in Martha Dickinson Bianchi, *Emily Dickinson Face to Face: Unpublished Letters with Notes and Reminiscences* (Boston: Houghton Mifflin Company, 1932), p. ix.

The Life and Mind of Emily Dickinson. The first of these gathers the alleged recollections of a lifelong resident of Amherst. Even as a child, Jenkins insists, he sensed Dickinson's special qualities. "Miss Emily," as he calls her, made children "feel near a thousand things we did not understand; she seemed to bring to us a world of fancy, a world of beauty, a world of hidden lovely things."[49] A charming but surely invented memory, which nonetheless documents the tug that Dickinson's personality exerted.

Pollitt's *Human Background*, though more substantial than Jenkins's, nonetheless relies on a small mixture of fact in a large quantity of fancy. Pollitt insists on reading Dickinson's mind, and inventing corresponding gestures, as in this quite typical example: "Throughout the winter Emily Dickinson seemed to herself to be passing a long graveyard. She was alone. A tombstone stood up whitely ahead of her in the winter light. She put her hands in her pockets and began to whistle, lovelier tunes than she had ever whistled before."[50]

Genevieve Taggard's *Life and Mind* is the first intellectually adventurous book-length study of Dickinson's work. An accomplished poet and a feminist essayist, Taggard recruited Dickinson as an heir to the English metaphysical poets, especially Donne. "Only John Donne, two hundred years before," Taggard wrote in defense of Dickinson's inward intensity, "had suggested multitudinous possibilities in line after line of rapid sketch."[51] Taggard's innovative inquiry was followed a few years later by George Whicher's *This Was a Poet* (1938), which remained the academic standard for several decades.

Aside from these personal memoirs and scholarly analyses, Dickinson was also the inspiration for Susan Glaspell's play *Alison's House* (1930). More homage than biography, the drama deserves attention as a pioneering effort by a woman writer to pay tribute to an earlier woman writer. After several years as a journalist in her native Iowa, Glaspell began publishing short fiction in such magazines as *McClure's* and *Harper's*. She wrote a number of moderately successful novels, but began writing plays when she and a number of other writers, including her husband, established the Provincetown Players at the time of the First World War.

[49] MacGregor Jenkins, *Emily Dickinson, Friend and Neighbor* (Boston: Little, Brown and Company, 1930), p. 22.
[50] Josephine Pollitt, *Emily Dickinson: the Human Background of Her Poetry* (New York: Harper & Brothers, 1930), pp. 164–165.
[51] Genevieve Taggard, *The Life and Mind of Emily Dickinson* (New York: Alfred A. Knopf, 1930), p. 232.

Her work, a series of one-act and full-length plays, shared the Provincetown stage with Eugene O'Neill's, and several critics judged her talent equal to his.

Produced by Eva Le Gallienne's Civic Repertory Theater, *Alison's House* was the surprising winner of the Pulitzer Prize for Drama in 1931. It takes place on a single day, December 31, 1899, eighteen years after the death of the poet, Alison Stanhope. Alison had renounced the love of a married man, and had spent much of her life in an upstairs room, dressed in white and quietly writing the poems that would bring posthumous fame. Like Dickinson, she had published almost nothing in her lifetime. The play's action is mainly talk, much of it intelligent: about Alison's work, about the strains through which the family has lived, and above all about the competing obligations of love and duty. The surviving family members have decided to sell the house, and their final day there – the final day of the nineteenth century as well – brings old history and long-standing tensions to the surface.

Alison's siblings have both faced the same choice she had to make. Her brother, John, remained faithful to a wife he did not love in order to hold his family together. Alison's younger sister, Edna, on the contrary, had refused self-denial and loneliness. Having fallen in love with a married man, she has defied convention, and her family, by moving in with him. Ostracized by John and by her aged aunt Agatha, she has returned on this fateful day to seek reconciliation.

Like many works set on a single day – O'Neill's much greater *Long Day's Journey Into Night* comes to mind – the action dramatized in *Alison's House* is both repetitive and decisive. The debates among the family's members have surely occupied them for years and decades. However, Edna's return and the impending sale of the house will change the family's life permanently. More dramatically, the combined shocks literally prove too much for Agatha, who dies while apparently trying to burn the house down.

In fact, as the somewhat agitated final scenes make clear, Agatha had been trying to burn a portfolio of Alison's poems. This small gathering of pages, tied together with a thread, contains poems that Alison never published, poems no one in the family has ever seen. They are "Alison – at her best," in John's view, but he believes they should be burned: they contain intimate revelations of her devastated passion.[52] Edna, on the other hand, argues that the poems belong to the future, not the past. The

---

[52] Susan Glaspell, *Alison's House*, a play in three acts (New York: S. French, 1930), p. 136.

play ends with John forgiving and embracing Edna, and yielding the decision about the poems to her.

When Pearl S. Buck received the Nobel Prize for Literature in 1938, the citation did not specifically mention her international bestseller, *The Good Earth*. Instead, the Academy saluted Buck "for her rich and truly epic descriptions of peasant life in China and for her biographical masterpieces." That final phrase referred to the book-length and separate biographies of her mother and father, *The Exile* and *Fighting Angel*, both published in 1936. Whatever the vicissitudes of Buck's reputation in the latter half of the twentieth century, these two books remain unparalleled accounts of the strange and terrible vocations pursued by generations of missionaries in China. The novelist John Hersey, himself a missionary child, has written that "As a China 'mishkid,' I still, to this day, reverberate with pity and horror to the memory of some of the images" in those books.[53]

Buck had written the first draft of *The Exile* fifteen years earlier, when she was still living in China, as a way of coping with her mother's death. Out of respect for her father, Absalom, who is treated harshly in the story, she waited to publish it until a few years after he died. Critics and public alike greeted the book with unanimous enthusiasm, which moved Buck immediately to write the companion volume, *Fighting Angel*, a biography of her father. This book, too, was met with strong reviews and sales; the paired biographies were quickly re-issued as a set, under the collective title, *The Flesh and the Spirit*. Through these books, Buck paid public tribute to her mother and settled old accounts with her father. In spite of her unconcealed partisan purposes, Buck created two of the most richly detailed and evocative narrative accounts ever written of the missionary world. *The Exile* and *Fighting Angel* are monuments to the story of Protestant evangelism in China, a vital chapter in American cultural history that continued to be neglected for decades.[54]

If homelessness and displacement stand among the major subjects of the violent twentieth century, *The Exile* is a neglected but important

---

[53] Letter from Hersey to the author, cited in my book, *Pearl S. Buck: A Cultural Biography* (New York: Cambridge University Press, 1996), p. xiii.

[54] Scholarly inquiry into the mission movement commenced in a major way with John King Fairbank, ed., *The Missionary Enterprise in China and America* (Cambridge, MA: Harvard University Press, 1974). More recent work is gathered in Daniel H. Bays and Grant Wacker, eds., *The Foreign Missionary Enterprise at Home: Explorations in North American Cultural History* (Tuscaloosa: University of Alabama Press, 2003).

document in the history of those experiences. In 1880, Buck's mother, Carie Stulting Sydenstricker, had accompanied her missionary husband to China, where she was homesick for the remaining forty years of her life. In her daughter's view, she was a woman whose life was shortened and embittered by her husband's single-minded and ultimately destructive devotion to his evangelical work. Carie Sydenstricker's emotionally impoverished marriage and her loneliness provided Buck with a tragic example of the price that women pay for loyalty to codes and customs that oppress them.

Wherever she lived in China, in Hangchow, Chinkiang, or Nanking, Carie Sydenstricker always made a flower garden. These were places of beauty and refuge, walled off from the Chinese streets that surrounded them. Carie's gardens, to which she was passionately devoted, and to which her husband was utterly oblivious, stood for Pearl Buck as a symbol of the distance between her parents. Significantly, throughout both of the biographies, she referred to herself as "Carie's daughter."

Fighting Angel, Buck's portrait of her father, uses biography to critique the entire missionary movement. Brought up in fundamentalist piety, Buck at a relatively early age found herself appalled by dogmatic Christianity. She despised the other-worldliness that could separate a man like her father from the needs and dignity of those around him. And she was incensed by the subordination of women that her father's version of religion entailed. Buck's debate with evangelism became a matter of public record, and of international comment, in 1932, shortly after the publication of *The Good Earth* had made her a literary celebrity. The occasion was a speech she gave in New York's Astor Hotel, at the invitation of a group of Presbyterian women, in which she undertook to answer the question: "Is There a Case for Foreign Missions?" Her answer was a qualified but unmistakable "No." To the presumable discomfort of the 2,000 men and women in her audience, she said that the typical missionary was "narrow, uncharitable, unappreciative, ignorant." She described missionaries to China as "so scornful of any civilization except their own, so harsh in their judgments upon one another, so coarse and insensitive among a sensitive and cultivated people that my heart has fairly bled with shame."[55]

Though it stirred up the fundamentalists – Buck was threatened with a trial for heresy – Buck's speech contributed to a rising chorus of discontent that had grown more vociferous throughout the twenties and

---

[55] Pearl S. Buck, "Is There a Case for Foreign Missions?" (New York: John Day Company, 1932), p. 8.

early thirties. Many Christians, some of them missionaries, had become disillusioned with the hundred years of Western evangelizing in China. Along with Buck's widely reported comments, the most decisive intervention was a book published at the same time, *Re-Thinking Missions*, the report of a Laymen's Inquiry Commission chaired by Harvard philosopher Ernest Hocking. Initiated to find strategies for the revival of missionary work, *Re-Thinking Missions* wrote the movement's epitaph: missionary activity was deemed obsolete, irrelevant at best, counterproductive at its typical worst.

Every Christian sermon was an insult. Regardless of the preacher's motives, regardless of the respect and even affection he might have for individual Chinese men and women, the doctrines he espoused were necessarily abusive to China's culture and traditions. George Santayana, one of the mission movement's most strenuous critics, understood the demeaning implications of preaching: "A missionary sermon is an unprovoked attack; it seems to entice, to dictate, to browbeat, to disturb, and to terrify."[56]

Drawn from this point of view, Buck's portrait of her father is remorseless: he emerges from her pages as a narrow-minded zealot, blinded by certainty, who spent over fifty years summoning Chinese farmers and merchants to a faith they treated with indifference or contempt. As he itinerated around the country, Absalom's safety depended on the power of imperialism, and the privileges of extra-territoriality; his preaching, in Buck's view, expressed a symmetrical "imperialism of the spirit."[57] He was insensitive to beauty, to human weakness, to the needs of his family, even to his own suffering. His wife's illnesses and loneliness were mere impediments to the evangelizing work, and his children – especially the girls – were merely nuisances.

Few biographies, in the 1930s or any other decade, were intended so purposefully as interventions in current debates as Buck's *Fighting Angel*. If we recall how important religion was (and remains) in the American imagination, it is clear that Buck was raising questions that spoke to literally millions of men and women: what is the truth of Christianity? What claims does it make on universal assent? What are the cultural implications of missionary activity? In Buck's view, the answers to all

---

[56] The passage, from Santayana's *Dominations and Powers*, is cited in Arthur Schlesinger, Jr., "The Missionary Enterprise and Theories of Imperialism," in Fairbank, ed., *The Missionary Enterprise in China and America*, p. 361.

[57] Pearl S. Buck, *Fighting Angel* (New York: John Day Company, 1936), p. 54.

these questions were to be found in the destructive consequences of evangelism for the Chinese people. The good that the missionaries did was social and secular: medical clinics, for example, or literacy, or relief in time of famine, or opposition to the barbaric practice of foot binding. For Absalom Sydenstricker, such work was subordinate and virtually irrelevant. His unyielding commitment was to an alien divinity.

Regardless of their political opinions, the great majority of Americans defined themselves as believers and churchgoers, though the beliefs they held and the churches they attended comprised a kaleidoscopic variety. In 1936, a government census enumerated 256 religious denominations.[58] The South and much of the Midwest were dominated by dozens of evangelical Protestant denominations. Fundamentalism (the term was invented in the 1920s), usually based on biblical literalism, traditional gender roles, and a suspicion of science, flourished in thousands of rural communities.

In March 1925, the Tennessee legislature passed a law prohibiting the teaching of "any theory that denies the story of the Divine Creation of man as taught in the Bible." Two months later, a high school teacher named John Scopes deliberately broke the law by including Darwin's theory of evolution in his science lesson. He was arrested, and his trial became a national sensation, with Clarence Darrow arguing for the defense and William Jennings Bryan for the prosecution. Scopes was convicted, but he and Darrow appeared to have triumphed in the court of public opinion. The intelligentsia misinterpreted the trial as a victory for enlightened ideas, but in fact the case provided a deep and powerful stimulus to the fundamentalist campaign. "Scopes" reverberates to this day.

Catholics, who made up nearly 20 percent of the population in the thirties, lived mainly in the cities of the East and Midwest. Catholicism had contributed to Al Smith's defeat in the 1928 election, but Catholics comprised a significant bloc in the successive elections of Roosevelt. Jews, a fraction of the population, also aligned themselves with Roosevelt. Still confined mainly to urban ghettoes, Jews found themselves beset by fashionable anti-Semitism in the North and rabid attack in the South, where the revived Ku Klux Klan had added both Catholics and Jews to their list of enemies. (When Father Coughlin moved to his tiny parish in suburban Detroit in the mid-twenties, he was greeted with a burning cross planted on his front lawn by the Klan.)

---

[58] Dr. T. F. Murphy, ed., *Religious Bodies: 1936*, vol. 1 (Washington, DC: Government Printing Office, 1941), p. 17.

The decade's most influential religious intellectual was undoubtedly Reinhold Niebuhr. After following his father into the pulpit of an evangelical country church, Niebuhr studied for two years at Yale's Divinity School, where he ingested a more liberal Christianity. After several more years leading a Midwestern parish, Niebuhr moved to a professorship at Union Theological Seminary in Manhattan. The most important of his many articles and books, *Moral Man and Immoral Society* (1934), argues the distinction summarized in the title: individual men and women are capable (only capable, to be sure) of ethically edifying behavior, including altruism and self-sacrifice, but groups, including nation states, will always act out of self-interest. Justice, not dreams of community, should be the goal of those who would lead society forward.

In a decade absorbed in the debate over inequality and the need for justice, Niebuhr's attempt to combine realism with hope possessed wide appeal. He acknowledged the prevalence of "coercion, self-assertion and conflict" in human affairs, and struggled to locate the means through which power could be turned to just purposes.[59] Neibuhr's realism reached to American race relations, which in his view fully exemplified his general theory. "Every effort to transfer a pure morality of disinterestedness to group relations has resulted in failure," he writes near the end of *Moral Man*. "The Negroes of America have practiced it quite consistently since the Civil War." Forgiveness and forbearance and religious virtues "did not soften the hearts of their oppressors" (p. 268).

The opinions of Reinhold Neibuhr, Ernest Hocking, and Pearl Buck were influential and approximately congruent. Each of them represented an effort to re-think Christianity in more modern terms, and thus move it away from the fundamentalism that fueled bigotry. Their work resembled the religious pragmatism of William James, and it followed in the wake of the Scopes Trial of 1925, which had been widely interpreted as a victory of rationality over superstition.

In fact, the thirties produced much evidence of both religious liberalization and conservative intransigence. In *The Common Faith* (1934), John Dewey's version of theology was sufficiently casual that he used the term "God" to suggest a vague idea of human fellowship rather than any being that resembled the Jewish or Christian deity. The influential clergyman Shailer Mathews, who spent his career defending what he called "modernism," published his autobiography under the suggestive title

---

[59] Reinhold Niebuhr, *Moral Man and Immoral Society: A Study in Ethics and Politics* (New York: Scribner, 1934), p. 234.

New Faith for Old in 1936.[60] At the same time, "something like a revival took place" among the Fundamentalists and the Holiness and Pentecostal churches, as the Depression added to the ranks of disinherited people.[61]

Despite the vigor of the debate between biblical literalism and liberal Christianity, the majority of Americans exhibited a degree of religious inertia. When the Lynds revisited "Middletown" in the mid-thirties, to find indicators of change since their landmark study of a decade earlier, they found new church buildings, but "the sense of expectancy over possible new vitality to be found here in the religious sector of the culture evaporated as one began again to attend church services and to read the sermons re-printed in the Monday-morning newspaper. Here, scattered through the pews, is the same serious and numerically sparse Gideon's band."[62] To quote again the result of a survey conducted in the middle of the decade: "Established values and desires persisted."[63]

Gertrude Stein's genre-bending *Autobiography of Alice B. Toklas* (1933) can provide a bridge between the biographies considered above and the autobiographies to follow. As she entered her sixties, Stein published two volumes of memoirs that finally brought her the public notice she had long sought. By 1937, in *Everybody's Autobiography*, she was able to declare, "It is very nice being a celebrity a real celebrity who can decide who they want to meet and say so and they come or do not come as you want them. I never imagined that would happen to me to be a celebrity like that but it did and when it did I liked it . . ."[64]

That celebrity had been conferred by her first memoir, *The Autobiography of Alice B. Toklas*, a self-portrait written from the assumed point of view of her companion.[65] Selected by the Literary Guild, *Alice* was also published in installments in the *Atlantic Monthly*, the latter fulfilling one of Stein's longstanding ambitions. The style of *Alice* is utterly unlike the experiments of her earlier work, precisely in its surface clarity and

[60] Paul K. Conkin, *When All the Gods Trembled: Darwinism, Scopes, and American Intellectuals* (Lanham, MD: Rowman & Littlefield, 1998), pp. 130–147.

[61] Sydney E. Ahlstrom, *A Religious History of the American People* (New Haven, CT: Yale University Press, 1972), p. 920.

[62] Robert S. Lynd and Helen Merrell Lynd, *Middletown in Transition: A Study in Cultural Conflicts* (New York: Harcourt, Brace and Company, 1937), p. 297.

[63] Terry A. Cooney, *Balancing Acts: American Thought and Culture in the 1930s* (New York: Twayne Publishers, 1995), p. 5.

[64] Gertrude Stein, *Everybody's Autobiography* (New York: Random House, 1937), pp. 3–4.

[65] Stein's pseudo-autobiography may have influenced the Chicago modernist Gertrude Abercrombie (1909–1977), an only child who painted her "Self-Portrait of My Sister," in 1941. Dizzy Gillespie called Abercrombie the "first bop artist."

accessibility. Furthermore, the voice that speaks throughout the book is quite close to Toklas's, as Toklas's own later publications would demonstrate. Using Toklas's point of view also permitted Stein to "have it both ways," as one of her biographers puts it: opinions about her own greatness or the weaknesses of others gain the appearance of greater legitimacy.[66]

Whether in Toklas's voice or not, many of the same preoccupations that marked Stein's previous essays and fictions can be discerned here as well. Stein exhibits something of her enduring fascination with psychology, and she repeats certain episodes and phrases, as a way of suggesting the interpretative dimension of conversations and events. The book proceeds by way of a semi-cubist series of suspensions and reconsiderations, in the manner of Conrad's narrative practice.

The most extravagant example is the famous banquet given in honor of Henri Rousseau in 1908, to which Stein returns at least three times, in each case revealing another level of meaning in the affair.[67] The stories of Matisse and his omelette, the exhibition of the Independents, Stein's purchase of Matisse's "Femme au Chapeau," the legendary Picasso portrait of Stein, are all told at least twice, the death of Apollinaire three times. There are even two versions of Stein's unforgettable dismissal of Hemingway: "remarks are not literature."[68] She explicitly annotates her method when she comments at one point, reporting a quarrel between Roger Frye and Wyndham Lewis: "They told exactly the same story only it was different, very different" (pp. 122–123).

Whatever its value as a specimen of Stein's prose, *Alice* has remained popular for its gossip and for its self-congratulatory but uncommonly shrewd artistic assessments. Every painter of consequence in modernism's first decade comes to visit at 27, rue de Fleurus, along with a score of expatriate American writers. If it is often comic in its egotism (Stein is one of only three geniuses that Toklas has ever met, the others being Picasso and Alfred North Whitehead), it is also a valuable trove of useful anecdote and circumstantial detail.

[66] James R. Mellow, *Charmed Circle: Gertrude Stein & Company* (New York: Avon Books, 1975), p. 422.
[67] The famous feast in honor of Rousseau has often been reported, analyzed, and parodied. It provides the entry and major motif for Roger Shattuck's indispensable cultural history of Paris in the early twentieth century, *The Banquet Years: the Arts in France, 1885–1918* (New York: Harcourt, Brace and Company, 1958).
[68] Gertrude Stein, *The Autobiography of Alice B. Toklas* (New York: Vintage Books, 1990 [1933]), pp. 76, 279.

The sixteen photographs that illustrate the book add their measure of significance. In the first, which serves as frontispiece, Alice B. Toklas stands framed by a door, at the entry of both the text and of the house she shared with Stein. Several document the rooms in which the two women lived, emphasizing the importance of place in Stein's imagination. And the last image follows the book's final page, with its celebrated conclusion: "About six weeks ago Gertrude Stein said, it does not look to me as if you were ever going to write that autobiography. You know what I am going to do. I am going to write it for you. I am going to write it as simply as Defoe did the autobiography of Robinson Crusoe. And she has and this is it." Facing that sly finale, with its reference to the autobiography of a fictional character, Stein has printed a photograph of the handwritten manuscript of the book's first paragraph. The circularity and repetition, the negotiations between writing and visual art, conclude with the transformation of word into image.[69]

Several other important women writers published autobiographies in the 1930s. Harriet Monroe's *A Poet's Life* was published in 1938, two years after her death. The book is poignantly if deliberately mistitled. Monroe persevered as a poet throughout much of her life, encouraged by a commission to write the official "Columbian Ode" for the World's Columbian Exposition of 1893 in Chicago. However, her claim on posterity's attention derived from her work as an editor. In 1912, she launched *Poetry: A Magazine of Verse*; for the next two decades, the magazine was among the most influential cultural publications in America. T. S. Eliot, Robert Frost, and Wallace Stevens were among the writers whose early work Monroe introduced; Ezra Pound served as her foreign correspondent. In the last decade of high modernism, one of its American founders reminded readers of the movement's origins.[70]

Edith Wharton's memoir, *A Backward Glance* (1934), is a more interesting book, from its remarkable first line: "There's no such thing as old age; there is only sorrow." Wharton's sadness was nourished by her loneliness: a lonely childhood, a loveless marriage that ended in divorce, a lifelong sense of dislocation. Early in the book, Wharton evokes the stultifying world of her early years: the upper (though not uppermost)

---

[69] Unfortunately, none of the subsequent paperback reprintings of *Alice B. Toklas* has included the photographs.

[70] Everything about modernism, including its circumscribing dates, remains controversial. Insofar as there is a consensus on this question, it would gather around the period from the late 1890s through the mid-to-late 1930s. *The Cambridge Companion to American Modernism* (2005), to give one recent example, uses the dates 1895 through 1939.

reaches of Old New York, with its antipathy to culture, its commitment to unreflective conformity, and its belief that a woman's vocation began and ended in marriage. "I was never allowed to read the popular American children's books of my day because, as my mother said, the children spoke bad English without the author's knowing it."[71]

Wharton's best novels – *The House of Mirth* (1905), *The Custom of the Country* (1913), *The Age of Innocence* (1920) – dramatize the unequal contests that pit frustrated women and limited men against the constraints of society's received codes and opinions, contests between freedom and disabling circumstance. Disappointment and even tragedy lie at the intersection of dissent and compliance, desire and adjustment. A discriminating if often ironic observer of the fates that befall her fictional victims, Wharton knew from personal experience the price that resistance to old orders entails. In *A Backward Glance*, she recalls her first effort at writing a novel. The opening sentence sets the scene: "'Oh, how do you do, Mrs Brown?' said Mrs Tompkins. 'If only I had known you were going to call I should have tidied up the drawing-room.'" The eleven-year-old Edith showed the manuscript to her mother, who responded, with crushing irrelevance: "Drawing rooms are always tidy" (p. 73).

Though her recollections of these humiliations were still fresh decades later, *A Backward Glance* reveals that Wharton's attitude toward the old world of convention had changed and ossified into a nostalgic conservatism. Instead of the ambivalence that animated her earlier fiction, her memoir is marked by an uncomplicated reverence for established beliefs, settled ideas, and customary patterns of behavior. The book discloses her respect for aristocratic rank and her suspicion of democracy, her scorn for "emancipated women" and her preference for the companionship and conversation of men, her fussy impatience with inefficient servants, and her defiantly old-fashioned opinions on art and culture (pp. 270, 238, 60, 273). Written when its author was separated from the USA by 4,000 miles and twenty years, *A Backward Glance* nonetheless added its voice to the thirties' dialogue, counseling caution in the face of change, and defending the dignity of the past.

Both Monroe and Wharton were in their early seventies, at the end of long careers, when they published their memoirs. Theodore Dreiser was younger, but had also produced most of his major work when he published the second of his memoirs, *Dawn* (1931). Here is the familiar hero of Dreiser's books, the young man from the sticks, possessed only of his

---

[71] Edith Wharton, *A Backward Glance* (New York: Charles Scribners Sons, 1934), p. 51.

ambition, talent, and sexual rapacity, who yearns to turn himself into a success. Dreiser was among the few major American writers who grew up in genuine poverty, and that experience shaped everything he believed and did throughout his life. Deploying the same technique that marks (and often mars) his fiction, Dreiser documents his ragged rural youth with a suffocating thoroughness. Poverty almost never generates nobility, as Dreiser knew and testified. In addition – and these episodes are among the most vivid in the book – young Dreiser was subjected to a pulverizing regime of Roman Catholic threat and punishment.

A seeker who combined hatred of the affluent with an envious desire for their glittering things, Dreiser tells us that the first book to influence him was *Hill's Manual of Etiquette and Social and Commercial Forms.*[72] Dreiser's unquenchable ambivalence is nicely captured in that single reference. Whatever his limits as a thinker and writer, Dreiser remained a revered pioneer for many of the younger writers of the 1930s. Sinclair Lewis, accepting the Nobel Prize for Literature in 1930, the first awarded to an American writer, famously named Dreiser as foremost among his countrymen who might have received the honor instead.

Dreiser's influence reached across generations and race, touching African-American writers such as Richard Wright and Langston Hughes. Hughes was still in his thirties when he wrote *The Big Sea* (1940), the first volume of his autobiography. Because it appeared at about the same time as Wright's *Native Son*, Hughes's book received less attention than it deserved.

The Big Sea opens with an emblematic scene. Hughes has signed on as a twenty-one-year-old seaman on the S. S. *Malone*, a rusty freighter bound from New York for Africa. As the ship passes Sandy Hook, he throws all his books overboard, the books he had bought as a student at Columbia: "like throwing a million bricks out of my heart."[73] With this gesture, Hughes introduces one of his principal themes, his choice of his African and African-American identity. His existential assertion receives an unexpected and rather comic rebuke when he arrives in Africa some weeks later: "The Africans looked at me and would not believe I was a Negro" (p. 11). Hughes, a brown combination of black and white, is

---

[72] Theodore Dreiser, *Dawn: A History of Myself* (New York: Horace Liveright. Inc., 1931), p. 104.

[73] Langston Hughes, *The Big Sea, an Autobiography* (New York: Hill and Wang, 1963 [1940]), p. 3. Hughes apparently adjusted the facts to meet his symbolic intentions: in an earlier version of the story, he confessed that he had reserved a volume of Walt Whitman's poetry from this watery destruction. See Arnold Rampersad, *The Life of Langston Hughes, Volume* 1: *1902–1941, I, Too, Sing America* (New York: Oxford University Press, 1986), p. 377.

simply not black enough to seem black to his African interlocutors. The juxtaposition of the solemn and ironic characterizes Hughes's strategy throughout his memoir.

Like all autobiography, *The Big Sea* is intended to conceal at least as much as it reveals. On the one hand, Hughes masks both his radical politics and his sexual orientation. On the other, he shares serious and even painful experiences, chief among them his teenaged realization that he hated his father. James Hughes "hated Negroes. I think he hated himself, too, for being a Negro" (p. 40). The elder Hughes had moved to Mexico to escape the daily humiliations suffered by African-Americans, and he prospered. But his greed, his cruelty, and above all his racial disloyalty – he invariably referred to black people as "niggers" – merely confirmed his son in his own commitments to his art and his race. His first published poem, "The Negro Speaks of Rivers," moves from the Mississippi to the rivers of Africa.

Hughes knew everyone in the black Renaissance, from entertainers like Bricktop and Josephine Baker to the writers and artists who had gathered in Harlem in the 1920s: Countee Cullen, Arna Bontemps, Aaron Douglas, Jean Toomer, and Zora Neale Hurston, with whom he attempted to collaborate on a play (the sunny beginnings of that venture, rather than its gloomy denouement, are featured in *The Big Sea*). In some external respects, Hughes's life fits the American pattern of success: from need and occasional destitution to an established reputation as a leading literary figure before his fortieth birthday.

Hughes knew, however, that no African-American could be the hero of a Horatio Alger novel. Despite its restraint and frequent good humor, despite its record of publications and prizes, every page of *The Big Sea* is shadowed by race, and the penalty that race inflicts on black people. The hotels and restaurants that refused him service, the jobs he couldn't get, the assumptions that ostensibly friendly whites made – about the inherent "primitivism" of blacks, for example – combine to frame Hughes's life in a cage of denial and diminishment.

Langston Hughes lived in and between ethnic and cultural worlds. So, too, did Nora Waln, the Quaker descendant of Philadelphia merchants, men who had been involved in America's China trade from its eighteenth-century beginnings. From an early age, she immersed herself in the records and objects that her ancestors had bequeathed, and decided, in 1920, at the age of twenty-five, to travel to China, where she spent the next twelve years. Initially, she lived with a gentry family in Hopei (Hebei) province, near the Grand Canal. Later, she lived with her husband, an English diplomatic officer posted to China. Based on the journals she kept during her long sojourn, Waln published a remarkable memoir, *The House of Exile* (1933).[74] The book's title has two meanings: it refers to Waln's own experiences, and also to the Chinese house in which she lived: several generations of the Lin family, numbering over eighty men, women, and children, residing in a compound that traced its origins back another thirty-five generations.

Unlike many of her contemporaries, Waln claimed neither a missionary nor a journalistic vocation: "I could not say that I had come to teach the Chinese people anything. Neither could I say that I had definite intent to learn anything from them."[75] Her report possesses an uncommon poise. She was content simply to live in China, first with the Lins, then with her husband, for over a decade. The first half or so of her book provides a thickly detailed account of life inside the compound of an affluent family. In particular, Waln reports at length on the custom and practices that defined women's lives in such settings. In addition, since the years of Waln's Chinese sojourn coincided with the tumultuous early period of the Republic, *The House of Exile* also provides a valuable record of the warfare and confusion that attended the shifting alliances and routine betrayals that eventually brought Chiang Kai-shek to power following the death of Sun Yat-sen in 1925. As a speaker of both Mandarin and Cantonese, and a woman with links to an important Chinese family with branches in several cities, Waln occupied a privileged if dangerous vantage point.[76]

The final two pages of the book record a remarkable transaction. Waln had received a proposal from Edward Weeks that she write a book about her experiences in China for the Atlantic Monthly Press – the book that would become *The House of Exile*. She submitted her manuscript to the Lin family for their approval. One says that the text is not literature, but "just the usual round of days in an ordinary family." The head of the family concludes that "There is no untruth in what she has put down, but

---

[74] Some years later, Waln wrote five chapters toward a sequel, "Return to the House of Exile." She abandoned the project, possibly to protect her Chinese friends from government reprisal. The chapters were included as a supplement to a 1992 re-printing of *The House of Exile* published by Soho Press.

[75] Nora Waln, *The House of Exile* (Boston: Little, Brown and Company, 1933), p. 80.

[76] Waln had a gift for putting herself in harm's way. Shortly after leaving war-ravaged China, she went to Germany and spent four years there, from 1934 to 1938. She fashioned those experiences into the book *Reaching for the Stars* (Boston: Little, Brown and Company, 1939), a somewhat surprising bestseller. Throughout the book, Waln tries to balance her rising disgust with Nazi behavior with her deep affection for her German friends.

there is no great truth in it either. There is no great Lin in these generations" (p. 336). Despite the objections of the family's oldest member, a ninety-six-year-old woman, who tells Waln that "Scholarship is useless to a woman" (p. 337), and then teaches her a recipe for honey ginger, the family consents to publication.

At about the same time that Nora Waln began her sojourn in Asia, Korean Younghill Kang migrated to America. Kang's "slightly fictionalized" memoirs, *The Grass Roof* (1931) and *East Goes West* (1937), were the first Korean-American autobiographies.[77] Born around 1900 (the precise date is not clear), Kang was old enough to recall the annexation of Korea by Japan in August 1910: "When the news reached the grass roof in Song-Dune-Chi, my father turned a dark red, and could not even open his mouth. My uncle *pak-sa* [senior scholar] became suddenly very old, and he shriveled and fainted in his own room."[78] For thirty-five years, the Japanese imposed a brutal regime, denying elementary civil and judicial rights, suppressing the Korean language, and compelling Korea's puppet rulers to sign extortionate commercial and trading agreements. The occupation ended only with Japan's defeat in World War II.

Korean resistance, always active underground, took a more public stance at the close of World War I. Like the Chinese, Koreans took seriously the meaningless promises of national self-determination pronounced by Western statesmen at the postwar peace conference. China's May Fourth Movement, provoked in 1919 by the betrayals of Versailles, and initiated by student protests in Peking, had a counterpart in Korea. Nationalists, outraged by the mysterious death of the ex-Emperor, declared Korea's independence on March 1919. Younghill Kang was among the students who organized a series of failed demonstrations against the Japanese, after which he fled the country to escape imprisonment and probable execution.

The Grass Roof takes the story to the point of Kang's journey to the USA. Filled with scenes of danger and violence, including Kang's multiple escapes from Japanese custody, *Grass Roof* instructed its Western readers in both the customs of an older Korea and the current catastrophe of the occupation. Given the invisibility of Korea to most Americans, today no less than seventy years ago, the lesson is exceptionally useful.

---

[77] Elaine H. Kim, *Asian American Literature: An Introduction to the Writings and Their Social Context* (Philadelphia: Temple University Press, 1982), p. 33.

[78] Younghill Kang, *The Grass Roof* (New York: Charles Scribner's Sons, 1931), p. 167. The episode occurs in a chapter called "Doomsday."

Looking back on his childhood in a small Korean village, Han Chungpa (as Kang calls himself in both books) recalls mainly the isolation and stability of his family's rural life. His recollections are affectionate but not sentimental: Kang leavens his descriptions with impatience for the backwardness of ossified customary behavior. Indeed, his enthusiasm for Western learning and science grows out of his accurate observation that modern technology has become the prerequisite for national survival. The Japanese invasion proved conclusively that reverence for classical scholarship is no match for well-armed soldiers. "Japan has conquered Korea by Western science," says one of Chungpa's teachers. "We must regain our freedom by a superior knowledge of that science" (p. 181).

Kang's admiration for Western science co-exists with his contempt for Western missionaries. There are two types of missionaries, he says, of which one was "educated and sincere," and "a rarity." The other "is the kind almost universally met with, the type that cannot get any job in the West so he comes to the East where he can live cheaply and have a cook and a waiter and a gardener and cherish a superiority-complex over 'heathen'" (p. 311).[79]

From Korea, Kang traveled to America: "It was my destiny to see the disjointing of a world."[80] *East Goes West* picks up Kang's memoir with his arrival in New York; he arrived, as he says, "just in time before the law against Oriental immigration was passed" (p. 5).[81] Less eventful than *Grass Roof*, Kang's second volume recounts the several years he spent trying to find a place for himself in his new world. Given the situation in Korea, which he rightly predicted would continue for another decade or more, Kang knows that he will not be returning – and indeed would feel like "an exile from America" if he did (p. 400). At the same time, while he continues to admire American energy and its pragmatic indifference to the past, he recoils from the materialism and machinery that seem to

[79] Lin Yutang was another Asian migrant whose transnational writing attracted considerable attention in the 1930s. Born in Fukien province, Lin was educated in a series of Chinese and foreign-language schools, including St. John's University in Shanghai, Harvard, and Leipzig. Returning to China, he worked as a teacher and journalist in China, emigrating to the USA in 1936 as the conflict between China and Japan escalated toward full-scale war. His first book, *My Country and My People* (1935), offered a series of personal impressions of China, intermingled with commentary on Confucian philosophy, history, and customs.

[80] Younghill Kang, *East Goes West: The Making of an Oriental Yankee* (New York: Charles Scribner's Sons, 1937), p. 4.

[81] The original Chinese Exclusion Act was passed in 1882, and renewed each decade thereafter for sixty years. Expanded to exclude other Asian nationals as part of the draconian legislation of 1924, the law was finally abolished in 1943, in the midst of a war in which the USA was allied with the Republic of China.

define American aspirations. Working at a large Philadelphia department store, with excellent chances for promotion, he finds the core of American values in movement and money:

This *is* American life, I said stubbornly. All day long the moving multitudes of humanity, with busy legs, constantly darting false smiles to cover their depressed facial expression, the worn-out machine bodies turning round in the aisles of unmoving glass and china sets, slowing figuring with shaking hands – haste and moving too many things made them so – now over the tally they go, recording 50 cents... then to run with the legs' tottering strength after a new customer, for fear of losing that sale to another salesman (there is a half per cent commission on that sale), at last the dead-tired body moving from the cloak-room to breathe the air – the street air, the dusty, respectable, stale air of staid Philadelphia. (p. 318)

The memoirs of Langston Hughes, Nora Waln, and Younghill Kang comprise an assortment of outsider reports on past and present. More explicitly ideological versions of such narratives were published in the thirties by two of the major radical figures of the early twentieth century, Lincoln Steffens and Emma Goldman. Between them, these books recalled an earlier era of protest and muckraking, and wrote the epitaph to a generation of dissent in the midst of another turbulent era.

A child of the middle class who had been educated at Berkeley and in German universities, Lincoln Steffens began his journalistic career in New York City as the protégé of Jacob Riis. Working as an editor and investigative reporter at *McClure's* magazine, he specialized in the corruption of city governments. The articles he wrote became chapters in his most important book, *The Shame of the Cities* (1904), an odorous and anecdotal survey of graft and malfeasance in six major cities. Over the next three decades, Steffens drifted in and out of public view, associating himself with the revolutions in Mexico and Russia, among other unpopular causes. He visited the Soviet Union in 1919 and greeted reporters on his return with the comment that would follow him for the rest of his life: "I have seen the future and it works." Art Young featured the remark in a 1932 *New Masses* cartoon, an intended compliment that Steffens did not reject; as late as 1936, an invalid near death, he could still rhapsodize: "Poetry, romance – all roads in our day lead to Moscow."[82]

Steffens's *Autobiography*, published when he was sixty-five years old, turned into an expectedly major event, and returned him for a brief

[82] Cited in Justin Kaplan, *Lincoln Steffens: A Biography* (New York: Simon and Schuster, 1974), p. 320.

season to prominence. Despite its length – nearly 900 pages – the book found its way onto college reading lists, and at least one abridged edition was published specifically for high school readers.[83] His timing was fortunate: appearing in the early years of the Depression, when the reforming urgency of the muckrakers and progressives was reviving from a decade of somnolence, the *Autobiography* provided a model of the activist writer.

In a memorable tribute in the *Nation*, Newton Arvin called the *Autobiography* "cartographic" – a map of its era – and compared Steffens to Mill and Tolstoy and Henry Adams, predecessors who had also embodied the spirit of a generation in their lives.[84] The book's success may also have something to do with its ultimately optimistic tone. Though Steffens had lived through wars and revolutions, and met corruption on unusually intimate terms, though he had suffered one ideological disappointment after another, he retained an indomitable belief in the future, in "the bright light to be seen through the darkness."[85]

Emma Goldman published her memoir, *Living My Life*, in two volumes in 1931; it is among the major autobiographical documents of the decade. Though Goldman had engaged in a lifelong argument with socialism and every other species of collectivism on behalf of her version of anarchism, she nonetheless shared a commitment to the two ideals that energized the radical Left in the early years of the century: "the autonomy of the intellectual and the self-liberation of the working class," in John Diggins's summary phrase.[86]

In the early years of the twentieth century, Goldman had become one of the most widely recognized dissident figures of her time: "Red Emma," pummeled in editorials and caricatured in cartoons, ultimately stripped of her citizenship and deported illegally during the Red Scare that followed World War I. Goldman believed restraint to be inherently corrupt, and

---

[83] William H. Cunningham's introduction to the 1937 high school version is rhapsodic in its estimation of Steffens's importance in the shaping of young minds. After calling the prose "lucid, fluent . . . poetic," Cunningham observes: "I can imagine no more pleasant and profitable method of obtaining an insight into the functioning of our society than an intelligent perusal of Steffens' in *Autobiography*." William H. Cunningham, "A Teacher Looks at Lincoln Steffens," in *The Autobiography of Lincoln Steffens, Abridged for High Schools* (New York: Harcourt, Brace and Company, 1937), p. v.

[84] Newton Arvin, "Epitaph for a Generation," *Nation* (April 15, 1931), pp. 415–416.

[85] Lincoln Steffens, *The Autobiography of Lincoln Steffens*, one-volume edition (New York: Harcourt, Brace and Company, 1931), p. 870.

[86] John P. Diggins, *The American Left in the Twentieth Century* (New York: Harcourt, Brace Jovanovich, 1973), p. 96.

she opposed virtually every customary and legal arrangement governing property, political power, and personal relations. Whatever was historically sanctioned was in her view automatically suspect. She regarded anarchism as the assertion of what she defiantly called "the New" against all of the claims of "the Old."[87]

Since all forms of government are ultimately grounded in violence – and the right to coerce individual compliance with government decisions – then all forms of government are inherently corrupt. Her scorched-earth commitments, forged in her hatred of Tsarist tyranny, were doomed in America's imperfect but undeniable democracy. In historian James Joll's view: "Anarchism is necessarily a creed of all or nothing," and thus given to the sort of apocalyptic ecstasy that could never make headway in America's middle-class polity.[88]

In the thousand pages of *Living My Life*, Goldman used the example of her own life to articulate her vision of the humane new world that men and women might build after they had freed themselves from the fetters of the past. The book is a frank and detailed chronicle of Goldman's public and private careers. It is also filled with the names and doings of other early twentieth-century radicals, and of their friends and opponents, and it has remained an indispensable sourcebook for some of the most agitated years of American politics. From the social workers to the "goo-goo's" to the Wobblies to the police, from Theodore Roosevelt to John Reed, Max Eastman and Bill Haywood, all the major actors, and a good many extras along with them, make their entrances and exits.

Somewhat ironically, the radical Goldman produced an autobiography of the most conventional and conventionally American kind. All the tropes and patterns that have characterized American memoirs from Benjamin Franklin's *Autobiography* to Booker T. Washington's *Up From Slavery* define the shape and tone of Goldman's book. *Living My Life* is the story of a conversion; of an education; of goodness endangered, repeatedly betrayed but endlessly resilient. It is an ideological re-casting of the rags-to-riches saga, the tale of a restless journey: the romance of the self, couched in the most familiar rhythms of the romance form. Goldman robed her remembered dreams of future perfection in the regalia of the past.

---

[87] Emma Goldman, "Anarchism: What It Really Stands For," in *Anarchism and Other Essays* (Port Washington, NY: Kennikat Press, 1969 [1910]), p. 53.

[88] James Joll, *The Anarchists* (Boston: Little, Brown and Company, 1964), p. 275.

An American Doctor's Odyssey (1936), by Victor Heiser, was the bestselling autobiography of the 1930s. Though it has long been out of print and is more or less forgotten today, the book sold upwards of 500,000 copies and received lead reviews in dozens of newspapers and magazines both in the United States and overseas. It was a Book-of-the-Month Club main selection, and was translated into a dozen languages. Why the exceptional interest in a man who spent his entire adult life as a health officer in Asia?

Sheer excitement, for one thing, beginning with the book's sensational opening chapter. As a teenager, Heiser barely survived the devastating Johnstown Flood of 1889, in which over 2,000 people died, out of a town population of 30,000. The victims included both of Heiser's parents. His account of the flood, and of his escape by clinging to the roof of a house as it careened downstream, immediately establishes Heiser's credentials as a storyteller and adventurer.

Both qualities mark the entire book. Put summarily, *Odyssey* is an epic, and Heiser is its self-authored hero. The enemy is disease, and the weapons are provided by the emerging science of public health. Recalling decades of travel in the Philippines, Japan, the Pacific islands, Ceylon (Sri Lanka), India, and several dozen other countries, Heiser combines scores of anecdotes, many fascinating and more than a few downright bizarre, with quite detailed and frequently revolting descriptions of hookworm, malaria, leprosy, tuberculosis, and their treatment. In his own account, he is routinely fearless, brilliant in diagnosis, skilled in languages, and expert in negotiation. He may have glamorized some of the episodes – his escape from a school of sharks, his capture of would-be bandits, his triumphant encounters with headhunting tribesmen in Borneo – but he did undeniably important work. His own research and clinical practice were multiplied by the health schools he helped to found and the dozens of younger physicians he recruited.

The scale of Heiser's achievement explains at least some of the interest his book elicited. He claims at one point to have saved 100,000 lives, a statement supported by the ascertainable facts. He first worked for the US government's Marine Hospital Service, treating veterans of the Spanish-American War. He then spent over a decade in the Philippines, establishing public health facilities that became models for other nations and Asian colonies. In 1915, Heiser was recruited by the Rockefeller Foundation to become Director of the East for the foundation's International Health Board; he held the post for the next fifteen years. In the course of his thirty years in the field, he traveled almost continuously around the islands and mainland countries of the Pacific. One of *Odyssey*'s strengths lies in Heiser's descriptive virtuosity: he brings to quite vivid life everything he recalls, from the jungles of Indonesia, to the temples of Angkor Wat, the overcrowded, oppressive slums of Manila, the Peak of Hong Kong, the native costumes of Korean farmers, the suffering of the patients in an airless and festering malaria ward in India.

Heiser occasionally resorts to the orientalist clichés that still defined Western perceptions of Asia in the 1930s. He invokes "Oriental guile" and "Oriental sophistry," insists that Sinhalese are "intractable" and Filipinos are "born actors."[89] He can refer, without irony, to the nobility of "the white man's burden" (p. 47). It should be added that he also engages in similar stereotyping with respect to Europeans: the Irish, Dutch, French are all abused in the course of the book, and the British are presented as especially blinkered and bigoted (p. 330).

Along with his intermittent condescension, however, Heiser consistently displays a good deal of respect for the people of Asia. He is humbled by Chinese generosity and delighted when a small Filipino child outsmarts a British major (p. 202). He takes pride in the exceptional skills of a Suva medical student (p. 375), and endorses the Javanese independence movement (p. 474). He is outraged by the disrespect symbolized in American legislation barring Japanese immigrants (p. 398). In matters of health, Heiser specifically embraces a fundamental equality. After an international health conference in Manila, he concludes that "yellow, brown and white had met in a common cause, and each had learned that the essentials of his problems were common to all" (p. 292).

Heiser reserves his most deliberated scorn for religion, both Asian and European. Roman Catholicism blights Filipinos with its "angry God" and "mediaeval atmosphere," and its belief that illness is a manifestation of divine wrath (p. 103). Heiser tells a hair-raising story to illustrate his point. A cholera outbreak is traced to Manila Bay. Two fishermen have reported bubbles rising in the water in the shape of a cross; hundreds of small boats bring Filipinos to the spot to drink. A local priest blesses the water and declares it a miracle. In fact, the city's main sewer line had ruptured; the miracle is the product of a flood of human waste, and scores of Filipinos were sickened and killed by the poison they drank (pp. 106–107).

Throughout *Odyssey*, Heiser ratifies his authority by incorporating quite technical descriptions of his therapeutic activities. It is a somewhat

---

[89] Victor Heiser, M.D., *An American Doctor's Odyssey: Adventures in Forty-five Countries* (New York: Grosset and Dunlap, 1936), pp. 30, 111, 334, 235.

risky rhetorical strategy, since lay readers may be overwhelmed by medical talk, as in this quite typical example:

I drew up a list of points on which further hookworm knowledge was desired, such as whether thymol or chenopodium was more efficient, the after effects of treatment, what kind of purge to use, the diet, the relation between the age of the patient and the severity of the infection, and whether necators were less resistant than ancylostomes. The final point was to determine to what degree uncinariasis infection was a menace . . . (p. 299)

However unexpected such paragraphs may be in a bestselling book, *Odyssey* is filled with them, in alternation with thickly textured and often appalling descriptions of the course of a dozen different diseases. In fact, the medical language epitomizes Heiser's design in the book. He subdues the terrors of lethal diseases through the instruments of modern science, a field whose arcane vocabulary infuses a kind of rational magic into the day-to-day work of improving medical conditions throughout the world.

In the midst of the Depression, when the machinery of politics had repeatedly failed to elevate the lives of ordinary citizens, *An American Doctor's Odyssey* offered an alternative, if only vicariously. The book seemed to affirm that trained intellect and hard work could still achieve remarkable success.[90]

Another of the decade's most popular self-portraits, Frank Lloyd Wright's *An Autobiography* (1932), was even more clamorous in its endorsement of self-reliance.[91] Wright's early triumphs – Unity Temple in Oak Park, Illinois (1904), the Larkin Building in Buffalo (1905), the Robie House in Chicago (1906), among many others – had been followed in the 1920s by a decade of decline. His book, written when he had "nothing to build at a very bad time in my life," represented a deliberate effort to reassert his claims on public attention.[92]

The *Autobiography* helped to launch what is usually called Wright's second career: the 1930s saw the completion of the headquarters of the S. C. Johnson & Company Administration Building in Racine, Wisconsin,

---

[90] A whole branch of scholarship has emerged that studies the interrelations between foreign policy and scientific medical research in Asia and Africa. For two examples, see Douglas M. Haynes, *Imperial Medicine: Patrick Manson and the Conquest of Tropical Disease* (Philadelphia: University of Pennsylvania Press, 2001), and Roy MacLeod and Milton Lewis, eds., *Disease, Medicine, and Empire: Perspectives on Western Medicine and the Experience of European Expansion* (London: Routledge, 1988).

[91] The book was re-printed in 1933 and again in 1938. A revised edition was published in 1943.

[92] Cited in Donald Leslie Johnson, *Frank Lloyd Wright versus America: the 1930s* (Cambridge, MA: MIT Press, 1990), p. 28.

and Fallingwater, a country house at Mill Run, Pennsylvania, often described as the most important residence built in the USA since Monticello (both 1936).[93] These buildings, along with the Usonian houses he designed for a middle-class market and his plans for a model city called Broadacre, established Wright as incontestably the most famous if not the most influential of American architects. Publication of the *Autobiography* coincided with the first international exhibition of modern architecture, at the Museum of Modern Art. In the catalogue of that exhibition, Henry-Russell Hitchcock pronounced Wright "one of the greatest architects of all time." Wright emphatically agreed, and his memoir was carefully orchestrated to support the proposition.

The *Autobiography* can be trawled for insights into Wright's theory and practice, though the contemporaneous *The Disappearing City* (1932) and especially *Modern Architecture* (1931) provide more useful sources.[94] The conspicuous task of the *Autobiography* is to present Wright as a heroic, authentically American genius, a man of large vision and equally large appetites. Wright relished his carefully disheveled long hair and his foppish clothing, evidence of his superiority and his exemption from convention. Candid about his sexual adventuring and his inadequacies as the father of his six children – "Is it a quality? Fatherhood? If so, I seemed to be born without it" – Wright takes it for granted that his devotion to his work offers full justification for his behavior.[95] In a famous anecdote, he boasts that he used his own height as the standard for his houses, and adds that if he had been taller the houses would be different (*Autobiography*, p. 139). Wright saw himself as literally the measure of all things.

He enjoyed brawling. Beating up a fellow worker in an impromptu boxing match (recalled at length in a section called "Combat") gave him as much satisfaction as insulting a group of rival architects at a dinner. He also enjoyed his self-appointed role as the nation's prophet and scold. In these moods, Wright's prose swells to oracular dimensions, rhapsodic

[93] It was a paradoxical decade in American architecture. Many architects went out of business when money for major projects – or even minor projects – dried up. On the other hand, the thirties saw the completion of several of the most important and indeed iconic projects in twentieth-century architecture. To Wright's masterpieces, add the Empire State Building (1932), the Chrysler Building (1931), and the complex at Rockefeller Center (1931–1940), all in New York City, and the Philadelphia Savings Fund Society (1932), long revered as the nation's first "International Style" office tower.

[94] *Modern Architecture* gathered the important Kahn Lectures that Wright delivered at Princeton in 1930.

[95] Frank Lloyd Wright, *An Autobiography* (New York: Longmans Green and Company, 1932), p. 111.

and often overheated. Bashing the styles and devices of eclectic architects, Wright asks:

What is your beauty – and yours – and yours – yes, and yours, my savant! I can't hear you but I imagine your answer. It would simmer down to a mere matter of "taste," if you spoke the truth. And "taste" is usually a matter of ignorance, or a personal idiosyncrasy, cultivated – overmuch.

Come to terms eclectism! None of the great architecture of the World ever grew up on any such flimsy basis as "taste." Even such rare taste as yours, my connoisseur. (p. 326)

In another passage, ostensibly eulogizing Louis Sullivan, but undoubtedly having himself also in mind, Wright celebrates the rare power of genius:

The effect of any genius is seldom seen in its own time. Nor can the full effects of genius ever be traced or seen. Human affairs are flowing. What we call life in everything is plastic, a becoming, in spite of all efforts to fix it with names, and all endeavors to make it static to man's will. As a pebble cast into the ocean sets up reactions lost in distance and time, so does any man's genius go on infinitely forever. For genius is an expression of principle. (p. 269)

Not everyone accepted Wright's self-promotion at his own high estimate, but John Dos Passos was among those who did. He included a sketch called "Architect" as one of the biographies in *The Big Money* (1936). Taking his cue from Wright's own beleaguered, misunderstood version of himself, Dos Passos salutes Wright as a prophet without honor in his own country, a man who drove his countrymen "toward the American future instead of toward the pain-smeared past of Europe and Asia."[96]

Along with its verve, the tribute is unintentionally ironic. While Wright did much to shape the aesthetic attitudes of the twentieth century, and while he greeted the future with exuberant optimism, he simultaneously clung with both hands to the past: the past of his own childhood and of nineteenth-century America. Europe, too: given the extent of Wright's unacknowledged debts to John Ruskin, William Morris, and the Arts and Crafts Movement.[97] Albert Bush-Brown, writing after Wright's death, was not the only critic to observe that Wright's "themes are nineteenth-century themes": individualism, heroism, nature, and pastoral.[98]

---

[96] John Dos Passos, *The Big Money* (New York: New American Library, 1979 [1936]), p. 439.
[97] I discuss these connections in some detail in *The Divided Mind: Ideology and Imagination in America, 1891–1917* (New York: Cambridge University Press, 1983), pp. 219–229.
[98] Albert Bush-Brown, "The Honest Arrogance of Frank Lloyd Wright," *The Atlantic* (August, 1959), p. 24.

Autobiography always lies at the intersection of fact and fiction. Frank Lloyd Wright's *Autobiography* re-writes not merely his own life story, but the sources and significance of his architecture. Another significant autobiography, published in the same year as Wright's, raises the questions of genre and authenticity in a quite different way. *Black Elk Speaks* (1932) is a translation and an act of multiple collaboration. John Neihardt, a Nebraska poet and historian, interviewed Black Elk, an aged holy man of the Oglala Sioux tribe; since neither man spoke the other's language, several different people served as interpreters.[99] Whose voice was actually recorded in the book?

A large number of purported Native American autobiographies had been published in the nineteenth and early twentieth centuries, all of which presented similar difficulties.[100] Books such as Sarah Winnemucca Hopkins's *Life Among the Paiutes* (1883), Simon Pokagon's *Life of O-Gi-Maw-Kwe-Mit-I-Gwa-Ki: Queen of the Woods* (1899), and "The Autobiography of a Fox Indian Woman" (1925)[101] transformed oral narratives into written versions that were undoubtedly shaped by the expectations and conventions of white authors and readers. Even the term "autobiography" bristles with definitional problems.

Despite its doubtful provenance, *Black Elk Speaks* has become the most widely read Native American memoir of the first half of the twentieth century. To begin with, Black Elk was witness to some of the most famous events in the history of Native American encounter with whites. Born in the late 1850s or early 1860s, he was present at the battle against Lieutenant Colonel George Custer and the US Cavalry at Little Big Horn in 1876. After a decade traveling with Buffalo Bill's Wild West Show, he then returned to the Dakotas and survived the massacre at Wounded Knee in 1890. Beyond that, Black Elk offers a self-portrait steeped in spiritual values and told in a prose of high formality. According to one source, *Black Elk Speaks* was recently included in a list of the ten most important spiritual books of the century.[102]

---

99   The many studies of the book's problematic authorship include Julian Rice, *Black Elk's Story: Distinguishing Its Lakota Purpose* (Albuquerque: University of New Mexico Press, 1991), and Brian R. Holloway, *Interpreting the Legacy: John Neihardt and Black Elk Speaks* (Boulder: University Press of Colorado, 2003).

100 Perhaps the earliest Native American autobiography was produced by Reverend Samson Occom, a Mohegan and a Christian convert, in 1768. Arnold Krupat, ed., *Native American Autobiography: An Anthology* (Madison: University of Wisconsin Press, 1994), p. 5.

101 "The Autobiography of a Fox Indian Woman" appeared in the 40th *Annual Report of the Bureau of American Ethnology* (1925), pp. 291–349.

102 Philip Zaleski, "*Black Elk Speaks* in the Top Ten Spiritual Books of the Century," *Neihardt Journal* (2000), p. 9.

Black Elk recalls in detail two visions he had as a child, along with his performance of the Horse Dance. Whether by his own choice or Neihardt's, he includes no mention of his conversion to Christianity, which took place decades before the interviews. Instead, he puts his visions of divinity at the center of his experience. At nine years old, he sees himself lifted up into the sky for a parley with six old men:

> I went in and stood before the six, and they looked older than men can ever be – old like hills, like stars.
> The oldest spoke again: "Your Grandfathers all over the world are having a council, and they have called you here to teach you." His voice was very kind, but I shook all over with fear now, for I knew that they were not old men, but the Powers of the World.[103]

Less memoir than the record of a spiritual quest, less ethnography than literary performance, *Black Elk Speaks* has nonetheless endured as a key text in the history of Native American culture and of relations between Native Americans and whites.

Several other volumes of Native American memoirs were published in the 1930s, including *We Indians: The Passing of a Great Race* (1931), the putative recollections of White Horse Eagle, and two books by Truman Michelson of the Bureau of American Ethnology, "The Narrative of a Southern Cheyenne Woman" (1932) and "The Narrative of an Arapaho Woman" (1933).[104] *Wah'Kon-Tah: The Osage and the White Man's Road* (1932), by John Joseph Mathews, lies between genres. Neither biography nor autobiography, the book transcribes the observations of Major Laban Stiles, a Quaker who was appointed federal agent to the Osages in 1878. Mathews embeds excerpts from Stiles's unpublished diary into a semi-fictional narrative; the collaborative portrait suggests that Stiles was a man who worked hard to secure equity for the Native Americans under his supervision. In a typical passage, he investigates a white assault on a band of Osage hunters and concludes: "there had been no provocation and no reason for the attack more than the desire of the white settlers to persecute the Indians."[105]

Like other of the biographies and autobiographies discussed in this chapter, Native American memoirs played an important part in the Depression decade's debate over the meaning of America.

---

[103] John Neihardt, *Black Elk Speaks: Being the Life Story of a Holy Man of the Oglala Sioux* (Lincoln: University of Nebraska Press, 1979 [1932]), p. 25.
[104] "The Narrative of a Southern Cheyenne Woman" was published in *Smithsonian Miscellaneous Collections* (1932); "The Narrative of an Arapaho Woman" appeared in *American Anthropologist* (1933).
[105] John Joseph Mathews, *Wah'Kon-Tah: The Osage and the White Man's Road* (Norman: University of Oklahoma Press, 1932), p. 38.

CHAPTER 5

The Southern past

Start with the end of the decade, and the publication of Wilbur J. Cash's controversial classic *The Mind of the South* (1941). Cash's influential book delivered the definitive rebuttal to the pious sentimentality of the Cavalier myth. Instead of resting on the virtues of honor and courage, according to Cash, Southern behavior and attitudes sprang from a "savage ideal," a code of conduct that drove the region's white inhabitants toward every form of social pathology.[1] In this reading, the South derived its distinctiveness and "separateness" from its history of poverty, disease,[2] military defeat, and segregation, not, as its apologists would have it, from the region's fidelity to agrarian values, personal loyalty, and tradition.[3] Much of the region's identity, and many of its problems, had roots in the past. This was the part of the country that had looked back throughout most of its history: to a barbarized chivalry in its antebellum years, and to the Lost Cause after the catastrophe of the Civil War.

In some measure, this unforgiving assessment of the South had been anticipated and indeed codified by the fiction produced during the 1930s, in the efflorescence of the so-called "Southern Renaissance." Among

---

[1] For a good brief discussion of Cash's influential book, see Daniel Joseph Singal, *The War Within: From Victorian to Modernist Thought in the South, 1919–1945* (Chapel Hill: University of North Carolina Press, 1982), pp. 373f.

[2] On the importance of disease in the making of Southern identity, see Thomas L. Savitt and James Harvey Young, eds., *Disease and Distinctiveness in the American South* (Knoxville: University of Tennessee Press, 1988). Throughout its history, right up through the thirties, the South was demonstrably the "sickest" of America's regions. Malaria, yellow fever, hookworm, and typhoid all claimed more victims in the South than elsewhere. With symptoms that included chronic fatigue, malaria, hookworm, and pellagra comprised what one historian has called "the Southern trilogy of 'lazy diseases.'" George Brown Tindall, *The Emergence of the New South, 1913–1945* (Baton Rouge: Louisiana State University Press, 1967), p. 227. See also John Ettling, *The Germ of Laziness: Rockefeller Philanthropy and Public Health in the New South* (Cambridge, MA: Harvard University Press, 1981).

[3] Not surprisingly, Cash included a compliment to Mencken's nasty polemic, "The Sahara of the Bozart": "while it all might be very wicked, it still had an uncomfortable lot of truth in it." Wilbur J. Cash, *The Mind of the South* (New York: Alfred A. Knopf, 1941), p. 325.

them, Erskine Caldwell's libidinous buffoons, Eudora Welty's grotesque and lonely outsiders, above all William Faulkner's gallery of idiots, con men, rapists, suicides, arsonists, and twisted souls, etched the lineaments of Southern identity in the acid of deviance, incest, violence, and death. The fictional portraits seemed to find documentary support in the photographs of the Farm Security Administration. Here, in the images of Dorothea Lange, Walker Evans, Arthur Rothstein, and others, was visual evidence of regional collapse.

The economic troubles that engulfed the country in the 1930s had bedeviled the South long before 1929. For three generations following the Civil War, America's gigantic industrial and urban growth had bypassed the South almost completely. The states of the old Confederacy continued to be rural, poor, agrarian, precariously tied to a single crop, and morally impoverished by a systematized racism. Because of the preponderantly agricultural basis of its economy, the "Depression was more devastating to the South than to any other region."[4] The South, in the memorable phrase of Franklin D. Roosevelt, was "the Nation's number one economic problem."[5]

One historian has recently concluded, "almost everywhere in this American subculture, conditions were uniformly miserable."[6] Such a generalization requires adjustment in favor of local difference. There were many "Souths," and they each had a distinctive set of customs, economic arrangements, and histories. Sherwood Anderson asked, "What is there in common between Savannah, Georgia, and Knoxville, Tennessee, between the North Carolina mill section and the sugar bowl of southern Mississippi?"[7] At the same time, more than any other region of the USA, the South nurtured a collective identity, if only as the site of defeat and resistance. It was also a particularly backward cluster of states, often willfully backward. For decades after the Civil War, literary culture was virtually non-existent. Ellen Glasgow, looking back on her childhood in late-nineteenth-century Virginia, later wrote, "southerners did not publish, did not write, did not read."[8]

[4] Charles Reagan Wilson, "Americanization," in Charles Reagan Wilson and William Ferris, eds., *Encyclopedia of Southern Culture* (Chapel Hill: University of North Carolina Press, 1989), p. 592.
[5] Cited in Patricia Sullivan, *Days of Hope: Race and Democracy in the New Deal Era* (Chapel Hill: University of North Carolina Press, 1996), p. 65.
[6] T. H. Watkins, *The Hungry Years: A Narrative History of the Great Depression in America* (New York: Henry Holt and Company, 1999), p. 371.
[7] Sherwood Anderson, *Puzzled America* (New York: Charles Scribner's Sons, 1935), p. 129.
[8] Cited from *The Woman Within* (1954), in Louis D. Rubin, *Writers of the Modern South: The Faraway Country* (Seattle: University of Washington Press, 1963), p. 5.

Glasgow herself would help initiate the change that turned a region known for its illiteracy into the headquarters of literary excellence in the first third of the century. The great literary achievement that became known as the Southern Renaissance became a self-conscious movement after the First World War, with the gathering of the Nashville Fugitives in and around Vanderbilt University. The magazine they put out, *The Fugitive*, first appeared in 1922 and was published for just three years. The group's members carried on, and they played seminal roles in the reassessment of the South's past and prospects that so conspicuously took place between the two world wars. They included the poets Donald Davidson, Allen Tate, and John Crowe Ransom, whose verses sought out the strength that might still reside in traditional values. In some cases, the tradition was "Southern" only by appropriation. Davidson's "On a Replica of the Parthenon in Nashville," for example, harshly condemns the busy materialism of modern city life by contrasting it with the tranquil simplicity of classical Greece. Davidson implies that the South is the only contemporary region in which that nurturing tranquility is likely to be rediscovered.

Much of Agrarian verse is filled with the retreating echoes of Civil War heroism. Plain soldiers and leaders are called up from the shadows, their images deckle-edged with authority and pathos. Davidson's best-known poem, "Lee in the Mountains," pictures the defeated general in retirement and idealizes him and the cause he fought for. Ransom's "Captain Carpenter" is treated with gentle irony as he goes down to defeat before the forces of modernity, but his outmoded gallantry is shown to be clearly preferable to the savage efficiency of his opponents. The most affecting of these historical meditations is Allen Tate's "Ode to the Confederate Dead," first published in 1926.

Agrarian themes were given expository statement in 1930 in a book called *I'll Take My Stand*. The dozen essays in this controversial volume range across economy and art, religion and race. Detailed, often sentimental sketches of rural life alternate with root-and-branch assaults on the technology and mass culture of the North. The book was subtitled "The South and the Agrarian Tradition." As Donald Davidson said in the introductory "Statement of Principles," all the essays in the book "tend to support a Southern way of life against what may be called the American or prevailing way; and all as much agree that the best terms in which to represent the distinction are contained in the phrase, Agrarian *versus* Industrial."[9] Agriculture was the only basis on which a coherent community could be

[9] *I'll Take My Stand*, By Twelve Southerners (New York: Harper Torchbooks, 1962 [1930]), p. xix.

honorably based. Fancying themselves heirs of America's authentic traditions, the essayists set themselves against the city and its alleged ugliness.

The polemical tone of the book is economically suggested by the titles of some of the individual essays: "Reconstructed but Unregenerate," "A Critique of the Philosophy of Progress," and "The Irrepressible Conflict." John Crowe Ransom described the South as anglophile, and traced his own conservative views in part to such writers as John Ruskin and Matthew Arnold.[10] In an unlikely act of appropriation, John Gould Fletcher reached further back, to Confucius, in demanding an educational system that fitted students for lives of virtuous submission to hierarchy and received values. Lyle H. Lanier lampooned Francis Bacon, John Dewey, and William James as apostles of scientific "progress" and therefore enemies of humane traditions.[11]

Aside from mystifying the land and the past, most of these writers shared retrograde attitudes toward blacks and women. Frank Lawrence Owsley, defending Southern resistance to Reconstruction, invoked the specter of "three millions of former slaves, some of whom could still remember the taste of human flesh and the bulk of them hardly three generations removed from cannibalism" (p. 62). In "The Hind Tit," Andrew Nelson Lytle offered a quite chilling defense of the South's commitment to property rather than currency in determining its wealth: "Stocks and bonds and cities did not constitute wealth to the planter. Broad acres and increasing slaves, all tangible evidence of possession, were the great desiderata of his labors" (p. 208).

In terms of twentieth-century politics, including racial politics, the Agrarians were fighting a rear-guard and losing action, and much of what they said seemed even at the time more quaint than pertinent. Rupert Vance, reviewing the volume in the *Mississippi Valley Historical Review* shortly after its publication, concluded, "a return to the agrarian tradition

---

[10] Stark Young, who contributed an essay called "Not in Memoriam, but in Defense," published a series of four loosely connected novels between 1926 and 1934, all set in Mississippi and all dedicated to the task of affirming Southern values against the urbanism, industrialization, and materialism of the North. The last and best of these books is *So Red the Rose* (1934), set in the Civil War.

[11] Commenting on nineteenth-century Britain, Bernard Knox offers an observation that also has relevance to the twentieth-century Agrarians: "One reason for this insistence on fake classical themes . . . must have been the overpowering ugliness of the Victorian industrial landscape . . ." "The Greek Conquest of Britain," *The New York Review of Books* (June 11, 1981), p. 27. American cities certainly housed their share of ugliness, but they were also, as Frederic C. Howe had pointed out in his landmark 1905 book, *The Hope of Democracy*. It was democracy more than any failure of aesthetics that provoked Agrarian opposition.

in the South is . . . a return to the abyss."[12] H. L. Mencken spluttered that *I'll Take My Stand* "has little more bearing upon life as men and women must now live it in the world than the Presbyterian metaphysics of Paul Elmer More . . ."[13]

If *I'll Take My Stand* substituted mythology for history, William Faulkner deployed history to demolish mythology. He was the region's preeminent fictional historian. Indeed, the stronger and defensible claim has been made that the "works of William Faulkner constitute the most splendid achievement of the historical imagination in twentieth-century American letters."[14] Though the fact is sometimes scanted, Faulkner produced most of his major novels and stories in the thirties. *Sartoris* and *The Sound and the Fury* (1929), which commenced the Yoknapatawpha saga, were followed by *As I Lay Dying* (1930), *Light in August* (1932), *Absalom, Absalom!* (1936), and *The Unvanquished* (1938); most of the stories in *Go Down, Moses* (1942) had been completed by 1940. Among American novelists, only Henry James sustained such a level of writing in so many books; only Melville pushed against the limits of fictional convention with such restless and prodigal fertility. And, unlike either James or Melville, Faulkner's great achievement was mainly the product of a single decade.

   Faulkner was noticed but devalued by most of the decade's critics, and by the small group of academics who addressed American writers in literary histories, surveys, and anthologies. In the years after the Second World War, that relative neglect has given way to ceaseless scrutiny. Using the evidence of scholarly publication as an index, Faulkner can probably be called the central fictional writer of the American twentieth century. Certainly no other American writer active in the thirties, not even Hemingway, has received a fraction of the critical and scholarly attention devoted to Faulkner over the past fifty years.

   Given the power and eccentricity of Faulkner's imagination, it is quite possible that the Yoknapatawpha saga would have emerged whether the country was struggling through the Depression or not.[15] He was attuned,

[12] Rupert B. Vance, review of *I'll Take My Stand, Mississippi Valley Historical Review* (June, 1931), p. 117.
[13] H. L. Mencken, "Uprising in the Confederacy," *American Mercury* (March, 1931), p. 380.
[14] Harry B. Henderson, III, *Versions of the Past: The Historical Imagination in American Fiction* (New York: Oxford University Press, 1974), p. 253.
[15] For one effort to connect Faulkner's work more directly with the national crisis of the 1930s, see Ted Atkinson, *Faulkner and the Great Depression: Aesthetics, Ideology, and Cultural Politics* (Athens: University of Georgia Press, 2006).

almost magically, to historical circumstance, but the root and branch of his concern was the history of his community and region. The South provided all of his subjects, source materials, and themes. He was more strongly connected to the past and the local than to the present and the national. Robert Penn Warren, one of Faulkner's most sympathetic readers, describes "the South which Faulkner had grown up in [as] cut-off, inward-turning, backward-looking. It was a culture frozen in its virtues and vices . . ."[16]

Faulkner rarely left the South. He went to Canada in the latter days of the First World War, in an unsuccessful effort to fly with the Royal Canadian Air Force, and he made an obligatory but unproductive sojourn in Europe in the early twenties. The national economic crisis of the 1930s intersected with Faulkner's sequence of fictions as a kind of larger validation: the deprivation and bewilderment that dogged the northern and western sections of the country had been smothering facts of ordinary life in the South for two generations and more.

Faulkner was an ambivalent heir of the Old South, whose legacy was a bankrupt economy, barbaric racial codes, inertia that alternated with spasms of cruelty, nostalgia for blighted honor, reverence for the unspoiled land, contempt for the intellect, and a passion for talk. Because his imagination was endlessly contemplating the past, and the events that linked the past ineradicably to the present, Faulkner's Yoknapatawpha, to use a phrase from *As I Lay Dying*, becomes a land of "weary gestures wearily recapitulant."[17]

Perhaps no novel so completely illuminates Faulkner's absorption in the past as *Absalom, Absalom!*, his dense meditation on race, history, family, sexuality, and death. Nor does any other novel so fully illustrate the interconnections between the tale and the telling. At the center of *Absalom* lies a mystery: why did Thomas Sutpen, the stupendously ambitious proprietor of a vast plantation, forbid the marriage of his daughter, Judith, to the handsome and apparently eligible Charles Bon? That act, which leads to Bon's murder by Judith's brother, Henry, is never definitively explained; the novel records the efforts of a sequence of narrators, each of whom is blinkered by personal need, by anger, desire, and loyalty, to search out the truth.

---

[16] Robert Penn Warren, "Faulkner: Past and Future," in Warren, ed., *Faulkner: a Collection of Critical Essays* (Englewood Cliffs, NJ: Prentice-Hall, Inc., 1966), p. 3.

[17] William Faulkner, *As I Lay Dying* (New York: Vintage Books, 1957 [1930]), p. 196.

As several commentators have observed, something like 90 percent of *Absalom* is talk (and therefore listening), ultimately comprising a shared act of seeking and questioning. The narrators are arranged in a pattern, beginning with the elderly Rosa Coldfield, a woman who knew Sutpen, was sister to his wife, and was the victim of his mortal insult. She is followed by Mr. Compson, who had the story from his father and passes it on to his own son, Quentin, who also spends an afternoon listening to Rosa. Finally, Quentin and his Harvard roommate, Shreve, take over the job of narration and explanation in the book's final chapters, implying that historical truth is a work of imagination as much as chronicle.

In that insight, Faulkner's views are congruent with those of several contemporaneous philosophers and historians. The English philosopher R. G. Collingwood's landmark essay, "The Historical Imagination," which was first published in the 1930s, bears a considerable resemblance to Faulkner's notions of the "constructed" nature of historical knowledge.[18] Early in the century, American historian Carl Becker argued, in "Detachment and the Writing of History" (1910), that "[t]he 'facts' of history do not exist for any historian until he creates them, and into every fact that he creates some part of his individual experience must enter."[19] Becker returned to the subject in another essay, "What Are Historical Facts?," which had appeared in the mid-1920s, and most famously in "Everyman His Own Historian," his 1931 presidential address to the American Historical Association. History, he argued there, is an "imaginative creation," fashioned by each of us out of "personal experience."[20] In 1932, Frederick Bartlett published his important book, *Remembering*, in which he concluded after numerous experiments: "remembering appears to be far more decisively an affair of construction rather than one of mere

[18] See, among other sources, Patricia Tobin, "The Time of Myth and History in *Absalom, Absalom!*," *American Literature* (May, 1973), pp. 252–270.
[19] Re-printed in Phil L. Snyder, ed., *Detachment and the Writing of History: Essays and Letters of Carl Becker* (Ithaca, NY: Cornell University Press, 1958), p. 12.
[20] Carl Becker, *Everyman His Own Historian: Essays on History and Politics* (Chicago: Quadrangle Paperbacks, 1966 [1935]), p. 243. Becker's "perspectival" view of historical writing closely resembled Ruth Benedict's proposition that all social scientists are captive to the assumptions and values they bring to their evidence. The difficulties of historical certitude, and the elusive quality of historical knowledge, have remained central subjects, attracting particular attention as a consequence of the intrusion of postmodernist and poststructuralist ideas into historical practice. Dominick Lacapra, Hayden White, and Paul Ricoeur, to name just three major figures, are among the historians, philosophers, and literary theorists who have pursued these questions. For a sensible treatment of these issues, see Joyce Appleby, Lynn Hunt, and Margaret Jacob, *Telling the Truth About History* (New York: W. W. Norton and Company, 1994).

reproduction."[21] *Absalom* brilliantly illustrates these contemporaneous conceptions; the "personal experience" of each narrator determines his or her imaginative creation.

At the center of each of those narrators' concerns stands Sutpen, whose history is gradually disclosed. He had settled for a time in Haiti, scene of Toussaint L'Ouverture's bloody and successful revolt against white overlords – an episode that would haunt the imagination of the white South for generations.[22] Charles Bon is (probably) the son whom Sutpen sired in Haiti with a black woman and then rejected, and marriage between Bon and Judith would therefore (probably) entail both incest and miscegenation. Henry, learning this tortured history, warns Bon away, then shoots him to prevent the unthinkable union of brother and sister, black and white. Sutpen's dynastic dreams disintegrate when one of his sons murders the other. The catastrophe that overtakes him has a logic that outstrips his capacity for comprehension: "You see," Sutpen tells Grandfather Compson, "I had a design in my mind. Whether it was a good or a bad design is beside the point; the question is, Where did I make the mistake in it . . ."[23]

Sutpen's self-inflicted tragedy is played out against the background of the Civil War – what Mr. Compson at one point calls that "horrible and bloody mischancing of human affairs" (p. 80). Early in the novel, Rosa Coldfield speculates on the link between Sutpen's outrages and the South's defeat: "Oh he was brave. I have never gainsaid that. But that our cause, our very life and future hopes and past pride, should have been thrown into the balance with men like that to buttress it – men with valor and strength but without pity or honor. Is it any wonder that Heaven saw fit to let us lose?" (p. 13).

Rosa is only half-right. Though Sutpen is not a traditional, slave-owning plantation master – indeed in some respects he more closely resembles a Northern opportunist than a Southern planter – his calamity inevitably echoes and encapsulates that of the South: rooted in the sins of racial injustice and sexual violence, "Sutpen's Hundred," like the entire region out of which it was carved, provides a lurid emblem of inhumanity and earned defeat.

---

[21] Cited in David Thelen, "Memory and American History," *Journal of American History* (March, 1989), p. 1120.

[22] African-American writers also produced an abundant but more positive response to Toussaint, some of which is described in chapter 6, Black memory.

[23] William Faulkner, *Absalom, Absalom!* (New York: Vintage Books, 1990 [1936]), p. 212.

Faulkner's childhood was spent in "the very midst of . . . radical racist hysteria."[24] He owned a copy of Thomas Dixon's *The Clansman* (1905), which is arguably the apotheosis of racial slander. He had almost certainly witnessed at least one lynching, and he would write about lynching in several of his stories and novels. In the political and ideological struggle over race, Faulkner equivocated. Two decades after *Absalom*, in the midst of the civil rights struggle, he announced his support for states' rights, including the prerogatives of state governments to maintain segregation by force.[25]

In Faulkner's fiction, however, some of the strongest characters are black. In *Go Down, Moses*, Lucas Beauchamp is the legatee of whatever courage and integrity have survived in the McCaslin family. And of Dilsey, Faulkner wrote with elliptical admiration, in the genealogy that he constructed as a putative commentary on *The Sound and the Fury*: "They endured." Sharing the paternalism that often poisoned white Southern attitudes, Faulkner nevertheless paid his tribute to the African-American stamina that had outlasted centuries of abuse and oppression.

Gone with the Wind (1936), published just three months after *Absalom, Absalom!*, can serve as a supremely informative guide to a contrary view of Southern history.[26] The only book Margaret Mitchell ever wrote, *Gone with the Wind* received the 1937 Pulitzer (the fourth Southern novel in six years to win the prize), was the bestselling novel of the thirties – 426,000 copies in the first ten weeks, according to Macmillan – and has remained one of the most popular American books of all time.[27]

---

[24] Joel Williamson, *William Faulkner and Southern History* (New York: Oxford University Press, 1993), p. 162.

[25] "[I]f it came to fighting I'd fight for Mississippi against the United States even if it meant going out into the street and shooting Negroes. After all, I'm not going to shoot Mississippians." William Faulkner, interview with Russell Howe, *Reporter* (March 22, 1956), p. 19. Faulkner later retracted the statement, insisting that he had been drunk at the time.

[26] *Absalom, Absalom!* was published in March, 1936, *Gone with the Wind* in July. Mitchell's novel sold over 200,000 copies in the first month, and has since sold tens of millions, in English and dozens of translations.

[27] The sales figure was contained in advertising copy that Macmillan ran in newspapers all over the country. As several critics have pointed out, most of the novels about the Civil War published in the 1930s were written by Southerners. Part of the reason was simply that the great majority of the war's battles were fought on Southern soil. More profoundly, the war's loss provided an unquenchable impulse to retrospection and historical re-creation. Along with *Gone with the Wind* and *Absalom, Absalom!*, the list includes Gwen Bristow's *Handsome Road* (1938), Clifford Dowdey's *Bugles Blow No More* (1937), T. S. Stribling's *The Forge* (1931), Andrew Lytle's *Long Night* (1936), Allen Tate's *Fathers* (1938), and Stark Young's *So Red the Rose* (1939). Pennsylvanian Hervey Allen's *Action at Aquila* (1938), discussed earlier, is among the exceptions. Margaret Sangster made this observation a century ago: "Far more has been told us concerning the South during the Civil

For over a thousand pages, *Gone with the Wind* follows its Southern characters from the eve of the Civil War, through the early years of Reconstruction. The main character is Scarlett O'Hara, a pretty and flirtatious young belle who lives with her father and mother and a group of slaves on Tara, the family plantation in Georgia. The war and its aftermath transform the girlish Scarlett into a grimly determined and shrewd woman. Stripped of her property, her possessions, and her family, she discovers reservoirs of courage and self-reliance. She is equally matched with the raffish Rhett Butler; their passionate relationship is the narrative armature around which the history of the entire region is wound.

J. Donald Adams, the editor of the *New York Times Book Review*, assigned *Gone with the Wind* to himself, and pulled out the stops: "I would go so far as to say that it is, in narrative power, in sheer readability, surpassed by nothing in American fiction."[28] *Time* magazine's reviewer called *Gone with the Wind* an "old-fashioned, romantic narrative with no Joycean or Proustian nonsense about it."[29] Indeed. The novel is also old-fashioned and romantic in its views of Southern history and its racial foundations. Where *Absalom* exposes the moral calamity that brought the South to its destruction, *Gone with the Wind* re-cycles the mythology of the Lost Cause. Gallant Ashley Wilkes, in a letter from the front to his wife Melanie, explains why he fights. He knows that he and his comrades have been betrayed by the "words and catch phrases, prejudices and hatreds" of their own leaders. When he goes into battle, Ashley says:

I see Twelve Oaks and remember how the moonlight slants across the white columns, and the unearthly way the magnolias look, opening under the moon . . . And I see Mother, sewing there, as she did when I was a little boy. And I hear the darkies coming home across the fields at dusk, tired and singing and ready for supper . . . And there's the long view down the road to the river, across the cotton fields . . .

War than concerning the North. Fiction has found the North a less romantic field, and the South has been chosen as the background of many a stirring novel, while only here and there has an author been found who has known the deep-hearted loyalty of the Northern States and woven the story into narrative form." Sangster, "Introduction," *Village Life in America, 1852–1872, Including the Period of the American Civil War as Told in the Diary of a School Girl* (New York: Holt, 1926 [1908]), p. x.

[28] J. Donald Adams, "A Fine Novel of the Civil War," *New York Times Book Review* (July 5, 1936), p. 1.

[29] "Backdrop for Atlanta," *Time* (July 6, 1936), p. 62.

But all those images are only "symbols," Ashley tells Melanie, "symbols of the kind of life I love. For I am fighting for the old days, the old ways I love..."[30]

Those "old ways," of course, included slavery. Stipulate that the enduring popularity of *Gone with the Wind* derives from its vivid scenes of warfare and suffering, the interactions between its feisty heroine and her virile lover, its panting eroticism, and its rhapsodic evocation of the land. Nonetheless, for Mitchell's contemporaries and for generations of readers, the novel also validated and reinforced a deeply contemptuous view of African-American humanity.

Appealing to a litany of defensive clichés, *Gone with the Wind* presents black people who are happily dependent in their bondage, sexually dangerous if not kept under restraint, and incapable of governing themselves, much less governing others. When blacks are emancipated and then quickly moved into positions of authority, the resulting pandemonium quite appropriately elicits the terror of the Ku Klux Klan and the ensuing process of disenfranchisement. "The scourge of war had been followed by the worse scourge of reconstruction" (p. 511). As always in the long history of anti-black propaganda, the specter of black rape hovers over the novel, which legitimates the lynch mob. One group that particularly vexes Southern whites, according to the novel's narrator, is the "unscrupulous adventurers who operated the Freedmen's Bureau" (p. 645).

In its presentation of Reconstruction, *Gone with the Wind* has its roots in such novels as Thomas Dixon's *The Clansman*, which had spawned D. W. Griffiths's enormously successful movie, *The Birth of a Nation* (1915). Mitchell also inherited some of her assumptions from the shelf of "reconciliation" novels that emerged in the 1880s and 1890s, in which South and North bury their decades of hostility, often through a marriage across the sectional divide. Winston Churchill's *The Crisis* (1901), to give a typical example, intermingles a romantic plot with its political and military events. Northerner Stephen Brice has fought on the Union side, gallantly to be sure, and treated his Southern adversaries as chivalric foemen, rather than renegades – conferring on them precisely the

---

[30] Margaret Mitchell, *Gone with the Wind* (New York: Avon, 1973 [1936]), p. 210. Stark Young's pro-Southern version of the Civil War, *So Red the Rose*, also insists on the essential virtue of the antebellum plantation culture. Evoking sympathy for the beleaguered planters whose graceful lives are being shredded by the war, Young lingers over each defeat as a sign of human tragedy. Sighing over the destruction of his acres and the loss of his slaves, owner Hugh McGehee clings to the proposition that democracy is "a good theory, a great human right, which works out none too well; slavery [is] a bad theory, a great human wrong, which works out none too badly." Stark Young, *So Red the Rose* (New York: Charles Scribner's Sons, 1934), p. 394.

romantic allure that satirists from Mark Twain to Ellen Glasgow diligently exposed. Stephen woos and wins Virginia Carvel, the articulate and independent daughter of a Southern Colonel who vociferously defends slavery and whose views she shares.[31] The marriage of Stephen and Virginia, and their subsequent happiness, enacts a domestic re-statement of the political theme.[32]

Margaret Mitchell's rehearsal of the white South's grievances during Reconstruction also found expression in H. J. Eckenrode's *Bottom Rail on Top: A Novel of the Old South* (1935). Eckenrode was Virginia's State Historian, author of a long list of books, among them biographies of Jefferson Davis and James Longstreet. The subtitle of his life of Rutherford B. Hayes, "Statesman of Reunion," accurately indicates his judgment about the proper resolution of Southern politics after the Civil War. One of his early books was called *The Political History of Virginia During the Reconstruction* (1904), a minutely detailed chronology of federal intervention and state constitutional debates in the years 1865–1868. Despite occasional expressions of sympathy for postwar African-American demands, Eckenrode consistently attacks the agents and instruments of Reconstruction, in particular the Freedmen's Bureau, as extremist and destructive. Radical politicians "inspired an ignorant and generally contented race with alluring and quite impossible hopes. They awakened desires in the colored race which could not then be attained and which left a fruit of desolating discontent."[33]

In the mid-thirties, three decades after he wrote those words, Eckenrode embraced an unchanged view of Reconstruction. *The Bottom Rail* traces the life of a white planter, William Carew (Buck) Musgrave, from his antebellum youth as a charming rapscallion, through a prison term (for theft), a brilliantly murderous career in the Confederate army – where his forty kills earn him the nickname "Death" – to his postwar efforts to rehabilitate his fortunes. Although he rejects any sentimental attachment to Southern values, and concedes the moral appeal of

---

[31] From the 1880s through the turn of the twentieth century, "American culture was awash in sentimental reconciliationist literature." David W. Blight, *Race and Reunion: The Civil War in American Memory* (Cambridge, MA: The Belknap Press of Harvard University Press, 2001), p. 216. Blight does not mention Churchill's novel.

[32] The novel finds common ground between Northern and Southern whites in their shared hostility for African-Americans. (That is probably the reason why Charles Waddell Chesnutt, as he wrote to Booker T. Washington, "started to read *The Crisis* but got switched off before I finished it.")

[33] Hamilton James Eckenrode, *The Political History of Virginia During the Reconstruction* (Gloucester, MA: Peter Smith, 1966 [1904]), p. 128. The book was originally published in the series, Johns Hopkins University Studies in Historical and Political Science.

egalitarian ideas, he calls the very notion of equality and cooperation between black and white "beautifully wrong. But wrong."[34] The burden of the past is simply too heavy. When the leading progressive tells him, "The past is dead," Buck responds, "Here in the South . . . the past is the only thing alive. We are only ghosts" (p. 169).

At one point, Eckenrode's narrator makes the latent parallel with the political doings of the 1930s explicit: the radicals, he says, "were the revolutionists of that day, as the communists are of ours, offering voters a new heaven and a new earth in exchange for ballots, precisely as revolutionists do now. Slogans are the only things that change in human life" (p. 214). Two targets with one shot: racial equality and communism, which were consistently linked in white supremacist propaganda in the thirties and throughout much of the twentieth century.

In the early 1930s, T. S. Stribling produced an ambitious trilogy of historical novels that traced the experiences of one Southern family, the Vaidens, from the antebellum years through the 1920s. *The Forge* (1931) covers the Civil War, *The Store* (1932), which won the 1933 Pulitzer Prize, carries the story through Reconstruction, and *The Unfinished Cathedral* (1934) concludes in the early decades of the twentieth century. Compared with writers such as Eckenrode or Mitchell or Bowers, Stribling's representation of the tumultuous changes re-shaping the South is fairly sophisticated. The relative balance of Stribling's attitudes can perhaps be traced to his origins: he was born in Tennessee to a mother whose family had fought for the Confederacy and a father with Union allegiances.

The Store, which *Time* magazine called "easily the most important US novel of the year," opens in 1884, the year in which Grover Cleveland won election as the first Democratic President since the Civil War.[35] Miltiades Vaiden, the chief character of *The Store*, had fought for the South in the war, earning the respect of his superiors and the honorary title of colonel upon his discharge. Returning to Florence, Alabama, Vaiden is beggared by the bankruptcy of a merchant, J. Handback, who bilked him of five bales of cotton. The novel's central plotline follows Vaiden from poverty to his criminal recovery of prosperity – he steals 500 bales of Handback's cotton, avoids prosecution, and invests the proceeds in property – and back to the brink of insolvency.

[34] H. J. Eckenrode, *Bottom Rail on Top: A Novel of the Old South* (New York: Greenberg Publisher, 1935), p. 260.
[35] "*The Store*," *Time* (July 4, 1932), p. 39.

Stribling's Florence is a squalid backwater, populated by losers and schemers, its blacks undone by oppression, its whites warped by racial hatred and soggy sentimental dreams of the Old South. Greed and revenge propel the novel's white characters toward an assortment of bad ends, but the principal cause of the final catastrophe is race: the lynching of Vaiden's unacknowledged, light-skinned son, Toussaint (a child borne by Vaiden's half-sister and former slave). Indeed, Stribling's major accomplishment in *The Store* is the chilling realism with which he captures the struggles of the novel's black characters to negotiate the ruthless apartheid that replaced slavery in the postbellum years. Each day brings its indignities and dangers. At Handback's store, African-Americans know they will only receive part of each pound of provisions they pay for. A black man who tries to break up a fight between two white men is beaten and arrested for touching one of the whites. A small black girl is reproved for referring to a newly married black couple as Mr. and Miss: terms reserved for whites. A black man who tries to vote in the crucial presidential election is physically ejected from the polling place.[36]

Few white Southern novelists had attempted to communicate the humiliation and frequent terror that African-Americans experienced in the South – and were still experiencing in the 1930s. Defending the accuracy of his fiction against charges that he was unfair to Alabama's whites, Stribling insisted: "My latest novel, *The Store*...deals with much the same situation as that going on right now in Alabama, where Negro 'share croppers' are being unmercifully bulldozed and persecuted."[37]

The 1939 film version of *Gone with the Wind* has probably done even more than the novel to cement regressive conceptions of race in the American imagination. Starring Clark Gable and Vivien Leigh, the movie was one of the major cultural events of the thirties decade, winning an unprecedented eight Academy Awards. Not everyone welcomed the film. The black poet and critic, Melvin B. Tolson, writing in the *Washington Tribune*, itemized the conclusions that audiences around the world would draw:

The North was wrong in fighting to free black men. The grand old Abolitionists were lunatics. Negroes didn't want to be free anyway. Slaves were happy. The greatest pleasure of the slave was to serve massa. Southern whites understand

[36] T. S. Stribling, *The Store* (University: University of Alabama Press, 1985 [1932]), pp. 91, 216, 376, 249.
[37] Ulysses Walsh, "Read and Write and Burn: An Interview with T. S. Stribling," *The Writer* (May, 1932), p. 127.

Negroes; that's the reason they treat them as they do. You need the Ku Klux Klan to keep Negroes in their place.[38]

The racial framework within which both Faulkner and Mitchell produced their meditations on the Civil War and Reconstruction had recently been reinforced by the publication of the immensely successful and systematically racist book, *The Tragic Era: The Revolution After Lincoln* (1929), by Claude G. Bowers. *The Tragic Era* rehearses every racial insult and repeats every racial slander. During the decade of Reconstruction, in Bowers's view, the good white people of the South, oppressed by a conspiracy of primitive blacks and unscrupulous Northern whites, "were literally put to the torture."[39] Led by such miscreants as "the mulatto orator," Frederick Douglass (p. 100), and "the bitter and abnormal" Thaddeus Stevens (p. 67), newly freed African-Americans inflicted untold hardships on their former masters. Poverty followed, since "the negroes would not work, the plantations could not produce" (p. 60).

Northern Carpetbaggers turned the "simple-minded freedmen" against the "native whites, who understood them best" (p. 198), and it took the good work of the Ku Klux Klan to produce "an improvement among" the blacks, "with more industry and less petty pilfering." The Klan satisfied the "desperate need for regulation" (p. 307).[40]

Bowers includes a classic episode, familiar from D. W. Griffiths's film, "The Birth of a Nation" (1915) and other fictional sources, purporting to represent black behavior in the South Carolina legislature:

---

[38] Melvin B. Tolson, "*Gone with the Wind* is More Dangerous than *Birth of a Nation*," in Robert M. Farnsworth, ed., *Caviar and Cabbage: Selected Columns by Melvin B. Tolson from the Washington Tribune, 1937–1944* (Columbia: University of Missouri Press, 1982), p. 215.

[39] Claude G. Bowers, *The Tragic Era: The Revolution After Lincoln* (Cambridge, MA: The Houghton Mifflin Company, 1929), p. vi. Not surprisingly, several of the Southern volumes in the American Guide series rehearsed the Southern party line on Reconstruction. According to the Alabama Guide, "William Hugh Smith, a scalawag, held the office of governor from 1868–1870 with the support of the carpetbaggers and a Negro general assembly. With Federal troops ready to enforce its actions with bayonets, this administration ratified the fourteenth amendment, encouraged an antagonistic attitude on the part of Negroes toward whites, and furthered an orgy of corruption, bribery, and speculation. Politically powerless, Southern white people resisted through determined organizations such as the Ku Klux Klan." *Alabama; a Guide to the Deep South* (New York: R. R. Smith, 1941), p. 53.

[40] The Klan also plays a major role in the early sections of *A Calendar of Sin* (1931), Evelyn Scott's mammoth, two-volume, multi-generational novel of Reconstruction and the Gilded Age. In *And Tell of Time* (1938), Laura Krey, a self-described and unreconstructed apologist for white supremacy, presents the Klan as an army of unsullied chevaliers, vigilantly protecting white womanhood and Southern honor.

We enter the House, where Moses, the Speaker, looks down upon members mostly black or brown or mahogany, some of the type seldom seen outside the Congo... A cozy atmosphere, too, with the members' feet upon their desks, their faces hidden behind their soles. Chuckles, guffaws, the noisy cracking of peanuts, and raucous voices disturb the parliamentary dignity of the scene. On one side a small group of whites, Democrats, representing the shadow of the old regime, "good-looking, substantial citizens... men of weight and standing in the communities they represent" sit "grim and silent"... Mingling with the negroes we see ferret-faced carpetbaggers, eager for spoils. (p. 353)

Enjoying exceptional popularity, *The Tragic Era* codified the prevailing view of Reconstruction, one that had received its definitive scholarly statement a decade earlier, in Ulrich B. Phillips's *American Negro Slavery* (1918). Phillips's denigration of black freedmen, and his defense of white reaction, would continue to dominate textbook history until the 1960s and even beyond.

David Brion Davis, looking back at his graduate school training, has recalled: "In the early to mid-1950s Phillips's book was still the standard work on the subject and appeared on course syllabi at Harvard and other leading universities... Phillips frankly affirmed that blacks were inferior to whites and that southern slavery had been a benign civilizing force..."[41] As Davis points out, the message that *American Negro Slavery* conveyed was reinforced by *Gone with the Wind* and by popular books such as W. E. Woodward's *New American History* (1936), with its admiring evocation of the plantation as a strict but effective training school for "African savages."

A similar theme lay at the center of Paul H. Buck's *The Road to Reunion, 1865–1900*, which won the 1937 Pulitzer Prize in history. Buck welcomed the movement toward regional reconciliation that followed the war, endorsing white Southern bitterness toward Reconstruction and tasking "arrogant" Northerners for immoderate intrusions into sectional autonomy.[42] Indifferent if not downright hostile to African-American

---

[41] David Brion Davis, *In the Image of God: Religion, Moral Values, and Our Heritage of Slavery* (New Haven, CT: Yale University Press, 2001), p. 6.
[42] Paul Herman Buck, *The Road to Reunion, 1865–1900* (New York: Little, Brown and Company, 1937), p. vii. Along with the usual array of historical sources, Buck deployed a large number of novels, plays, newspapers, and magazines in his survey. Horatio Alger, David Belasco, George Cable, Kate Chopin, Rebecca Harding Davis, J. W. De Forest, Edward Eggleston, Ralph Waldo Emerson, Clyde Fitch, Joel Chandler Harris, Bret Harte, Sarah Orne Jewett, Sidney Lanier, Henry Wadsworth Longfellow, James Russell Lowell, Thomas Nast, Thomas Nelson Page, Edgar Allan Poe, William Gilmore Simms, Mark Twain, and Constance Fenimore Woolson, among others, are enrolled in the argument that literature both reflected and helped to nurture reconciliation. In particular, chapter 9, "The

demands for equality, Buck insisted that the great story in the years following the Civil War was reunification: "The central theme of American life after the war, even in the years of political radicalism, is not to be found in a narrative of sectional divergence. It was national integration...that marked every important development" (p. vii). Reconstruction had been a failed experiment. The reconciliation enabled by the Compromise of 1877 was sealed in blood when Northern and Southern veterans fought side by side in the Spanish-American War. By the end of the nineteenth century, Americans had secured one of the "noblest achievements when within a single generation true peace had come to those who had been at war" (p. 307).

As for the African-Americans at whose expense this alliance was forged, Buck summed up his opinion in the title of the penultimate chapter: "The Negro Problem Always Ye Have With You." The condescending Biblical allusion implies that black inequality will be a permanent feature of Southern life, a problem best addressed by unfettered Southern discipline.

The nation's leading school text reinforced the same message. According to one student of the subject: "For nearly half the [twentieth] century, a high percentage – perhaps even a majority – of American school children learned American history from a single book: David Saville Muzzey's *American History*."[43] Muzzey, as it was universally called, was a bestseller when first published in 1911, and it was still selling strongly in the 1950s. Briskly written and confidently patriotic, the book deployed an assortment of racist stereotypes, attacked Reconstruction, and supported the so-called Compromise of 1877.

Obsolete conceptions of Reconstruction exerted their authority through the thirties for several reasons, among them the inertial power of consensus, and the continued lack of interest on the part of white writers and readers in the claims that African-Americans were making on historical legitimacy. Beyond that, however, the diminishment of Reconstruction dovetailed with the needs of a nation under special stress in the 1930s. Aided by new technologies, including magazines such as *Time* (1925) and *Life* (1936), national radio networks, and the movie newsreel, the country was undergoing another and decisive stage in its shift from

North Feels the Power of the Pen," proposes that Southern literature found its proper role when it (allegedly) shed localism for nationalism (pp. 220–235).
[43] Frances Fitzgerald, *America Revised: History Schoolbooks in the Twentieth Century* (New York: Little, Brown, 1979), p. 59.

sections to nation.[44] Emphasizing the rightness of reconciliation after the Civil War, even at the expense of black rights, contributed to this transformation.

The definitive answer to Phillips and Muzzey and Bowers and Eckenrode and Paul Buck came in 1935, in W. E. B. Du Bois's *Black Reconstruction*, which is discussed in the next chapter.

In the 150 years since the raid on Harper's Ferry in 1859, John Brown has proven one of the most durably contentious figures in American history. Both among professional historians, and in popular culture, Brown's violence has engendered two opposing interpretations. To some, he was a saint, a man whose deeds hastened the Civil War and the end of slavery, and whose execution "made the gallows glorious like the Cross" (in Emerson's famous apostrophe). To others, Brown was a bloodthirsty fanatic, whose massacre of five men at Pottawatomie, Kansas, in 1856, initiated a brief but incendiary career of murder that had no demonstrable effect on subsequent events.[45]

Writers have devoted continuous attention to Brown. The first decade of the twentieth century had seen two major biographies, both of which honored Brown as an abolitionist hero. W. E. B. Du Bois, in his *John Brown* (1909), declares that Brown was "the man who of all Americans has perhaps come nearest to touching the real souls of black folk."[46] In 1910, Oswald Garrison Villard, a prominent journalist and reformer, published a more comprehensive but equally fervent study, *John Brown, 1800–1859: A Biography Fifty Years After*.[47] Brown's biographical opponents included Robert Penn Warren, whose extended attack of 1929, *John Brown: The Making of a Martyr*, will be discussed below. That would be

---

[44] For fifteen cents, newsreel houses offered everybody fairly direct access to national and even international events: Fox Studio's *Movietone News*, which commenced in 1929, and *Time* magazine's *The March of Time*, first exhibited in theaters in 1935, provided graphic scenes of the Dust Bowl, Japanese pilots strafing and bombing Chinese civilians in Shanghai, and battles between strikers and police.

[45] The acrimonious debate that Brown's career has fueled continues. See, most recently, David S. Reynolds, *John Brown, Abolitionist: the Man Who Killed Slavery, Sparked the Civil War, and Seeded Civil Rights* (New York: Alfred Knopf Company, 2005). The title makes Reynolds's position clear.

[46] W. E. Burghardt Du Bois, *John Brown* (Philadelphia: G. W. Jacobs, 1909), p. xxv. In the words of Eric Sundquist, Du Bois's life of Brown is rendered as "a parable of puritanic righteousness." Sundquist, *To Wake the Nations: Race in the Making of American Literature* (Cambridge, MA: The Belknap Press of Harvard University Press, 1993), p. 597.

[47] Katherine Mayo, whose novel, *General Washington's Dilemma*, is discussed in an earlier chapter, worked for Villard as a research assistant on the John Brown book.

Illustration 9. Horace Pippin, "John Brown on the Way to His Hanging"
Pennsylvania Academy of the Fine Arts

followed in 1942 by James C. Malin's *John Brown and the Legend of Fifty-Six*, a more systematically documented sequence of accusations. In 1936, the Federal Theatre Project commissioned a sympathetic version of Brown's life, *Battle Hymn*, written by Michael Blankfort and Michael Gold.

In 1932, the state of West Virginia erected a plaque near the site of Brown's scaffold in Charles Town, near Harper's Ferry. In 1935, a large bronze statue of Brown was installed in North Elba, New York, where he had lived for the last ten years of his life. The West Virginia volume in the American Guide series took a pro-Brown position, quoting Du Bois on Brown's effort to blaze a trail "from slavery to freedom."[48] Brown has also been the subject of countless paintings, among them Thomas Hovenden's "The Last Moments of John Brown" (1884), in which a saintly Brown pauses on his way to the gallows to kiss a black child, and Horace Pippin's

---

[48] *West Virginia: A Guide to the Mountain State* (New York: Oxford University Press, 1941), p. 226.

"John Brown on the Way to His Hanging" (1942), which pictures the condemned man riding to his death with stoic dignity.[49]

The most memorable representation of John Brown was produced in the late 1930s, John Steuart Curry's large mural, painted in 1937 for the Kansas State House. Curry's title, "Tragic Prelude," distills the history of what was called Bleeding Kansas. The Kansas–Nebraska Act of 1854 dictated that the voters would decide whether those territories would enter the union as free or slave states. Through the violent years of the mid-1850s, pro- and anti-slavery settlers in Kansas battled for control of that decision. In May 1856, in retaliation for a pro-slavery attack on Lawrence, Brown and his sons took five pro-slavery men from their huts on the Pottawatomie Creek and murdered them.

"Tragic Prelude" is the culmination of Curry's lifelong fascination with Brown, an interest that was almost personal: the painter was born in a town not too many miles from the site of the Pottawatomie massacre. The huge canvas neither attacks nor defends Brown; instead, the focus concentrates on the sheer scale of Brown's intervention in history. Standing nearly twelve feet tall, and surrounded by men and women half his size, John Brown erupts out of the canvas like a Biblical prophet – his bearded face clearly modeled on Michelangelo's "Moses." His arms are spread out, a Beecher Bible clutched in his left hand, a rifle in his right, a sheathed sword hanging from his belt. Underneath him, soldiers face each other under the opposing flags of Union and Confederacy. A black rifleman leads the Northern forces, while black captives cower under the rifles of the South.

Two of the soldiers lie at Brown's feet. In the distance, one of Curry's trademark tornadoes fills the left quarter of the canvas, now a political symbol rather than a mere fact of the unforgiving climate of the Midwest. A raging brushfire sweeps across the other side of the background, another emblem of the internecine bloodshed to come. In the middle distance, suggestions of continuity and hope: the covered wagons of settlers moving west, and a handful of wild flowers growing in the lower left corner. A scene of uncommon energy and portent, "Tragic Prelude" is also a comment in the debate over painting. Curry embraces all the pictorial and narrative conventions of history painting in the grand manner. Like the Bible Brown holds, his painting tells an epic story, of

---

[49] For a superb account of Pippin's accomplishment as a historical painter, see Steven Conn, "The Politics of Painting: Horace Pippin the Historian," *American Studies* (Spring, 1997), pp. 5–26.

Illustration 10. John Steuart Curry, "Tragic Prelude"

war and nation-making, a sequence of events and complex entanglements that remain timely eight decades later.

Robert Penn Warren, like most white Southerners of his generation, took a dim view of Brown, and he laid out his case in the first book he published, *John Brown: The Making of a Martyr*. This acid, ungenerous biography debunks both the moral and political value of Brown's career, and in particular his legendary raid on Harper's Ferry.[50] For Warren, Brown's abortive attack was not only tactically stupid. Far more importantly, it proved again that violence is presumptively self-defeating, and that the temptations of power always lead to disaster. In Warren's opinion, as he said in a long note analyzing earlier biographies of Brown, those books had typically neglected "one of the most significant keys to John Brown's character, his elaborate psychological mechanism for justification which appeared regularly in terms of the thing which friends called Puritanism and enemies called fanaticism."[51]

On several occasions, Warren acknowledges Brown's courage, but that is the only virtue he allows. In Warren's view, Brown was a lying self-promoter, an opportunist, a traitor to his nation, and a murderer whose crimes deserved the punishment they received. Brown's lifetime of failure inflamed his ambition to perpetrate some legendary deed, and that desire led "to meanness, to chicanery, to bitter querulous intolerance, to dishonesty, to vindictive and ruthless brutality" (p. 350). Brown's supporters are also treated with contempt, especially New England "romantics," and above all Emerson, "a man who lived in words, big words, and not in facts" (p. 245). Emerson's praise of Brown's famous final speech draws this rebuke from Warren: "Perhaps Emerson was right on the matter of rhetoric; and matters of fact, the questions of truth or falsehood, were often perfectly inconsequential to the sage of Concord. The sage of Concord gracefully transcended such things" (p. 414).[52]

Warren's antipathy for Brown was also grounded in his more or less benevolent view of slavery. "The slave himself," he writes at one point,

---

[50] "With very few exceptions the twenty or more books about John Brown published before Warren's work were devoted in some degree to the making or the perpetuation of his name as a hero and a martyr." C. Vann Woodward, "Introduction" to the Southern Classics Series edition of Warren's *John Brown* (Nashville, KY: J. S. Sanders & Company, 1993), p. xi.

[51] Robert Penn Warren, *John Brown: The Making of a Martyr* (New York: Payson & Clarke, Ltd., 1929), p. 446.

[52] For many Southerners, the image of John Brown as hero was proof of Northern contempt for their whole region. In Clifford Dowdey's *Bugles Blow No More*, one Virginian says to another: the Northerners "must hate us very deeply to make a hero out of a maniac who wanted to murder us in our beds" (Boston: Little, Brown and Company, 1937), p. 12.

"was at the same time more realistic and more humane" than Brown. He "never bothered his kinky head about the moral issue, and for him the matter simply remained one of convenience or inconvenience. . . [S]ince immediate contact existed between master and slave, an exercise of obligation reached downward as well as upward and the negro's condition was tolerable enough" (p. 332). In other words, Warren assented to the views famously codified by Ulrich B. Phillips in such influential works as *American Negro Slavery* (1918) and *Life and Labor in the Old South* (1929), books that were generally sympathetic to slaveholders, emphasizing the financial security and ties of personal loyalty that slavery allegedly conferred on its victims. Such an ideology was certain to offer John Brown no quarter.[53]

John Brown anticipated many of the themes that would continue to attract Warren throughout his long career, among them his fascination with history, his axiomatic suspicion of abstract idealism, and his resistance to progressive notions of human perfectibility. In some ways, as he noted himself in a later interview, the biography of Brown also reaches forward to his first novel, *Night Rider*, published ten years later.[54]

Warren was born in Guthrie, Kentucky, in the heart of the tobacco belt; in later recollections he recalled the Black Patch as "a world of violence," a place where "you accepted violence as a component of life" (Watkins *et al.*, eds., *Talking with Warren*, p. 18). Warren grew up hearing stories of the tobacco wars from men and women who had taken part in them. Out of those materials he fashioned *Night Rider* (1939).[55]

At the turn of the twentieth century, the tobacco business, along with much of the rest of the American economy, was being transformed by the emergence of industrial concentration and cartel. Traditionally, the tobacco industry had consisted of individual deals between thousands of small farmers and one or another of dozens of tobacco product manufacturers. Most of the growers were poor, but they retained a modicum of independence and at least the chance of choosing among competitive bids for their leaf. With the rise of the American Tobacco Company in the 1890s, the monopoly power of big business pushed the farmers further

---

[53] Leonard Ehrlich produced a less memorable but more balanced account of Brown in his novel, *God's Angry Man* (1932). Rather like the Brown of John Steuart Curry's paintings, Ehrlich's protagonist is marked by the stature of a world historical figure, driven by a mixture of motives.

[54] "It hadn't occurred to me till later, long years after. But in reviewing *Night Rider* a Frenchman said it was the John Brown story over again." In Floyd C. Watkins, John T. Hiers, and Mary Louise Weaks, eds., *Talking with Robert Penn Warren* (Athens: University of Georgia Press, 1990), p. 137.

[55] Warren originally intended to call his book *John Brown's Body*, but that title was preempted by Stephen Vincent Benet for a long poem he published in 1927.

into dependence and penury. As prices slid below the cost of production, the rural populations of Tennessee and Kentucky, the heart of the tobacco region known as the Black Patch, found themselves in a spiral of intolerable debt.

Facing the combined hostility of buyers, state governments, and the courts, growers banded together in cooperatives and semi-secret associations, determined to bargain on a more equal basis over the sale price of their crops. The ensuing tensions eventually erupted in the tobacco wars, a violent though little-known chapter in American history. When persuasion and boycott failed, a small but significant number of growers turned to vigilante action, first burning out the crops of their recalcitrant neighbors, then attacking the warehouses in which the companies stored the leaf. Making their first appearance in the fall of 1905, the "night riders" engaged in a series of spectacular raids, usually quite well-planned, that destroyed many thousands of pounds of tobacco. By 1909, the vigilantes had been effectively suppressed; American Tobacco continued to meet resistance, but never again on such a scale.[56]

The story is told mainly through the consciousness of Percy Munn, a successful young lawyer who allies himself with the growers and eventually becomes one of the leading figures both in the legal organization – the Association of Growers of Dark Fired Tobacco – and in the criminal activities of the vigilantes – somewhat euphemistically called the Free Farmers Brotherhood for Protection and Control.

Munn's motives are never made fully clear: his own livelihood is not directly at stake in the confrontation between growers and buyers, and he never articulates a developed political or philosophical point of view. He may be interested in justice or equity, but he seems rather to drift into his commitments. Nor does he share the excitement of other Association men, or their optimism that a voluntary organization of small farmers can effectively resist the encroaching domination of big business. Warren described Munn as "an idealist trapped by his own ideals" (Watkins *et al.*, eds., *Talking with Warren*, p. 263), but he is talking about another character than the one he created. Munn is a skilled recruiter, and a brave man, but he takes on each assignment rather mechanically. His death on the book's final page – shot down, ironically, by soldiers who are hunting

---

[56] For useful surveys of these events, see Tracy Campbell, *The Politics of Despair: Power and Resistance in the Tobacco Wars* (Lexington: University Press of Kentucky, 1993), especially chapter 5, "Night Riders," and Christopher Waldrep, *Night Riders: Defending Community in the Black Patch, 1890–1915* (Durham, NC: Duke University Press, 1993), especially chapter 6, "Night Riders."

him for a murder he did not commit – is close to suicidal: Munn deliberately puts himself in the line of fire.

From its opening pages, an atmosphere of fatality pervades the novel. The growers will never have enough power to oppose the collective force of money and government. As in so many of Warren's other books, from *All the King's Men* (1946), to the long narrative poem *Brother to Dragons* (1953), to the semi-documentary *Flood, a Romance of Our Time* (1964), individual will is unequal to inexorable historical forces.

In a somewhat murky meditation halfway through the novel, Munn finds himself wondering whether his will even exists. He has just threatened an Association member named Bunk Trevelyan, a man whom Munn successfully defended in a murder trial but who has now betrayed the Association's secrets. As he rides away from Trevelyan's dilapidated farmhouse, Munn thinks: "[I]s it a different thing . . . part of the same motion fulfilling a single act of will? But not his own will, it occurred to him. Not entirely his own. In this, now, there is no will, not mine nor anybody's, for there is no will in the act in memory, for it is complete and is in one time out of time . . ."[57]

The best parts of *Night Rider*, and they are many, are those in which significance is embedded in description, action, and dialogue. Midnight raids, secret meetings, long twilight conversations in which farmers and their wives record their deprivations, renderings of the land in all its moods and seasons: these engage our attention through the energy and specificity with which Warren evokes them, and they serve as well more general emblematic purposes as well. The novel's opening scene exemplifies Warren's practice. Percy Munn is traveling to Bardsville for the first rally of the Association. The train is packed and sweltering, and Munn finds himself unable to move except as the crowd pushes him along. It is a splendid device, a convincing representation of the heat and discomfort of a Kentucky summer afternoon, but also a prophecy of Munn's entire career.

In phrases Warren surely intended to refer to himself, he described Conrad as a "philosophical novelist, or poet . . . one for whom the documentation of the world is constantly striving to rise to the level of generalization about values, for whom the images strive to rise to symbol . . . for whom the urgency of experience, no matter how vividly and strongly experience may enchant, is the urgency to know the meaning of

[57] Robert Penn Warren, *Night Rider* (New York: Vintage Book edition, 1979 [1939]), p. 155.

experience."[58] In all of Warren's work, including *Night Rider*, the "meaning of experience" is the unalterable weight of history, pressing down on both individual and regional identity.

Through most of its history, Florida and its past had remained invisible to the literary imagination. That neglect ended with the publication of Marjorie Kinnan Rawlings's *The Yearling* (1938), a story of the Southern past. Rawlings, a Phi Beta Kappa graduate of the University of Wisconsin, did her apprentice writing as a journalist, in New York City, Louisville, and upstate New York. She wrote *The Yearling* after years of painstaking research in Florida's isolated north central wilderness, research that included countless hours of listening to the talk of the region's plain people.

The novel's main characters, Penny Baxter, his wife, Ora, and their son, Jody, poor whites who inhabit Florida's swamps, are hardworking, honest, and loyal. Told from twelve-year-old Jody's point of view, *The Yearling* follows the family through one year of hunting, farming, surviving: grubbing out a bare living from their unpromising circumstances, sometime in the 1880s. Jody adopts an orphaned fawn, who grows into the yearling of the title. The bond between boy and animal occupies the center of the novel, and the book's final crisis occurs when the young deer has to be shot to protect the family's meager crops.

In the postwar years, *The Yearling* has been relegated to middle school and high school reading lists, where indeed it is still much read. When it was published, however, the novel elicited exceptionally strong reviews, often including suggestions that Rawlings bore comparison with Mark Twain, in her creation of her boy hero, and with Thoreau, in her rendering of the Florida countryside. While those accolades went too far, the novel's subsequent neglect has obscured its considerable strengths. The plot is merely charming: a more or less formulaic portrait of a boy's growth toward adulthood. The major characters, though patiently drawn, remain rather too simplified to be convincing: Penny is almost impossibly noble, brave, and resourceful, while his wife Ory is a maternal symbol coined out of courage, love, and common sense. Jody himself is more precociously alert, introspective, and sensitive than a twelve-year-old boy has any right to be.

---

[58] Robert Penn Warren, "'The Great Mirage': Conrad and *Nostromo* [1951]," in *Selected Essays* (New York: Random House, 1958), p. 58. Several scholars have noted similarities between Percy Munn and the main characters in *Nostromo* and *Lord Jim*. I would add to the list the resemblance between the cold-blooded vigilante strategist of *Night Rider*, Dr. MacDonald, and the unnamed Professor in Conrad's *The Secret Agent*.

When those characters speak, on the other hand, the novel comes to life. Rawlings had an uncommon capacity for reproducing the idiosyncratic dialect of rural Florida's poor whites. These are unlettered people, but their speech conveys their humor and dignity. Penny, in particular, produces hunting tales and aphorisms in abundance, using a rhythm and vocabulary always suited to the point. Explaining to Jody the propensity of men to fight, Penny tells him: "They's no end to what a man'll fight for. I even knowed a preacher takened off his coat and fit ary man wouldn't agree to infant damnation. All a feller can do, is fight for what he figgers is right, and the devil take the hindmost."[59] Both Penny and Ora respect book learning, and both want Jody to get more education than the year or two of schooling they had. But the novel, in the Emersonian grain, affirms the value and often the superiority of the practical wisdom these country folk have accumulated over the years. Penny has a vast knowledge of the animals he hunts, the crops he farms, and the weather that controls his life. Ora manages the household with shrewd economy.

What these characters know becomes the texture of the narrative, which weaves the wildlife and plant life, the geography and atmosphere, of this Florida outback into a buzzing mosaic of sights and sounds. The heat of summer, for example, continues into the early days of September, but with a

vague change, as though the vegetation sensed the passing of one season and the coming of another. The golden-rod and asters and the deer-tongue thrived on the dryness. The poke-berries ripened and the birds fed on them along the fence-rows. All the creatures, Penny said, were hard put to it for food. The spring and summer berries, the brierberries, the huckleberries, the blueberries and choke-berries and the wild gooseberries, were long since gone. The wild plum and the mayhaw had had no fruit for bird or beast for many a month. The 'coons and foxes had stripped the wild grapeberries.

The fall fruits were not yet ripe, papaw and gallberry and persimmon. The mast of the pines, the acorns of the oaks, the berries of the palmetto, would not be ready until the first frost. The deer were feeding on the tender growth, bud of sweet bay and myrtle, sprigs of wire-grass, tips of arrow-root in the ponds and prairies, and succulent lily stems and pads. (p. 221)

Every chapter of *The Yearling* is saturated in such detail; over the novel's 400-plus pages, the Baxter homestead and its surroundings emerge with tangible particularity. The close observations are sinewed by a clear-eyed

---

[59] Marjorie Kinnan Rawlings, *The Yearling* (New York: Charles Scribner's Sons, 1938), p. 187.

view of nature as a place of perpetual violence. There is nothing sentimental about the lessons Jody learns.

Out in the scrub, the war waged ceaselessly. The bears and wolves and panthers
and wild-cats all preyed on the deer. Bears even ate the cubs of other bears, all
meat being to their maws the same. Squirrels and wood-rats, 'possums and
'coons, must all scurry for their lives. Birds and small furred creatures cowered in
the shadow of hawk and owl. (p. 142)

In the course of the novel, Rawlings describes hog-butchering, bear-
skinning, and snake-bite, along with hunger, hurricane, and drought. If
Jody is an idealized little boy (according to one of Rawlings's biographers,
she harbored a "deep-seated yearning for a little boy of her own: a desire
never fulfilled"), the world in which he grows up is a place of raw brutality.[60] One of the book's female reviewers saluted Rawlings's "virile
talent," her willingness to find a worthy subject in human and natural
violence.[61] An odd mixture of treacle and steel, *The Yearling* offers a more
dimensional account of its setting than its people. It also provides an
invaluable lesson in the history of a little-known region of nineteenth-
century America.[62]

Caroline Miller's *Lamb in His Bosom* (1933), which also won the
Pulitzer Prize and the French Prix Femina and went through nearly forty
editions in the fifty years after its publication, bears fairly close comparison with *The Yearling*. Once again, the characters are the poor whites
of the rural South, in this case people of rural Georgia in the antebellum
years. Cean Carver is the book's central figure, a young girl when the
novel opens in the 1830s, who will marry twice and bear fifteen children in
the next three decades. Life is hard on the swampy Georgia frontier: the
novel transcribes a crushing sequence of deaths and losses. Pregnant with
her first child, Cean is bitten by a rattlesnake; though she survives, the
frightening and nearly fatal episode stands as a forecast for the punishments that lie ahead.

Cean will eventually bury half-a-dozen of her children, who die of fever
and fire and warfare. Her oldest child, a daughter named Maggie, dies
giving birth to her own first child, Cean's first grandchild. (The grandchild

[60] Samuel I. Bellman. "Rawlings, Marjorie Kinnan"; www.anb.org/articles/16/16-01348.html;
American National Biography Online, February 2000.
[61] Mary M. Colum, "Life and Literature," *Forum and Century* (May, 1938), p. 280.
[62] The bestselling novel of 1938, *The Yearling* won the Pulitzer Prize for fiction. Several years later,
the book was adapted as an MGM film that earned seven Academy Award nominations, including
best film, best actor for Gregory Peck, and best actress for Jane Wyman.

dies as well.) Cean's first husband dies of gangrene after half-severing his foot with an axe. Her house burns down, and most of her possessions with it. Less mortally but typically, one of her sons has a finger bitten off by a snapping turtle.

Lamb creates a world of such systemic poverty and pain that the Civil War, which overtakes Cean and her family late in the book, merely passes like a shadow. These are people who do not lose much in the war, because they have just about nothing to lose. They endure. The book's strength consists in its unblinking portrait of life near the bottom, a mixture of bad choices, bad luck, and weariness. *Lamb* includes a detailed recipe for making soap from animal fat that serves as an emblem at once of self-reliance and need.

Elizabeth Fox-Genovese has written that *Lamb in His Bosom* may be the fullest and most accurate representation of non-slaveholding poor whites in the years before the Civil War.[63] Part of that accuracy lies in the casual racial prejudice that Cean and her neighbors feel for African-Americans. Neither Cean nor the other women in her region have ever seen a black person (the men have, when they travel for trade to the larger towns). Nonetheless, Cean is convinced that blacks belong in slavery, and she daydreams that she would have a black servant if she had the money. As she works in the fields under the blinding Georgia sun, Cean thinks:

Lord! What wouldn't she give for some niggers now! You could buy them at the Coast . . . Coast planters . . . bought wenches and bucks and mated them, and let them breed, and in a few years there were crops of fine, fat blacks to pick cotton and grind cane and shuck corn and plow; or the owners could sell them off around the country for a profit. Oh, Cean knew there was no chance of that for her. She could work her fingers to the bone in the field . . . and she'd never live like the Coast ladies.[64]

Ugly as these attitudes are, they contribute to the authenticity of the novel's evocation of its characters. So, too, does the pervasive appeal to religion. Beaten down by her losses, Cean's few moments of happiness occur when she is transported by religious visions, such as this one: "She was walking up a green slope, and her body was feather-light, so that walking was no labor. She knew herself to be beautiful and strange-appearing, [her body] molded of cloudlike, shining substance, soft to the touch" (p. 320).

---

[63] Elizabeth Fox-Genovese, "Afterword" to Caroline Miller, *Lamb in His Bosom* (Atlanta, GA: Peachtree Publishers, 1993), p. 350.
[64] Caroline Miller, *Lamb in His Bosom* (New York: Harper & Brothers Publishers, 1933), pp. 189–190.

Aside from its own celebrity, at least according to a well-established anecdote, *Lamb in His Bosom* also led to the "discovery" of *Gone with the Wind*. After he read Miller's novel, Harold Latham, senor editor at Macmillan, organized a "scouting trip" to the South "to see if there were any more Caroline Millers down there." Soon after the search began, Latham signed a contract with Margaret Mitchell.[65]

---

[65] See Finis Farr, *Margaret Mitchell of Atlanta: The Author of Gone with the Wind* (New York: William Morrow & Company, 1965), p. 91.

CHAPTER 6

Black memory

Much of the literary and artistic work of the white 1930s documents the racism that continued to deform American society in the period, dramatizing the pervasive power of America's apartheid. In March, 1931, nine young African-American men, one of them thirteen years old, another fourteen, were arrested for the rape of two white women. The alleged crime was committed on a train traveling through Alabama, and the men were taken to a prison in Scottsboro. In less than three weeks, the young men were tried, convicted, and sentenced to die. The evidence made it transparently clear that they were being victimized for the crime of their color. The infamous "Tuskegee study," which commenced in 1932, denied treatment to black men infected with syphilis. The Georgia volume in the American Guide series (1940) reported, in a matter-of-fact tone: "Negroes have no direct influence and virtually no part in Georgia politics. Most of them are virtually disenfranchised by the white primary system and discriminatory party rules."[1] Similar systems of exclusion and subordination prevailed across the South, and oppressive if slightly more subtle patterns could be found in most parts of the North as well. These constitute the present within which the past was framed.

For many black Americans, the Crash intensified hardships they had long known. Competition for jobs intensified, and racial scapegoating become fiercer. In Harlem,

the crashing drop of wages drove Negroes back to the already crowded hovels east of Lenox Avenue. In many blocks one toilet served a floor of four apartments... Without exception these tenements were filthy and vermin-ridden. Along Fifth Avenue, between 135th and 138th streets, were flats with old-fashioned toilets which rarely flushed and, when they did, they often overflowed

---

[1] *Georgia: A Guide to Its Towns and Countryside* (Athens: University of Georgia Press, 1940), p. 84.

on the floors below. In the winter the gaping holes in the skylights allowed cold air to sweep down the staircase, sometimes freezing the flush for weeks.[2]

Similar tales of deprivation could be multiplied across the country.

Black intellectual response to the Depression took shape as a debate between those who kept racial questions at the center of their analysis and those who adopted a Marxist viewpoint and shifted their emphasis from race to economics and class structure. Without insisting on perfect symmetry, this was an alternative way of encoding the struggle between the past and the future.[3] The flourishing interest in African-American folklore, for example, yielded an energetic effort both to reclaim and to re-define the shared black past of stories and song. Classically trained William Levi Dawson, Professor of Music at Tuskegee (and a teacher of Ralph Ellison), arranged dozens of African-American spirituals; his *Negro Folk Symphony* (1934) was given its premiere by Leopold Stokowski and the Philadelphia Orchestra.

The same impulse motivated scholar-writers such as Zora Neale Hurston to trace, record, and tap into the long racial memory that folk tales and music preserved. Hurston was a student of Franz Boas, who had spent decades, beginning in the 1890s, building a counter-system to the evolutionary determinism common in the study of human society in the late nineteenth century. His commitment to particularity and relativism, according to one historian of the field, "controlled the intellectual direction and social organization of North American anthropology at least until the end of the Second World War."[4]

Most relevant for the discussion in this chapter, Boas was a path-finding and often brave opponent of racism, which he likened to superstition. Whether directed at Jews, African-Americans, or "primitive peoples," theories of racial superiority could not, according to Boas, find support in a rigorous science. Thus, while the 1930s continued to nurture deep-rooted prejudice and discrimination, it was also in that decade that the pseudo-scientific bases on which racism was grounded were decisively

[2] Roi Ottley and William J. Weatherby, eds., *The Negro in New York, an Informal Social History* (New York: New York Public Library, 1967), p. 266.
[3] The arguments were often bitter, and the poets and novelists who engaged in them reflected the same divisions as the historians and political scientists. Documenting this debate, one scholar has quoted William Pickens, an influential officer of the NAACP in the twenties and thirties: it would take "a miracle of God to make twelve Negroes pull in the same direction [and] a miracle beyond God to bring all Negro and pro-Negro organizations under one direction." Cited in James O. Young, *Black Writers of the Thirties* (Baton Rouge: Louisiana State University Press, 1973), p. 237.
[4] Regna Darnell, *Invisible Genealogies: A History of Americanist Anthropology* (Lincoln: University of Nebraska Press, 2001), p. 33.

confounded. The trend was undoubtedly hastened by revulsion against Hitler's racialist policies and their lethal consequences.[5]

One of Boas's prominent students produced one of the decade's most influential books. Indeed, Ruth Benedict's *Patterns of Culture* (1934) proved to be one of the significant books of the century, continuously in print with over a million copies sold. Tracing the dominant psychological foundations that shape the structures into which cultures are configured, Benedict insisted on a comparative and relativist perspective. Different peoples and their customs need to be understood, not arrayed in hierarchical order. The diversity of cultural practices proves humanity's "plasticity," its ability to choose its religious and social norms from numberless alternatives. This equivalence has been obscured, in Benedict's view, by the extent to which Western norms have achieved the status of universal standards. The consequences have been tragic, not only for the inhabitants of "primitive" societies, but also for victims of racism and anti-Semitism. "Social thinking," she says near the conclusion of *Patterns*, "has no more important task before it than that of taking adequate account of cultural relativity."[6] Benedict's achievement, in the view of her biographer, was to demonstrate the congruence of cultural tolerance with "the old goals and values of American society."[7]

A similar ambition impelled Zora Neale Hurston. Racial conflict is not typically at the center of her work because she chose to create narratives of self-contained black experience, stories that tell of life within black communities, and her testimony has proved valuable, enduring, and fertile. She made distinguished contributions to black folklore studies, recording and analyzing folk customs and tales across the South and in the Caribbean.[8]

---

[5] For a detailed survey of these developments, see Elazar Barkan, *The Retreat of Scientific Racism: Changing Concepts of Race in Britain and the United States Between the World Wars* (New York: Cambridge University Press, 1992). See also George M. Frederickson, *Racism: A Short History* (Princeton, NJ: Princeton University Press, 2002), pp. 115–117. Neither Barkan nor Frederickson discusses the important contribution Edward E. Evans-Pritchard made in the 1930s to the discussion of these developments. In his book, *Witchcraft, Oracles, and Magic Among the Azande* (1937), Evans-Pritchard showed decisively that tribal magic had its own internal logic and system, and was not merely some sort of irrational mumbo-jumbo. One of the more interesting documents in the history of relativizing anthropology in the 1930s was Julius Lips's *The Savage Hits Back* (New Haven, CT: Yale University Press, 1937). The book surveys how the strange customs and beliefs of white explorers and anthropologists appear to native peoples around the world.

[6] Ruth Benedict, *Patterns of Culture* (New York: Houghton Mifflin Company, 1934), p. 278.

[7] Margaret Caffrey, *Ruth Benedict: Stranger in This Land* (Austin: University of Texas Press, 1989), p. 210.

[8] The decade's burgeoning interest in folklore was matched by investigations and uses of folk music. *Porgy and Bess*, perhaps the most famous example, derived from folk sources. John Lomax

The essays in *Mules and Men* (1935) and the recollections in her autobiography, *Dust Tracks on a Road* (1942), are rich with the evidence she gathered of African-American culture. She brought her considerable social-scientific skills to her fiction. She had a remarkable ear for the varieties of speech, and one of the particular strengths of her novels and her non-fiction is her use of dialect with convincingly human, rather than merely eccentric, effect. Hurston's first novel, *Jonah's Gourd Vine* (1934), follows an itinerant preacher named John Buddy "Jonah" Pearson, whose sermons are almost verbatim transcriptions of material Hurston had gathered in her research. Plot and character virtually disappear beneath the re-creation of vernacular talk.

Her second novel, *Their Eyes Were Watching God* (1937), was one of the more significant books of the Depression decade. The novel follows the life of its central character, a black woman named Janie, from childhood into middle age. The past here is personal, taking the form of a fictionalized autobiography: the portrait of the African-American artist as a young woman. Despite Richard Wright's strictures, the novel is not racially indifferent.[9] During the hurricane in *Their Eyes*, white people occupy the safer, higher ground, while blacks are forced to huddle below. And after the disastrous flood, Hurston includes a chilling scene of the segregated burial of blacks and whites, an episode that eloquently condemns the lunacy of racism.

Such scenes recall an America – both South and North – when segregation was enforced with pathological consistency. Whether in times of domestic emergency, or in wartime, for example, the Red Cross of the thirties and forties refused to accept blood from African-American donors. This demeaning and biologically preposterous gesture was intended to protect whites from receiving those drops of black blood that so terrorized them.

transcribed and recorded the sources themselves. Lomax had grown up in rural Texas in the decades after the Civil War, and exhibited a lifelong interest in the music of the frontier and small town: cowboy songs, African-American spirituals, traditional ballads, and work hollers. His first major collection, *Cowboy Songs and Other Frontier Ballads*, had appeared in 1910. Throughout the Depression, Lomax, his wife, Ruby, and his son, Alan, traveled across the country, supplying materials for the Archive of American Folksong at the Library of Congress. A man of dubious scholarly standards, Lomax's principal legacy consisted in the thousands of hours of tape recordings he made, often the only surviving evidence of the art of scores of American musicians. Among the treasures of the Lomax tapes are unique recordings of Lead Belly (Huddie Ledbetter) and Woody Guthrie. Lead Belly, who spent years in Louisiana prisons, introduced African-American folk music to middle-class audiences in the 1930s; Guthrie survived a disastrous childhood to write and perform some of the most important protest songs of the decade.

[9] Richard Wright, "Between Laughter and Tears," *New Masses* (October 5, 1937), p. 22, 25.

Moses Man of the Mountain (1939), Hurston's third novel, and her longest, takes the ancient past as its explicit subject. *Moses* elaborates one of the principal mythic themes in African-American culture, the parallels between enslaved American black people and the Israelites held in bondage in Egypt. Hurston would have found the connection everywhere in her own fieldwork: "The single most persistent image the slave songs contain...is that of the chosen people."[10] The image is not only pervasive in songs, but in stories and fables, and in twentieth-century literary texts, from Paul Laurence Dunbar's "Antebellum Sermon" to Richard Wright's "Fire and Cloud," to James Baldwin's *Go Tell It on the Mountain*. The identification was recycled in political discourse as well. Booker T. Washington, for example, figured himself as the man ordained to lead his people out of the wilderness. In *Up from Slavery* (1901), Washington approvingly quotes this journalistic account of his Atlanta Exposition speech of 1895: "While President Cleveland was waiting at Gray Gables today, to send the electric spark that started the machinery of the Atlanta Exposition, a Negro Moses stood before a great audience..."[11]

Moses also occupied a central place in Caribbean folklore. In *Tell My Horse* (1938), a somewhat slipshod report on politics and voodoo in the West Indies, Hurston had noted the deference paid to Moses as a father of magic in Africa.[12] Joining these continental and island traditions, *Moses* re-tells the story of *Exodus* with the analogy between Israelites and African-Americans explicitly at the novel's center.[13] Hurston shifts between standard English and dialect as a way of re-creating the Biblical story while at the same time superimposing it on the experience of American blacks under slavery. While she remains relatively faithful to the sequence of Biblical events, Hurston's Moses is a combination prophet and hoodoo man, the leader of the Hebrew people and a democratizing champion of black rights: "He was wishing for a country he had never seen. He was seeing visions of a nation where there would

---

[10] Lawrence Levine, "Slave Songs and Slave Consciousness," in Tamara K. Hareven, ed., *Anonymous Americans: Explorations in Nineteenth-Century Social History* (Englewood Cliffs, NJ: Prentice-Hall, Inc., 1971), p. 111.

[11] Booker T. Washington, *Up from Slavery* (Garden City, NY: Doubleday, Doran, 1944 [1901]), p. 238.

[12] See Robert Hemenway, *Zora Neale Hurston: A Literary Biography* (Urbana: University of Illinois Press, 1980), p. 258.

[13] The Exodus was put to quite different uses in Robert Nathan's *Road of Ages* (1935), a novelistic fable in which all the Jews of the world are driven into exile in the Gobi Desert.

be more equality of opportunity and less difference between top and bottom."[14]

Despite its ambitions and its occasionally memorable set pieces, *Moses* never embodies its provocative apparatus in credible characters, and it has received relatively little scholarly attention. Indeed, a recent commentary begins with the declaration that "[c]ritics have avoided Zora Neale Hurston's 1939 novel, *Moses, Man of the Mountain,* like the ten plagues of Egypt."[15] Ralph Ellison's earlier condescension was too dismissive – "this work sets out to do for Moses what 'The Green Pastures' did for Jehovah; for Negro fiction it did nothing" – but even Hurston was disappointed by the distance between the novel's premises and its achievement.[16]

Wallace Thurman's *Infants of the Spring* (1932) lampoons Zora Neale Hurston in the character of Sweetie May Carr, and attacks Countee Cullen under the thin disguise of DeWitt Clinton. Richard Wright was especially offended by what he viewed as the subservience of many Renaissance writers to white standards and patronage. In an important essay called "Blueprint for Negro Writing" (1937), Wright described the Renaissance writers as

prim and decorous ambassadors who went a-begging to white America . . . They entered the Court of American Public Opinion dressed in the kneepants of servility, curtsying to show that the Negro was not inferior, that he was human, and that he led a life comparable to that of other people. For the most part these artistic ambassadors were received as though they were French poodles who do clever tricks.[17]

According to Wright, in the 1930s the job of the black writer was to identify himself with the masses and then use literature to "create values by which his race is to struggle, live and die" (p. 43). Wright adhered to a more or less dogmatic Marxism for only a few years, but during the late thirties he regularly measured black literature by the yardstick of revolutionary utility. He elaborately praised Arna Bontemps's *Black Thunder*

[14] Zora Neale Hurston, *Moses Man of the Mountain* (Urbana: University of Illinois Press, 1984 [1939]), p.100.
[15] Ronnie Scharfman, "Africa Has Her Mouth on Moses: Zora Neale Hurston Rewrites the Exodus Narrative," in Judith Misrahi-Barak, ed., *Revisiting Slave Narratives* (Montpellier: Université Montpellier 111, 2005), p.37.
[16] Ralph Ellison, "Recent Negro Fiction," *New Masses* (August 5, 1941), p. 211.
[17] Richard Wright, "Blueprint for Negro Writing," reprinted in Ellen Wright and Michel Fabre, eds., *Richard Wright Reader* (New York: Harper & Row, Publishers, 1978), p. 37.

(1936), for example, a good political novel that Wright valued as the first fictional product of a black proletarian impulse.

When he wrote *Black Thunder*, Arna Bontemps was living in a small room in his parents' house in California. It is his finest novel and one of the important books of the decade. It was also the first novel based on a slave revolt written by an African-American.[18]

Black Thunder tells the story of a slave uprising in Virginia in 1800 from the point of view of the slaves. Gabriel, an uneducated but charismatic slave, is owned by a young man named Thomas Prosser, a sadist who flaunts his cruelty when he murders another of his slaves, an elderly drunk named Bundy, in the novel's opening scenes. Gabriel's insurrection fails through a combination of betrayal and a furious storm that makes a coordinated revolutionary action impossible. The uprising is put down before it really begins, the ringleaders eventually rounded up and hanged. Bontemps wrote *Black Thunder* with the Scottsboro case much on his mind, and he saw parallels between the fate of Gabriel Prosser and the Scottsboro defendants.

Bontemps effectively reproduces the political atmosphere that inspired Gabriel's conspiracy. "The dozen years following 1790," in the judgment of one scholar, "formed a period of more intense and widespread slave discontent than any that had preceded (with the possible exception of the much shorter period from 1737 to 1741)."[19] It was an Age of Revolution. Toussaint L'Ouverture, whose military victories had established the independence of Haiti in the 1790s, is invoked several times in the novel as a hero and model. The French Revolution, with its assertions of equality, is also much discussed. (One of the characters is a French printer, accused of radical ideas.) But America's own Revolution provides an even greater stimulus, as Gabriel and his allies appeal to the new nation's own founding rhetoric as their justification. Gabriel, in the words of one scholar, represents those "who, not remarkably, first imbibed and then came to articulate the belief that the rights of the revolutionary era belonged to them as well."[20]

---

[18] Arnold Ramperad, "Introduction," Arna Bontemps, *Black Thunder* (Boston: Beacon Press, 1992), p. vii.

[19] Herbert Aptheker, *American Negro Slave Revolts* (New York: International Publishers, 1969 [1943]), p. 209.

[20] Eric J. Sundquist, *To Wake the Nations: Race in the Making of American Literature* (Cambridge, MA: The Belknap Press of Harvard University Press, 1993), p. 55. For an extended study of the revolt, see Douglas R. Egerton, *Gabriel's Rebellion: The Virginia Slave Conspiracies of 1800 and 1802* (Chapel Hill: University of North Carolina Press, 1993).

Religious sentiments also played a role in Gabriel's vision: *Black Thunder* includes long passages from scripture in support of freedom: "Therefore thus saith the Lord: Ye have not harkened unto me, in proclaiming liberty, every one to his brother, and every one to his neighbor: behold, I proclaim a liberty for you, saith the Lord, to the sword..."[21] and so on for several paragraphs: a Bible defense of slave revolt.

Bontemps uses African-American dialect in a generally successful attempt to create characters whose speech can rise from the colloquial to the prophetic. When the judge at his trial insists that white radicals must have tutored him, Gabriel responds:

"I tell you. I been studying about freedom a heap, me. I heard a plenty folks talk and I listened a heap. And everything I heard made me feel like I wanted to be free. It was on my mind hard, and it's right there the same way yet. On'erstand? That's all. Something keeps telling me that anything what's equal to a gray squirrel wants to be free. That's how it all come about... I ain't got no head for flying away. A man is got a right to have his freedom in the place where he's born. He is got cause to want all his kinfolks free like hisself." (p. 210)

Both mainstream newspapers and the African-American press gave *Black Thunder* good notices. In the *New York Times*, Lucy Tompkins favorably compared Bontemps's story of slave revolt to *Man's Fate*, André Malraux's novel of China's civil war. Both novels, Tompkins said, present "the spectacle of human dignity as manifest in the revolutionary spirit..."[22]

A few years later, Bontemps returned to the theme of black revolution with his next novel, *Drums at Dusk* (1939). Based on Toussaint's uprising in Haiti, *Drums* is a more studiously programmatic book, less complex in its characterization, and ultimately less successful in projecting the air of reality that Bontemps achieved in *Thunder*. The difference may lie in the attitude Bontemps takes toward his central figures: while Gabriel was a historical personage, little was known about him and Bontemps was compelled to let his imagination work freely in dramatizing this early nineteenth-century slave. Toussaint, on the other hand, is embedded in both abundant documentation and an iconic reputation as one of the major black heroes in the history of the Americas.

By a coincidence of chronology, W. E. B. Du Bois published his magisterial study *Black Reconstruction* in 1935, just a year before *Gone with the*

[21] Arna Bontemps, *Black Thunder* (Boston: Beacon Press, 1968 [1936]), p. 45.
[22] Lucy Tompkins, "Slaves' Rebellion," *New York Times Book Review* (February 2, 1936), p. 7.

Wind appeared. Du Bois had been contemplating a substantial study of Reconstruction for over thirty years. "Of the Dawn of Freedom," an essay defending the Freedmen's Bureau that became the second chapter of *The Souls of Black Folk* (1903), had been published at the turn of the century. Another essay, "Reconstruction and Its Benefits," had appeared in the July 1910 issue of *The American Historical Review*.

Other projects intervened, but the combined stimulants of a research grant and the publication of the immensely successful and systematically racist book, *The Tragic Era*, by Claude G. Bowers, discussed in the previous chapter, spurred Du Bois to complete his book. As we have seen, *The Tragic Era* gave pseudo-scholarly support to the derisory images of African-Americans that pervaded *Gone with the Wind*. And both books reinforced the inclinations of popular culture. To take a single but key example: for several Depression years, *Amos 'n' Andy* was the most popular show on radio, with a nightly audience estimated at forty million listeners.[23]

Throughout the early 1930s, "millions of radios... resounded every evening at seven o'clock with the voices of Freeman F. Gosden and Charles J. Correll, better know as Amos 'n' Andy; 'I'se regusted' and 'Check and double-check'... made their way into the common speech."[24] Louisiana's Governor, Senator, and presidential candidate, Huey Long, took his nickname, "The Kingfish," from the show. Advertising innovator William Benton was blessed by a mercantile inspiration provoked by the program. Walking home one hot May night, "I heard these colored voices leaping out into the street, from all the apartments. I turned around and walked back up the street. There were nineteen radios on and seventeen were tuned to '*Amos and Andy*.' This is probably the first audience research survey in the history of radio broadcasting."[25]

[23] *Amos 'n' Andy* was not the only white appropriation of African-American life and speech in the 1930s. Du Bose Hayward's *Porgy* (1925) was adapted by George and Ira Gershwin as the "folk opera" *Porgy and Bess*, in 1935. The popular white novelist Roark Bradford specialized in stories and novels featuring African-American protagonists, usually as comic and sentimental figures. The stories in Bradford's *Ol' Man Adam and His Chillin* (1928) were adapted by Marc Connelly as the Pulitzer Prize-winning play, *Green Pastures*. Bradford's *Kingdom Coming* (1933) is a more serious historical novel, dealing with black experiences before and during the Civil War. Though marred by stereotype, the book takes a generally sympathetic view of black aspirations for freedom, and provides a well-informed fictional account of the Underground Railroad.
[24] Frederick Lewis Allen, *Only Yesterday: An Informal History of the Nineteen-Twenties* (New York: Harper & Brothers Publishers, 1931), p. 352.
[25] William Benton, interviewed in Studs Terkel, *Hard Times: An Oral History of the Great Depression* (New York: Pantheon Books, 1970), p. 71.

It seemed that every radio was tuned to the show: "Movie theaters played it in their lobbies; Atlantic City merchants broadcast it on the boardwalk. Utility companies reported drops in water pressure as people flushed toilets after the show ended, and one sponsor, Pepsodent tooth-paste, saw a massive rise in sales."[26] References to the program turn up in unexpected places, as in this account of the death of Djuna Barnes's father: "On 21 May 1934, Wald [Barnes] died laughing, apparently of a heart attack, as he rose in his seat while listening to *Amos 'n' Andy* on the radio."[27]

To be sure, some African-Americans approved of *Amos 'n' Andy*. In August 1931, Gosden and Correll were the guests of honor at a picnic organized by Chicago's black newspaper, *The Defender*, and they were greeted with cheers from the huge crowd. The reception "was the most dramatic of many signs that the two men's portrayals of African-Americans in the big city had a large following among blacks themselves."[28]

However, large numbers of black men and women protested the vul-garity and stereotypes in which the program wallowed. Pittsburgh's African-American *Courier* led a long editorial campaign against the show, likening it to *Birth of a Nation* and other popular but insulting pictures and books. Black journalist George Schuyler catalyzed a nation-wide black protest against the program, assailing the show's crude caricatures of African-American life.[29]

In short, Du Bois faced a nearly united front of bigotry and precon-ception as he developed his revisionist interpretation of postbellum American history. The book he produced, *Black Reconstruction in America*, was a landmark and a model of archival research, argumentative power, and intellectual integrity.[30] The subtitle suggests the methodo-logical as well as the thematic focus of the study: "An Essay Toward a History of the Part Which Black Folk Played in the Attempt to Recon-struct Democracy in America, 1860–1880." In seventeen chapters that take

[26] Jim Cullen, *The Art of Democracy: A Concise History of Popular Culture in the United States*, second edition (New York: Monthly Review Press, 2002), p. 173.
[27] Phillip Herring, *Djuna: The Life and Work of Djuna Barnes* (New York: The Viking Press, 1995), p. 49.
[28] Melvin Patrick Ely, *The Adventures of Amos 'n' Andy: A Social History of an American Phenomenon* (Charlottesville: University Press of Virginia, 1991), p. 5.
[29] Through years and even decades of debate, the program continued to attract listeners – and viewers, with a television series (starring an African-American cast) that commenced in 1950.
[30] For a superb summary of the composition and significance of *Black Reconstruction*, see David Levering Lewis, *W. E. B. Du Bois: The Fight for Equality and the American Century, 1919–1963* (New York: Henry Holt and Company, 2000), pp. 349–378.

up more than 700 pages, *Black Reconstruction* painstakingly sets out the economic and political circumstances of both blacks and whites in the Civil War and the postwar South, tracing the provisional triumphs of emancipated African-Americans and the concerted opposition that ultimately defeated any possibility of an alliance between black and white workers.

Despite its occasional flights of high rhetoric – Du Bois could never resist the temptation to pile capitalized adjectives and nouns on top of each other – and its reliance on an intermittent and idiosyncratic Marxism, *Black Reconstruction* was and remains a masterpiece: a book that convincingly replaces the passive and two-dimensional "Sambo" of mainstream historiography with a full-blooded cast of African-American human beings, disadvantaged by poverty and illiteracy, to be sure, but responding quickly to the legal opportunities that emancipation brought.

Du Bois also understood that the alleged gallantry of white Southern military men, both regular army and irregular raiders, was the noisome counterpart of anti-black racism. African-Americans were invariably presented as physically unclean and morally unfit, while the generals and cavalrymen of the Confederacy and later the Klan were daring and also brilliantly groomed men, almost as notable for their snappy uniforms as their valor. To take an example, almost literally at random, Thomas Robson Hay, a distinguished historian who had won the American Historical Association's Johnston Prize in Military History, had this to say in a review of John W. Thomason, Jr.'s adulatory biography, *Jeb Stuart* (1930): "Jeb Stuart, the dashing cavalryman, the hard-fighting soldier, the skilled tactician, clad in his gray uniform and golden sash, with his scarlet cape over his shoulder and his feathered hat on his head, moves swiftly through the glamorous pages. It is an enthralling story . . ."[31]

One of the most provocative sections of *Black Reconstruction* is the final chapter, "The Propaganda of History." Here Du Bois argues that the historical truth of the postbellum American South has been held hostage to the ideology of white supremacy.[32] Referring back and forth to each other, choosing gossip and diaries over government reports and financial and demographic data, studies of Reconstruction in the first third of the

[31] Thomas Robson Hay, review of *Jeb Stuart*, in *The Mississippi Valley Historical Review* (June, 1931), p. 96.
[32] Not surprisingly, *The Tragic Era* is one of Du Bois's examples of deformed history; he calls it "an excellent and readable piece of current newspaper reporting, absolutely devoid of historical judgment or sociological knowledge." W. E. B. Du Bois, *Black Reconstruction in America* (New York: Russell & Russell, 1935), p. 721.

twentieth century have become nothing more than an echo chamber droning with repeated anecdotes, unsupported claims, and downright lies.

In order to paint the South as a martyr to inescapable fate, to make the North the magnanimous emancipator, and to ridicule the Negro as the impossible joke in the whole development, we have in fifty years, by libel, innuendo and silence, so completely misstated and obliterated the history of the Negro in America and his relation to its work and government that today it is almost unknown. (p. 723)

Du Bois, whose early faith in the liberating power of truth had been shaken by decades of experience, nonetheless continued to believe that only a rigorous and unbiased search for truth could provide the foundation for racial justice. The object of history, he insisted, was "simply to establish the Truth, on which Right in the future may be built." And such truth will not be possible until "we have in our colleges men who regard the truth as more important than the defense of the white race, and who will not deliberately encourage students to gather thesis material in order to support a prejudice or buttress a lie" (p. 725).

Seventy years after its publication, in the early twenty-first century, many of the positions Du Bois argued in *Black Reconstruction* have become mainstream. Above all, his fierce determination to document the full human capacity of black people, and their claims to recognition as historical actors, has influenced several generations of historians. At the same time, in the contest for legitimacy in the broader American imagination, *Black Reconstruction* continues to struggle against the inherited inclinations that re-emerge every time *Gone with the Wind* is shown on television or in a theater.

The aging Thomas Dixon was among the unreconstructed Southerners who responded vehemently to Du Bois's revised history. More than three decades after *The Clansman* had codified the terms of white supremacy, Dixon published *The Flaming Sword* (1939), explicitly as a rebuttal of *Black Reconstruction*. The title comes from a passage in Du Bois's book – "Across this path [toward equality] stands the South with flaming sword" – that Dixon gleefully used as his novel's epigraph. His intention, Dixon declared, was to defend America from "that blazing manifesto of communism" and its alleged call for race mixing.[33] Despite that avowed intention, the novel's action is not set in the Reconstruction period, but

---

[33] Cited in John David Smith, Introduction to Thomas Dixon, *The Flaming Sword* (Lexington: University Press of Kentucky, 2005 [1939]), p. xviii.

in the first four decades of the twentieth century. Aside from Du Bois, his many targets include the Scottsboro defendants, James Weldon Johnson (for writing poetry that motivated African-American discontent), Oswald Garrison Villard and other white leaders of the NAACP, and Eleanor Roosevelt. In the novel's apocalyptic finale, an alliance of African-Americans and communists successfully revolts against the government, and the United States surrenders its governance to the Soviet Union.

Such a book, as Du Bois well understood, merely proved that the legacy of the "peculiar institution" continued to thrive in the rank soil of Southern racism. Like Faulkner, Du Bois knew that in the South the past was not past. In the opinion of the most distinguished historian of the South, Jim Crow's suffocating segregation, with its tangle of prohibitions and cruelties, had actually "reached its perfection in the 1930s."[34]

Black history provided the materials for several plays in the 1930s, including Sheppard Randolph Edmonds's *Nat Turner* (1935), which recreates Turner's 1831 rebellion, and May Miller's *Harriet Tubman* (1935), which dramatizes a single episode in Tubman's long career as an organizer of the Underground Railroad. These plays, and eleven others, were published in a volume called *Negro History in Thirteen Plays*, an anthology of commissioned work aimed at instructing both white and black audiences in the accomplishments of Africans and African-Americans. The book's introduction was written by Carter G. Woodson, founder of the *Journal of Negro History* and recognized in the 1930s as the dean of black historians.[35] Woodson argued for theater that would present "the vision of the Negro in the new day," and declared that the work in *Thirteen Plays* dramatized the Negro "as a maker of civilization in Africa, a contributor to progress in Europe, and a factor in the development of Greater America."[36]

Langston Hughes's *Emperor of Haiti* (1936) was probably the most important African-American historical drama of the decade. *Emperor* is based on the struggles of black Haitians to liberate themselves from French rule at the end of the eighteenth century and the beginning of

---

[34] C. Vann Woodward, *Thinking Back: The Perils of Writing History* (Baton Rouge: Louisiana State University Press, 1986), p. 87.
[35] Two of Woodson's historical studies appeared in the 1930s: *The Mis-Education of the Negro* (1933), and *The African Background Outlined* (1936).
[36] Carter G. Woodson, "Introduction," in Willis Richardson and May Miller, eds., *Negro History in Thirteen Plays* (Washington, DC: The Associated Publishers, Inc., 1935), p. v.

Black memory   197

the nineteenth.[37] Independence was an achievement that reverberated for generations, inspiring – among many others – the painter Jacob Lawrence and the writer Arna Bontemps, whose responses to Toussaint L'Ouverture are discussed elsewhere. Among black Americans, interest in Haiti was especially high in the early twentieth century. The United States had invaded the country in 1915, arguing under the Monroe Doctrine that the island's internal turmoil gave America the right to intervene and restore order. US Marines remained stationed in Haiti for nearly twenty years, being recalled only in 1934.

The rebellion began in 1791, inspired in part by the French Revolution and its militant claims for human equality and the rights of man. After more than ten years of struggle, Haiti declared its independence in January, 1804, and in doing so became the first black republic in the world. Toussaint did not live to see independence: he died in a French prison in 1803. Jean-Jacques Dessalines succeeded him in command, first as President of the new nation, then as Emperor.[38] The civil war devastated the country, and brought it to the edge of anarchy. Following a campaign aimed at eliminating whites from the country, Dessalines was assassinated in 1806.

Hughes's *Emperor* was first performed at Cleveland's pioneering Karamu House. Its three acts spotlight just the beginning and end of Dessalines's career.[39] In Act one, set in 1791, he and other slaves gather in secret to plot their revolt. The second and third acts leap forward to Dessalines's final days. He has proclaimed himself Emperor (taking the idea from Napoleon) and has fallen into incompetent and narcissistic luxury. He has renounced the black woman of his early life and taken a light-skinned mulatto woman as his Empress. He showers titles on his courtiers, using nomenclature that is twisted by Hughes into deliberate and accusatory absurdity: The Duke of Marmelade, Lady Fifi Beauregard, Baron Congo, the Grand Alimony, the Chief Bugle-Blower, and so on.

Though no white characters appear in the play, Hughes provides ample evidence of French colonial brutality. Dessalines bares his whip-scarred

[37] The Federal Theatre Project also produced a play called *Haiti* (1938), by a white, Southern journalist named William Dubois.

[38] For a reliable summary of the Haitian uprising, see C. L. R. James, *The Black Jacobins: Toussaint L'Ouverture and the San Domingo Revolution*, second edition, revised (New York: Vintage Books, 1963), pp. 224ff.

[39] A revised version, re-named *Drums of Haiti*, was produced in Detroit in 1937. The play was revised again in 1949, this time as an opera called *Troubled Island*, in collaboration with composer William Grant Still.

back on more than one occasion, and another character has had one arm cut off for striking his master. But the play's structure italicizes the ineptitude and self-destructiveness of its black characters. In the end, Dessalines is betrayed by a combination of his own appetite for power and the treachery of the island's elite mulattoes, many of whom have never known slavery.[40]

The poor of Haiti remain poor, having exchanged one form of tyranny for another. Dessalines, like other despots, presumes to identify his own success with that of his people. In a conversation with an old man, Martel, the only one brave enough to tell him the truth, Dessalines insists: "I've created the first black Empire in the world, so why shouldn't I glory in it, Martel? I'm the king! I'm on top! I'm the glory of Haiti":

MARTEL: The glory of Haiti lies in no one man, Jean Jacques.
DESSALINES: Where does it lie?
MARTEL: In the people's love for freedom.
DESSALINES: Too much freedom – if they no longer obey me, their liberator; I'm their freedom – and this Court's their glory.[41]

Dessalines dies as he lived, murdered by conspirators who take advantage of his bravado and lure him into an ambush. In a sly Shakespearean allusion, one of the assassins looks down at the dead man and pronounces him "food for worms" (p. 72). So had Prince Hal greeted the death of Hotspur, another reckless overreacher, at the end of *I Henry IV*. Dessalines's death concludes the play with a foretaste of the civil strife that will torment the island nation for generations.

"The struggle over slavery's memory has been almost as intense as the struggle over slavery itself."[42] One of the major chapters in that contest was written in the 1930s. Between 1936 and 1938, under the auspices of the Works Progress Administration, a miscellaneous group of writers, journalists, and teachers conducted over 2,000 interviews with ex-slaves in seventeen states. It was the most ambitious attempt ever made to gather

---

[40] A useful discussion of the play can be found in Joseph McLaren, *Langston Hughes: Folk Dramatist in the Protest Tradition, 1921–1943* (Westport, CT: Greenwood Press, 1997), pp. 101–106.
[41] Langston Hughes, *Emperor of Haiti*, in Errol Hill, ed., *Black Heroes: Seven Plays* (New York: Applause Theatre Book Publishers, 1989), p. 39.
[42] "Introduction: Slavery as Memory and History," in Ira Berlin, *et al.*, *Remembering Slavery: African Americans Talk About Their Personal Experiences of Slavery and Freedom* (New York: The New Press, 1998), p. xiii.

first-person accounts of individual experiences under slavery.[43] The resulting transcripts comprise an unprecedented if much-contested exercise in African-American memory.

A set of fixed questions was developed to guide each interview, so that comparative information could be gathered on such questions as work, punishments, diet, and marriage. Despite these preparations, the transcripts make clear that the discussions often went in unpredicted directions. Since most of the men and women were in their eighties and nineties at the time of the interviews, often with wobbly memories, the reliability of their testimony has long been the focus of a lively debate.[44] Furthermore, where it has been possible to compare original transcripts with the copies filed in Washington, the latter sometimes "showed a pattern of editing that resulted in a more positive view of the 'peculiar institution' than was present in the original interviews."[45] Finally, even if the interviews are presumed to be accurate, they record only the particular experiences of individuals; they do not offer a comprehensive account of slavery, which differed in different times and places, and they rarely include useful quantitative information.

These limitations, together with the fact that almost all the interviewers were Southern whites, typically local and sometimes descended from slave-owners, may explain at least in part the unmistakable note of nostalgia that seeps into many of the interviews.[46] Charity Anderson, who gave her age as 101 years, was interviewed in April, 1937. Recalling her life as the slave of Mr. Leslie Johnson, she said:

Missy, peoples don't live now, and niggers ain't got no manners, and don't know nothin' about waitin' on white folks. I kin remember de days when I was one of de house servants. Dere was six of us in de ol' marster's house, me, Sarai, Lou, Hester, Jerry and Joe. Us didn't know nothin' but good times den. My job was lookin' a'ter de corner table whar nothin' but de desserts sat. Jo and Jerry were de

[43] Earlier interviews had been conducted, on a smaller scale, mainly by black scholars in the 1920s. Some of the transcripts were published in the *Journal of Negro History*.

[44] As long ago as 1941, B. A. Botkin, chief editor of the WPA Writers' Unit, acknowledged the "obvious limitations" these materials presented: "bias and fallibility of both informants and interviewers, the use of leading questions, unskilled techniques, and insufficient controls and checks." Introduction to the microfiche edition of the typescript of *Slave Narratives: a Folk History of Slavery in the United States from Interviews with Former Slaves*.

[45] George Rawick, "General Introduction," in Rawick, general editor, *The American Slave: A Composite Autobiography*, Supplement, Series 1 (Westport, CT: Greenwood Press, 1977), pp. xi–xii.

[46] The Florida section of the project, which vigorously recruited African-American interviewers, was an exception to the general practice. Zora Neale Hurston was among the most active interviewers in the Florida section.

Illustration 11. Charity Anderson

table boys, and dey ne'ber touched nothin' wid dere hans', dey used de waiter to
pass things wid. My! dem was good ol' days.

My old Marster was a good man, he treated all his slaves kind, and took care
of dem . . .[47]

---

[47] *The American Slave.* Cited from the Library of Congress WPA Slave Narrative project: http://
memory.loc.gov/ammem/snhtml/.

Tempe Herndon Durham, who claimed to be 103 at the time of her interview, also testified that life was better under slavery:

Freedom is all right, but de niggers was better off befo' surrender, kaze den dey was looked after an' dey didn' get in no trouble fightin' an' killin' like dey do dese days. If a nigger cut up an' got sassy in slavery times, his Ole Marse give him a good whippin' an' he went way back an' set down an' 'haved hese'f. If he was sick, Marse an' Mistis looked after him, an' if he needed store medicine, it was bought an' give to him; he didn' have to pay nothin'. Dey didn' even have to think 'bout clothes nor nothin' like dat, dey was wove an' made an' give to dem. Maybe everybody's Marse and Mistis wuzn' good as Marse George and Mis' Betsy, but dey was de same as a mammy an' pappy to us niggers.[48]

Despite their age and occasional absent-mindedness, despite whatever intimidation may have been brought to bear on them by their interviewers, many of the ex-slaves provided testimony that was neither affectionate nor even conciliatory. Another centenarian, Mary Reynolds of Dallas, Texas, told her interviewer that

Slavery was the worst days was ever seed in the world. They was things past tellin', but I got the scars on my old body to show to this day. I seed worse than what happened to me. I seed them put the men and women in the stock with they hands screwed down through holes in the board and they feets tied together and they naked behinds to the world. Solomon the overseer beat them with a big whip and massa look on. The niggers better not stop in the fields when they hear them yellin'. They cut the flesh most to the bones and some they was when they taken them out of stock and put them on the beds, they never got up again.

After describing more of the cruelty she and other slaves endured, Reynolds gave thanks for abolition: "I think Gawd done took that burden offen his black chillun and I'm aimin' to praise him for it to his face in the days of Glory what ain't so far off."[49]

---

[48] *The American Slave.* Cited from the Library of Congress WPA Slave Narrative project: http://memory.loc.gov/ammem/snhtml/. Other former slaves reported similar judgments. Charles Spurgeon Johnson interviewed members of over 600 African-American families in Macon County, Alabama in the early 1930s. One of them, an aged man named Zack Ivey, told Johnson: "I done had a harder time since I been free than when I was a slave. I never had such a hard time in my life as I'm having now." *The Shadow of the Plantation* (Chicago: University of Chicago Press, 1934), p. 19. Looking back to the Civil War from the late 1930s, the former slave Geneva Tonsill recalled standing near a Virginia battlefield, "with my mind on my master, praying for him to come back safe, although he and the rest were fighting to keep me under bondage. I love him just the same." Tom E. Terrill and Jerrold Hirsch, eds., *Such As Us: Southern Voices of the Thirties* (Chapel Hill: University of North Carolina Press, 1978), p. 18. *Such As Us* is the belated sequel to *These Are Our Lives* (1939), an earlier and influential gathering of WPA interview material.

[49] *The American Slave.* Cited from the Library of Congress WPA Slave Narrative project: http://memory.loc.gov/ammem/snhtml.

As this small sampling indicates, the narratives can be used to provide evidence for "almost anything about slavery," in C. Vann Woodward's summary. "A paradise and a hell on earth," Woodward continues, "food in plenty and daily starvation, no punishment at all and brutal beatings for no reason at all, tender care and gruesome tortures, loving family ties and forced breedings, gentle masters and sadistic monsters" – these are among the dichotomies that emerge, and sometimes in the same interview.[50]

Notwithstanding the difficulties that hedge the narratives, they remain uniquely valuable: "indispensable," in the words of another scholar.[51] No other sources provide such intimate access to the daily life of men, women, and children under slavery.

The 1930s was the scene of a flowering of African-American history painting. Horace Pippin, whose painting of John Brown was mentioned earlier, served in the First World War with the legendary, all-black 369th Infantry. In 1918, his right arm was shattered, a crippling injury that would affect his painting for the rest of his life. He brought the authority of his experience to bear on "The End of the War: Starting Home" (1931), a look back to the war that is among the most poignant images of the terrible realities of the trenches.

Along with Pippin, two of the most gifted historical painters of the Depression decade were Aaron Douglas and Jacob Lawrence. Douglas had established his reputation in the 1920s, through his illustrations for Alain Locke's landmark anthology, *The New Negro* (1925), James Weldon Johnson's *God's Trombones* (1927), Langston Hughes's *Fine Clothes to the Jew* (1927), and other books. He worked in a distinctive manner, a combination of art deco and cubism, situating silhouetted figures dramatically against stylized backgrounds and swirling geometric shapes. In the 1930s, Douglas completed a number of important murals. The first, a group of paintings commissioned by Fisk University and called a "symbolic history series," tell "the story of the Negro's progress from central Africa to present day America," as Douglas explained it.[52]

[50] C. Vann Woodward, "History from Slave Sources," in Charles T. Davis and Henry Louis Gates, Jr., eds., *The Slave's Narrative* (New York: Oxford University Press, 1985), p. 53.
[51] Paul D. Escott, "The Art and Science of Reading WPA Slave Narratives," in Davis and Gates, *The Slave's Narrative*, p. 40.
[52] Cited in Jeannine DeLombard. "Douglas, Aaron"; www.anb.org/articles/17/17-00233.html; *American National Biography Online*, February 2000.

In 1934, Douglas was invited by the 135th Street Branch of the New York Public Library (now the Countee Cullen Branch Library) to complete a sequence of large murals that have become his most famous work.[53] Comprising four panels, the piece was called "Aspects of Negro Life," a subject that Douglas develops historically. The first panel, "The Negro in an African Setting," places two dancing figures in the midst of drummers and spectators. An African sculpture symbolizes both the African heritage of American black people, and the role of African precedent in the making of Modernism. "An Idyll of the Deep South," the second panel, puts a group of musicians at the center, surrounded by other men and women variously singing and working.

The third panel, "Slavery Through Reconstruction," is the most historically circumstantial: Ku Klux Klansmen, wielding clubs, enter the scene from the left; soldiers – presumably Union troops – depart to the right, to the sound of a trumpeter's retreat. A large male figure in the center, with his back to the viewer, points to a city in the distance, while around him black laborers lean to their cotton picking. The idyllic overtones of the second panel (which seem ironic in any case) here give way to the lethal dangers of Klan violence. At the center of "Song of the Towers," the final panel in the series, Douglas has placed a man with a saxophone, crossing a wheel-like bridge to the skyscrapers of New York (the Statue of Liberty is visible in the distance). A second man follows, suitcase in hand, apparently fleeing the fires and hooded shapes behind him.

Jacob Lawrence also found many of his most important subjects in African-American history. Lawrence early on developed the style that would serve him through a long career, a thinly painted, dramatically colored collage cubism that he put at the service of narrative, stories of the African-American present and past. In the course of just four years, he produced five exceptionally important historical sequences: "The Life of Toussaint L'Ouverture," (1938, forty-one paintings), "The Life of Frederick Douglass" (1939, thirty-two paintings), "The Life of Harriet Tubman" (1940, thirty-one paintings), "The Migration of the Negro" (1941, sixty paintings), and "The Life of John Brown" (1941, twenty-two paintings).

Lawrence was, in effect, creating a counter-narrative to the received, textbook versions of history – an epic of black life in America. He

---

[53] "Aspects of Negro Life" was commissioned by the Public Works of Art Project of the United States Treasury.

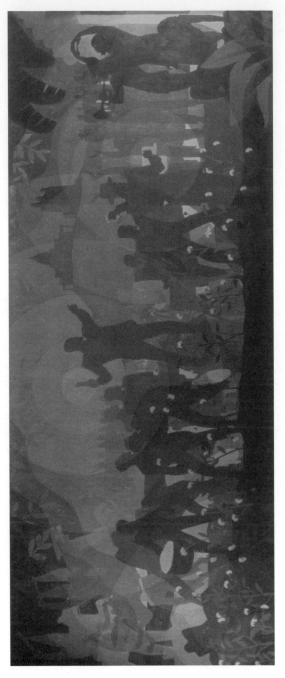

Illustration 12. Aaron Douglas, "Slavery through Reconstruction"

intended these series not only as acts of historical recovery, but also as interventions in the racial politics of the 1930s. Discussing the Toussaint sequence, he wrote:

Having no Negro history makes the Negro people feel inferior to the rest of the world. I don't see how a history of the United States can be written honestly without including the Negro. I didn't do it just as a historical thing, but because I believe these things tie up with the Negro today. We don't have a physical slavery, but an economic slavery.[54]

Instead of titles, Lawrence numbered the paintings in his series, and provided brief captions. The tenth image in the Toussaint series, which shows a white overseer beating a manacled black slave, bears the caption: "The cruelty of the planters led the slaves to revolt, 1776. These revolts kept cropping up from time to time – finally came to a head in the rebellion."

Though each painting makes its narrative contribution to the various lives Lawrence represents, many are also effective as individual images. The twenty-second painting in the Frederick Douglass series, for example, shows Douglass, in jacket and tie, writing in a study, with books lined up on the table and on a shelf behind him. Lawrence captures the centrality of literacy and writing to Douglass's mission: author of the most influential slave narrative of the nineteenth century, and editor of the abolitionist newspaper, *North Star*, Douglass lives because he etched his name and accomplishments on the American memory. The seventh image of Harriet Tubman pictures a large, square-shouldered black woman sawing on a wooden log: Tubman as an icon of strength, doing whatever needed to be done in the cause of freedom.

Perhaps the most moving single painting in all these series is the fifteenth in "The Migration of the Negro." The caption tells us: "Another cause [of the migration] was lynching. It was found that where there had been a lynching, the people who were reluctant to leave at first left immediately after this." The painting is radically simplified. In the left center, a black figure crouches on a rock, turned away from the viewer. Hovering over the figure's head, a single, bare tree branch points like a finger or dagger. From the branch, an empty noose dangles. A single, barely discernible figure, a stylized tree branch, a noose: out of these few

---

[54] Cited in Patricia Hills, "Jacob Lawrence's Expressive Cubism," in Ellen Harkins Wheat, ed., *Jacob Lawrence: American Painter* (Seattle: University of Washington Press, 1986), p. 16.

Illustration 13. Jacob Lawrence, "Another Cause was Lynching"

elements Lawrence constructs a shattering portrait of the physical and emotional reality of lynching.

In 1937, John Dollard mapped the contemporary state of Southern race relations in his book, *Caste and Class in a Southern Town*. A combination of social statistics and extensive interviews with both black and white informants, and deeply influenced by Freudian psychoanalysis, *Caste and Class* described the deformations of a society governed by racial hierarchy. The so-called "etiquette" of race conferred every economic, social, and sexual privilege on whites, while confining blacks inside a system of oppression. The universal message was black inferiority, enforced by constant white violence, including lynching.[55] Caste was, in effect, the South's efficient substitute for slavery.

Dollard's use of a single town, Indianola, Mississippi, for his source material, has provoked controversy, as has his explanatory apparatus.[56] His book's strength lies rather in the multiplication of anecdotes, by turns

[55] Though the incidence of lynching declined in the 1930s, an estimated 100 persons were lynched in that decade, almost all of them African-American. Franklin Roosevelt, as part of the devil's bargain he had struck with the Southern Senators and Representatives who controlled both houses of Congress, refused to support an anti-lynching bill throughout the thirties.
[56] Hortense Powdermaker's *After Freedom* (1939) was also based on field work in Indianola.

grotesque and barbaric, that illustrate the inhumanities of Southern racism. What Dollard called "the emotional structure" of the society is anchored in hatred, mutual suspicion, and white violence. A young black man, whose car is hit by a white man's car, is jailed and beaten, despite the fact that the white man caused the accident.[57] A black man accused of winking at a white woman is whipped by a mob (p. 336). The countless individual incidents create an atmosphere of dread that pervades African-American daily life.

As Dollard makes repeatedly clear, his survey of contemporary attitudes and behaviors also encompasses a history of the South: "[t]he subservience of the Negro is obviously a heritage from slavery days" (p. 186).[58] Sociology is history: the dehumanizing culture of apartheid had its sources in centuries of carefully nurtured bigotry, reaching across the divide of emancipation through the legalized devastations of Jim Crow.

[57] John Dollard, *Caste and Class in a Southern Town* (Garden City, NY: Doubleday Anchor Books, 1957 [1937]), p. 288.
[58] For another local study of the debilitating consequences of slavery for the African-American community, this time in Macon County, Alabama, see Charles S. Johnson, *Shadow of the Plantation* (Chicago: University of Chicago Press, 1934).

CHAPTER 7

History and the party line

The American Left declined to a despised handful of true believers in the 1920s. The inflamed patriotism that accompanied American participation in World War I, and the selective but flamboyant prosperity of the succeeding decade, reduced the influence of left-wing dissent to the vanishing point.[1] A movement that had shown strength in the early twentieth century was decimated by the war and its political aftermath.[2] At the beginning of the twenties, the imprisoned Eugene V. Debs might have served as an emblem of the beleaguered state of postwar American dissent. Debs, who had polled nearly a million votes in 1912 as the Socialist Party's candidate for President, was convicted of violating the Espionage Act in 1919, and was sentenced to ten years in the Atlanta penitentiary; he would serve nearly three, before he was pardoned by President Warren G. Harding.

The political preface to the 1920s was written in Debs's trial and conviction, and in the similar harassment of thousands of other alleged subversives who were imprisoned or deported in the closing days of Woodrow Wilson's presidency. The first major "Red Scare" of the century disclosed a habit of suppression that would be revealed again in some of the most notorious political episodes of the 1920s decade, including the Scopes trial in 1925, and especially the execution of Sacco and Vanzetti two years later. Daniel Bell has described the twenties as "the melancholy intermezzo" in the history of the American Left.[3] Exhausted by official

[1] One of the best and most frightening evocations of the tyranny that a murderous jingoism imposed on civil liberties during the war can be found in Katherine Anne Porter's *Pale Horse, Pale Rider* (1939).
[2] Daniel Aaron's *Writers on the Left* (New York: Oxford University Press, 1973 [1961]) remains the most circumstantial account of the personal histories of literary radicals in the early twentieth century. The abundance of testimony and details Aaron summons confirms the ideological dreariness of the 1920s, at least from the point of view of the Left.
[3] Daniel Bell, *Marxian Socialism in the United States* (Princeton, NJ: Princeton University Press, 1973 [1952]), p. 117.

persecution, public hostility, and internal factionalism, the assorted socialist and communist parties, splinter groups, associations, and collectives rapidly lost membership and influence. The presidential election of 1928 offered a telling measure of the left's fallen fortunes. Socialist Party candidate Norman Thomas received fewer than 270,000 votes, the lowest socialist total since 1900.

The early years of the Depression temporarily re-vitalized the Left. The mainly local and marginal resistance that had survived the twenties now attracted men and women who had previously stood aside from political questions, a cross-section of writers, artists, and other professionals, as well as working people, who sought an alternative ideology. If only fleetingly, the remnant began to seem a vanguard.

Eager to honor radical commitment and to re-orient literary value judgments, recent scholarship on the 1930s has transformed a host of once-obscure novelists, critics, and poets into allegedly substantial figures. Essays, chapters, and entire books are given over to investigations of V. F. Calverton, Meridel Le Sueur, Tillie Olson, Tom Kromer, Anna Louise Strong, *New Masses*, Michael Gold, Josephine Herbst, the John Reed Clubs, Kenneth Fearing, and the 1935 anthology *Proletarian Literature in the United States*. There is often more than a hint of nostalgia and advocacy in the way these writers and texts are treated, since their vanished dreams of dissent rhyme with contemporary discontents and aspirations.[4]

For their part, though they anatomized the present on behalf of an idealized communist future, proletarian novelists and poets frequently joined other writers of the 1930s in acts of historical reconstruction. Prophecy was embedded in the past. *New Masses* argued that the "reinterpretation of our history is not a matter of academic interest but an immediate political need."[5]

The historical undertaking was guided by a fundamental distinction: the Depression was to be understood not as an anomalous or inexplicable

---

[4] To give just a few recent examples: Laura Browder, *Rousing the Nation: Radical Culture in Depression America* (1998); James Edward Smethurst, *The New Red Negro: the Literary Left and African American Poetry, 1930–1946* (1999); Robert Shulman, *The Power of Political Art: the 1930s Literary Left Reconsidered* (2000); Cary Nelson, *Revolutionary Memory: Recovering the Poetry of the American Left* (2001); Alan M. Wald, *Exiles from a Future Time: the Forging of the Mid-twentieth-century Literary Left* (2002); Janet Galligani Casey, ed., *The Novel and the American Left: Critical Essays on Depression-era Fiction* (2004); Andrew C. Yerkes, *Twentieth-century Americanism: Identity and Ideology in Depression-era Leftist Fiction* (2005).

[5] Cited in Richard H. Pells, *Radical Visions and American Dreams: Culture and Social Thought in the Depression Years* (Middletown, CT: Wesleyan University Press, 1984 [1973]), p. 314. Pells's book, which is marked by a consistent balance and common sense in its assessments of American culture in the 1930s, continues to be a valuable resource for any student of the period.

misfortune but as a symptom and proof that America's long-held beliefs were misconceived. In short, in the view of left-wing commentators, the Depression confirmed the moral and not merely the economic bankruptcy of traditional political assumptions and the institutions they authorized. The solution to the problem of the present depended, at least in part, upon correcting the intellectual errors of the past. Describing the radical use of history in the French Revolution, Jan Starobinski has written that those who would "invent the future" must locate themselves in the terrain of the past: "only when one's purpose was fixed, by examples from the past, could the future be shaped with a determination to impose new purpose."[6] The American radicals of the 1930s agreed; history needed to be re-written.

Some context is needed here. The crisis in historical studies long predated the economic turmoil of the 1930s. In the years following World War I, an energetic debate over historical truth had become increasingly prominent in discussions of history; some of this debate was summarized in an earlier chapter. Throughout the 1920s, both the academic and popular press had contained articles and editorials that by turns celebrated or denounced the flagging allegiance of historians to nineteenth-century notions of detached, impartial, and even "scientific" objectivity.[7] Indeed, the science on which "scientific" history was allegedly based was itself undergoing transformation from the hard-edged positivism of the nineteenth century. At the same time, the "Whig interpretation," which discerned inevitable progress in the chronicle of America's past, lost a good deal of its credibility. According to John Higham, it had already become evident in the twenties that "history had somehow gone wrong."[8] The thirties merely seemed to confirm that diagnosis.

In effect, the muckraking of the prewar years was extended in the twenties and thirties to the revered institutions and iconic figures of the nation's history. Indeed, the intellectual consequences were more significant than those entailed by muckraking, since many of those turn-of-the-century investigative journalists had been steadfast in their admiration

---

[6] Jan Starobinski, *1789: The Emblems of Reason* (Charlottesville: University of Virginia Press, 1982), p. 104.

[7] Peter Novick, *That Noble Dream: The "Objectivity Question" and the American Historical Profession* (Cambridge: Cambridge University Press, 1988), especially chapter 6, "A Changed Climate." See also Cushing Strout, *The Pragmatic Revolt in American History: Carl Becker and Charles Beard* (New Haven, CT: Yale University Press, 1958).

[8] John Higham, *History: Professional Scholarship in America* (New York: Harper & Row, 1973 [1965]), p. 198.

for the virtuous political behavior of the earlier Republic.[9] They sought to return the country to "what used to be." The debunking historians and biographers, by contrast, set out to raze the founding myths themselves. The Puritan settlers, Jefferson and Jackson, even Washington and Lincoln, were subjected to a season of exposure by such talented nay-sayers as James Truslow Adams, Albert Beveridge, and Thomas Abernethy.[10] In the disillusioned opinion of these and like-minded writers, the "course of America's progress was strewn with too many mistakes, failures, and illusions to have unfolded with the neat, intrinsic logic that Turner and Beard had sketched" (Higham, *History*, p. 198).

At the same time, professional historians played only a minor role in the particular work of left-wing historical revision in the thirties. According to Peter Novick, "[n]ot much Marxist historical work of any kind appeared during the 1930s." Novick identifies only three books published in the decade that might accurately be called Marxist: Roger Shugg's *Origins of Class Struggle in Louisiana* (1939), economist Louis Hacker's *Triumph of American Capitalism* (1940), and W. E. B. Du Bois's landmark *Black Reconstruction* (1935), discussed in the previous chapter. (*That Noble Dream*, p. 249n).[11] The general resistance of the historical profession to Marxist re-interpretations of the past may be an example of cultural lag, or of scholarly conservatism (or of common sense). It is also the case, however, that Marxism, especially as professed in the 1930s, demanded consent to an axiomatic set of doctrines, which made it in some obvious sense incompatible with the relativizing tendencies of the interwar period. Historians who were shaking off one version of absolutism were understandably reluctant to adopt another.

In any case, the job of trying to capture America's history for the Left fell, by and large, to novelists, poets, playwrights, and journalists. In 1932,

---

[9] On the nostalgia of the muckrakers and of early American radicals in general, see Justin Kaplan, *Lincoln Steffens: A Biography* (New York: Simon and Schuster, 1974), and Peter Conn, *The Divided Mind: Ideology and Imagination in America, 1898–1917* (New York: Cambridge University Press, 1983), especially chapter 3, "Restoration as Reform."

[10] James Truslow Adams, *The Founding of New England* (1921), the first volume in his three-volume history; Albert Beveridge, *Abraham Lincoln: 1809–1858*, two volumes (1928); Thomas P. Abernethy, *From Frontier to Plantation in Tennessee: A Study in Frontier Democracy* (1932). Of course, more traditionally reverential views survived and co-existed with newer revisionist interpretations. To give just two examples, discussed in some detail in an earlier chapter, Carl Sandburg's six-volume biography of Lincoln, and Marquis James's two-volume life of Jackson presented essentially heroic portraits of their central figures. And even the debunkers made distinctions: if James Truslow Adams pilloried the Puritans, he still regarded Washington as a hero.

[11] Novick's list of three might better be reduced to two. At a minimum, the description *of Black Reconstruction* as "Marxist" needs to be hedged with distinctions.

several dozen of the country's most prominent writers announced this project when they joined together as signatories of *Culture and the Crisis*, a thirty-two-page manifesto that called for revolution and endorsed the presidential campaign of Communist Party candidate William Z. Foster.

The pamphlet had a two-fold significance. First, it demonstrated the dramatically expanded constituency of left-wing protest by bringing together over fifty writers whose backgrounds were unusually diverse. The signers included whites and African-Americans, women and men, Harvard graduates and high school dropouts, immigrants and the native born. In addition, their prior political experience and commitments differed extensively; while some of the writers who attached their names to this pamphlet had embraced radical dissent before the Crash, others were enrolling in the ranks of the Left for the first time. They aligned themselves with the communist cause because the Left seemed to offer a coherent explanation of what had gone wrong, and a prescription for radical change.

Culture and the Crisis was also significant because it announced an unprecedented alliance of intellectuals and workers. For literally the first time in American history, a substantial number of those who worked with their pens called for solidarity with those who worked with their hands and backs. In the somewhat condescending terminology of the manifesto, the "brain workers" declared that they intended to make common cause with the "muscle workers."[12] Neither in 1932 nor at any later date would the "muscle workers" show much reciprocal interest, but the call for united and perhaps violent action at least offered the intellectuals an outlet for their honorable if diffuse proletarian sympathies.

From its opening lines, the pamphlet is informed by an apocalyptic urgency that announces the opening of a new historical era: "When we look backward, we see our American past like a great tidal wave that is now receding... When we look ahead, we see something new and strange, undreamed of in the American philosophy... The great wave piled up too much wreckage – of nature, of obsolete social patterns and institutions, of human blood and nerves"(p. 3). Like its economy, the nation's system of beliefs, including its reverent view of its own history, was declared bankrupt. The "Hooverville," a "new No Man's Land of tin and paper covered shanties" (p. 9), has become the architectural emblem

[12] *Culture and the Crisis: An Open Letter to the Writers, Artists, Teachers, Physicians, Engineers, Scientists and Other Professional Workers of America* (New York: Workers' Library Publishers, 1932), p. 3.

for the nation's condition. Under capitalism, the United States is "like a house that is rotting away" (p. 6).

On the far side of dissolution lies a future untrammeled by the obsolete institutions of the American past. The reconstructed society that comes into being will engender a new art as well as a new set of political arrangements, "a new cultural renaissance" (p. 30). Since "the cultural crisis . . . grows directly out of the economic crisis" (p. 29), the revolution will require a liberation from received myths and the creation of a new history. Furthermore, as these pugnacious remarks suggest, the project of reconstruction would reach out to embrace the entire cultural apparatus – including the religious and artistic heritage – through which the ruling class legitimized its authority.

Clifford Odets's *Waiting for Lefty* (1935) includes a scene that economically summarizes the proletarian revolt against the canonical past. The sixth major sequence in the play is called "The Interne Episode"; in it, the distinguished Dr. Barnes explains the corrupt facts of modern medical life to the younger, Jewish, Dr. Benjamin. Those facts include the privileges of influence, the subordination of medical ethics to opportunism, and anti-Semitism. Barnes's indictment reaches back to embrace the nation's founding documents:

Doctors don't run medicine in this country. The men who know their jobs don't run anything here, except the motormen on trolley cars. I've seen medicine change – plenty – anaesthesia, sterilization – but not because of rich men – in *spite* of them! In a rich man's country your true self's buried deep . . . . See this ankle, this delicate, sensitive hand? Four hundred years to breed that. Out of a revolutionary background! Spirit of '76! Ancestors froze at Valley Forge! What's it all mean? Slops! The honest workers were sold out then, in '76. The Constitution's for rich men then and now. Slops![13]

The historical distinction here is significant. Dr. Barnes doesn't call for improvements or reforms that would re-establish the integrity of the nation's founding principles. Rather, the Constitution itself is exposed as

---

[13] Clifford Odets, *Waiting for Lefty*, in *Three Plays* (New York: Covici-Friede, 1935), p. xx. *In Johnny Got His Gun*, discussed above, Dalton Trumbo's narrator makes a similar comment on the true significance of 1776. "America fought a war for liberty in 1776. Lots of guys died. And in the end does America have any more liberty than Canada or Australia who didn't fight at all? . . . . So maybe a lot of guys with wives and kids died in 1776 when they didn't need to die at all . . . If they weren't fighting for liberty they were fighting for independence or democracy or freedom or decency or honor or their native land or something else that didn't mean anything" (*Johnny Got His Gun* [Philadelphia: J.B. Lippincott, 1939], pp. 111–112).

a conspiracy against democracy, an instrument of control that was designed to institutionalize and perpetuate the domination of the poor and working classes by the rich.[14] The current crisis has merely stripped away the encrusted layers of pious deceit that have hidden the truth of America's political past from its own citizens.

Alfred Hayes strikes a similar note in his long poem, "In a Coffee Pot," a verse monologue spoken by an exhausted, unemployed casualty of the Depression. The man has been mis-educated in America's schools and is re-learning the lessons of history through hard experience:

> They taught me what to read and what to say
> The nobility of man my country's pride
> How Nathan Hale died
> And Grant took Richmond.
> Was it on a summer or a winter's day?
> Was it Sherman burned the Southland to the sea?
> The men the names the dates have worn away
> The classes words the books commencement prize
> Here bitter with myself I sit
> Holding the ashes of their prompted lies.[15]

Sitting through the night drinking coffee in a diner, the speaker rehearses the fate that has overtaken all the "bright boys" he went to school with, who learned the same irrelevant and lying history, believed in the same ersatz heroism and long-gone trivia.

Muriel Rukeyser's "City of Monuments" is a meditation on the public memorials of Washington, DC. The occasion behind the poem was the savage attack by Federal troops on the Bonus Army that had encamped in

---

[14] Though I am not interested in adjudicating or even tracing the countless doctrinal disputes that roiled the Left in the 1930s, the theoretical position Odets occupies in the play is problematic. *Waiting For Lefty* was warmly received by most of the communist press; the editors of *Proletarian Literature*, who included a long section in the anthology, called it "a milestone" that added "stature to revolutionary drama." However, Odets's economic insights were probably as much "Beardian" as "Marxian." The distinction, often ignored in the 1930s, was important. According to Charles Beard himself, *An Economic Interpretation of the Constitution* (1913) was based on ideas of class struggle and economic determination that long antedated Marx's theories. In a preface he wrote for the 1935 re-print of the landmark book, Beard wrote that "the germinal idea of class and group conflicts in history appeared in the writings of Aristotle, long before the Christian era, and was known to great writers on politics during the middle ages and modern times. It was expounded by James Madison, in Number x of the *Federalist*, written in defense of the Constitution of the United States, long before Karl Marx was born" (New York: The Free Press, 1935), pp. xii–xiii. Michael Gold accused Beard of being a Marxist, but one who was afraid to admit it. See Aaron, *Writers on the Left*, p. 187.

[15] Alfred Hayes, "In a Coffee Pot," in Joseph Freeman, *et al.*, eds., *Proletarian Literature in the United States: An Anthology* (New York: International Publishers, 1935), p. 162.

the Anacostia Flats in the summer of 1932. Those veterans become, in Rukeyser's response, the "still unemancipated slaves," whose fate condemns the misplaced patriotism that has accompanied all of America's military history: "Give over Gettysburg! A word will shake your glory." The futility of contemporary politics also illuminates the irrelevance or falseness of past glories. Rukeyser conflates the heartless, current leaders of the nation with the carved likenesses of earlier heroes: all the generations of politicians are "marble men," who "rejoice / careless of torrents of despair." In a striking final image, the marble of the monuments is split "by a tendril of revolt": the revolution is implicitly defined as an act of nature, brought on by the inevitable rhythms of the natural world in response to the oppression and deceits of the status quo and its underlying mythologies.[16]

One of the most melodramatic examples of historical revisionism undertaken by a proletarian writer can be found in H. T. Tsiang's *The Hanging on Union Square* (1935). Granville Hicks described the novel as "a kind of Communist Pilgrim's Progress." Though Tsiang denied that he had ever read Bunyan's work, Hicks's remark is suggestive.[17] Tsiang's hero is a man named "Nut," whose experiences with a variety of allegorically named capitalists and radicals in New York City (e.g., Miss Stubborn, Mr. Wiseguy, Mr. Would-Be-Bureaucrat) leads him eventually to embrace revolutionary consciousness.

The story's title refers to its climactic action. On a dark winter night, Nut wanders around the empty Union Square and notices the flag post at the center:

At the bottom of the Flagpost was a brass tablet with the Declaration of Independence inscribed on it. A brisk wind rattled the ropes of the Flagpost and the ropes called: "Come to me, you Nut! You would be a better Flag to hang up on me. You would be the Flag of Starvation Amid Plenty! You would be the Flag of So-Called Civilization." (p. 180)

Nut tries to commit suicide by hanging himself from the flag post. His body would be the Republic's true flag; his death, which would appear to

---

[16] Muriel Rukeyser, "City of Monuments," in Janet E. Kaufman and Anne F. Herzog, eds., *The Collected Poems of Muriel Rukeyser* (Pittsburgh: University of Pittsburgh Press, 2005), pp. 51–52.

[17] Hicks's comment is taken from one of several pre-publication letters reprinted as part of the novel's prefatory material. H. T. Tsiang [Chiang His-tseng], *The Hanging on Union Square* (New York: published by the author, 1935), p. [5]. In a footnote, Tsiang insists: "Since I didn't attend high school in this country, I read *Pilgrim's Progress* only after receiving G.H.'s letter." The other letters are from Louis Adamic, Thomas H. Uzzell, and Carl Van Doren.

provide his only escape from oppression, would rebuke the promises of the Declaration of Independence.[18] Union Square was a principal assembly place for the Left in the 1930s, and the setting for much pro-letarian fiction – a "historical spot," as one of Tsiang's characters quite accurately puts it (p. 197).[19] In Tsiang's use of it, the square also provides the location for an embittered rejection of two of America's most sacred emblems.

Poems and novels such as these propose contrary readings of American history and its icons: the flag, the military heroes, the carved heroic statuary are each challenged in turn. Theodore Dreiser joined in the root-and-branch attack on American values. Through the first fifty or so years of his life, Dreiser had shown little interest in the details of either politics or economics. He had formulated his world view by combining his own experience of poverty with his unguided reading in Nietzsche, Darwin, and Herbert Spencer; from these sources he generated ill-formed and contradictory notions of supermen and determinism. It was not politics but a compulsive desire to represent the urges of appetite, and the fatality of choice, which had impelled his great fictions, *Sister Carrie* (1900) and *An American Tragedy* (1925).

In the late 1920s, he moved fitfully but volubly leftward, purporting to find in the Soviet Union, which he visited in 1927, better solutions to poverty than those capitalism offered. He was among those who signed the manifesto *Culture and the Crisis*. At about the same time, he wrote in support of the "Scottsboro boys," and he traveled to Harlan County, Kentucky, in express solidarity with striking coal miners. He was indicted in Kentucky, on trumped-up charges of sexual misconduct, and was defended by the American Civil Liberties Union and the National Committee for the Defense of Political Prisoners.[20]

Out of his rising discontent, Dreiser cobbled together *Tragic America* (1931), a 400-page mélange of communist pamphlets, genuine outrage, and notes provided by research assistants. Written in a turgid prose,

---

[18] The novel's plot evades the "defeatism" of suicide, as party apparatchiks would call it, when Nut is rescued and eventually revenges himself violently on Mr. Wiseguy and Mr. System. The contrived sequence of events does not alter the ideological significance of Tsiang's use of the Flag and the Declaration of Independence.

[19] Albert Halper's *Union Square* (1933) is the best known of the novels that employ the square as a major setting. Isabel Bishop's strange painting, "Dante and Virgil in Union Square" was discussed in a previous chapter.

[20] The Harlan County strikes produced some of the most violent labor confrontations of the decade. The events were commemorated in song by Florence Reece and Aunt Molly Jackson, described in prose by Dreiser, Sherwood Anderson, Malcolm Cowley, and others.

lurching between revolutionary slogans and celebration of the individual, and flawed by numberless repetitions and inaccuracies, the book is a sustained rant against businessmen, politicians, the courts, the American Federation of Labor, teachers, and the Catholic Church, among others. Neither subtlety nor fine discriminations were part of Dreiser's repertoire. Every indictment is uttered in a shout:

The most meaningless thing which the trudging American of to-day possesses is his right to vote. The ballot! The value he sets on it – the numskull of the country store, the village corner, the farmers' grange! His senator! His governor! His President! Bah! And that in the face of the ills they have not only permitted but aided to descend upon him! Of all the farces in the world to-day, and especially in connection with the marching mobs who endure anything without a murmur, the vote is the greatest!...Oh, the glories of theoretical justice! Would that I might stir even a few with the actualities![21]

Dreiser's anti-democratic tendencies were at least coherent with his contempt for the plain people he claimed to represent. For our purposes, the main point of his diatribe is its putative exposure of the emptiness of America's democratic traditions.

Most of the decade's radical writers proceeded in a more complex way. Though they often denied it, they understood the essentially conservative nature of popular sentiment, which was nourished by widely shared assent to an entire structure of belief, memories, and even shared prejudices. Despite the polemics of radical critics, ordinary citizens are typically reluctant to abandon their loyalty to things as they are. Religious and cultural history would have to be contested if the proletarian challenge to American mythology was to succeed.

Understanding the power of American myths and heroes in the popular imagination, left-wing novelists and poets sensed that the struggle for the present entailed a contest over the past. Thus, the idea of heroism figured prominently in radical writing. Insofar as American notions of heroism and nationalism were intertwined, proletarian logic might have obliged simple resistance to the American heroic ideal. After all, as Gary Wills has pointed out, "hero worship is elitist...[and] suggests that individual talent is a more important force than large economic processes."[22] The heroes in the American pantheon represented the apotheosis of bourgeois individualism. Despite the revisionist efforts of

[21] Theodore Dreiser, *Tragic America* (New York: Horace Liveright, Inc., 1931), p. 312.
[22] Gary Wills, *Cincinnatus: George Washington and the Enlightenment* (Garden City, NY: Doubleday & Company, 1984), p. 109.

the historians mentioned earlier, America's heroes continued to symbolize for most citizens idealized icons of human will untainted by ulterior motives or material circumstance.

In fact, however, rather than merely rejecting America's popular heroes, left-wing writers set out to reinterpret and to possess them. Washington was sometimes pressed into service, as in this flourish which likens the Chinese Red Army to the soldiers of the American Revolution: "The hardships of camps and marches in cold and hunger remind one of Washington's winter at Valley Forge . . ."[23]

Abraham Lincoln provides the most important example of this ideological cross-dressing – predictably, perhaps, given his own "proletarian" origins and his apparent identification with the common man and woman. In Josephine Herbst's *Rope of Gold* (1939), for example, Lincoln is "Father Abraham," whose memory is treasured by the Bonus Marchers and other protestors who have come to Washington in 1932. In a section of the novel called "Abraham's Bosom," and set in front of the Lincoln Memorial, a generalized voice of the people prayerfully summons Lincoln as a prophetic progenitor: "How lovely the lights shine on the water and light old Abe, of Springfield. You going to let us down, Father Abe? We're still here, another batch of men, wearing different skins, different clothes. We never forgot what you said. We're making the same old fight, property versus human rights."[24]

Especially after 1935, left-wing writers often endorsed Earl Browder's fatuous but conciliatory slogan, "Communism is Twentieth-Century Americanism." The "Star Spangled Banner" sometimes replaced the "Internationale" at American Communist rallies,[25] and songs about Roosevelt, Jefferson, and Lincoln were heard more often than those about Lenin, Marx, and Stalin.[26] "Abe Lincoln," a song written by Alfred Hayes and Earl Robinson, included passages from Lincoln's speeches in its choruses.[27]

Life imitated art. Communist apparatchik Earl Browder claimed descent from Littleberry Browder, a soldier in the Continental army; and the Young Communist League led the 1937 celebration of Paul Revere's

[23] Robert Morss Lovett, "Introduction," Agnes Smedley, *China's Red Army Marches* (New York: International Publishers, 1934), p. viii.
[24] Josephine Herbst, *Rope of Gold* (New York: Harcourt, Brace, 1939), p. 81.
[25] R. Serge Denisoff, *Great Day Coming* (Urbana: University of Illinois Press, 1971), p. 56.
[26] Richard A. Reuss, with JoAnne C. Reuss, *American Folk Music and Left-Wing Politics, 1927–1957* (Lanham, MD: Scarecrow Press, 2000), p. xx.
[27] Waldemar Hille, ed., *The People's Songbook* (New York: Oak Publications, 1961 [1948]), pp. 50–51.

ride.[28] There was a loopy pragmatics in this effort to recruit American myth to left-wing purposes. Citizens of Dubuque or even New York were unlikely to embrace imported political nostrums, especially those that entailed the repudiation of patriotic assumptions. As one student of the subject has said, accurately if a bit awkwardly: "proletarian culture was doomed to fail in the United States . . . [because] its imported images, styles, and subcultural signs cut against the vernacular grain of nativist popular culture so that it often simply repulsed noninitiates."[29]

In addition to adopting some of America's canonical figures, the Left also tried to create what might be called a counter-history, a proletarian pantheon enshrining the men and women who had given their lives to the cause of American radicalism.[30] "The hero is the people," Walter Benjamin famously pronounced; but "the people" do not provide the dramatic satisfaction that the imagination seems to require. Heroes there must be, whatever the cost in proletarian logic. The radical investment in heroism may represent a small paradox, but it grew out of the recognition that popular movements need to be embodied in popular and preferably outsized figures. Furthermore, left-wing writers insisted on the American identities of their heroes: the Haymarket anarchists, Mother Bloor and Mother Jones, John Reed,[31] the Ludlow miners, and Bill Haywood, Joe Hill, and Wesley Everest of the Industrial Workers of the World (I.W.W.). The task of radical literature was to imply that the impending communist revolution had an indigenous American lineage, and was not merely a foreign import.

Instinct as much as calculation encouraged the radicals to celebrate their American antecedents. The Soviet Union did play an undeniably major part in the symbolic politics of the 1930s, serving as the allegedly achieved example of socialist revolution, the model state – the future that

---

[28] Robert Bendiner, *Just around the Corner: A Highly Selective History of the Thirties* (New York: Harper & Row, 1967), pp. 98–99.
[29] Walter Kalaidjian, *American Culture Between the Wars: Revisionary Modernism and Postmodern Critique* (New York: Columbia University Press, 1993), p. 61.
[30] Eric Hobsbawm gets it half-right when he observes that "Revolutions and 'progressive movements' which break with the past, by definition, have their own relevant past, though it may be cut off at a certain date, such as 1789." Hobsbawm, "Introduction," in Hobsbawm and Terence Ranger, eds., *The Invention of Tradition* (New York: Cambridge University Press, 1983), p. 2. As this chapter has demonstrated, revolutionary movements also try to domesticate and re-direct the mainstream national past as well.
[31] In a section of *Writers on the Left* called "Reviving John Reed – Hero," Daniel Aaron writes, "Reed in 1929 had already become a legend" (p. 213). That legend was inflated and turned to doctrinaire communist purposes in the 1930s.

worked, in Lincoln Steffens's legendary miscalculation. But individual Soviet leaders, Stalin in particular, were treated with conspicuous ambivalence by the American left. Langston Hughes's "Ballads of Lenin" is more goodhearted than militant:

> Comrade Lenin of Russia,
>   High in a marble tomb,
> Move over, Comrade Lenin,
>   And give me room.[32]

Instead of Lenin or Marx, a figure like Joe Hill satisfied the desire of Depression radicals to find heroic American predecessors. Hill's revolutionary credentials were impeccable, but so too was his status as an ordinary American citizen, a child of the Middle West, a worker among workers. Furthermore, Hill had a particular appeal to writers in the thirties since he had been a poet himself, the chief literary voice of the I. W.W. His songs had become the cherished patrimony of the radical labor movement, and his death in front of a Utah firing squad had sanctified his memory.

Hill is the subject of one of the best poems of the radical 1930s, Kenneth Patchen's "Joe Hill Listens to the Praying." Set at the moment of Hill's death in 1915, the poem is polyphonic in its structure, combining narrative, dialogue, political comment, quotations from Hill's songs, and fragments of the sermon preached at his execution by an unnamed minister.[33]

Like the radical writers of the 1930s, Joe Hill had conceived of art as a weapon in the class struggle, often the only weapon the powerless had. Like those later writers, too, Hill wanted to inscribe his revolutionary themes in forms that would make them accessible – and acceptable – to the broadest range of people. Toward that end, he devised an apparently simple strategy: he wrote new lyrics for traditional songs, among them the anthems and hymns of Christian churches. Thus, "What a Friend We Have in Jesus" becomes "Dump the Bosses Off Your Backs," "Sweet Bye and Bye" is turned into "The Preacher and the Slave," and "There is

[32] Langston Hughes, "Ballads of Lenin" in Arnold Rampersad, ed., *Collected Poems of Langston Hughes* (New York: Alfred A. Knopf, 1994), pp. 183–184.
[33] In its emphases and techniques, "Joe Hill Listens to the Praying" bears strong resemblances to John Dos Passos's sketch in *Nineteen Nineteen* (1932). Given the novel's wide circulation, and Dos Passos's popularity among left-wing intellectuals in the early thirties, it seems reasonable to identify *Nineteen Nineteen* as a source of Patchen's poem.

Power in the Blood" undergoes a Wobbly metamorphosis into "There is Power in the Union."

By superimposing his radical message upon the most familiar and orthodox tunes, Hill wanted to make his revolutionary songs easy for working men and women to learn. Beyond that, he was tacitly acknowledging that such music constituted a principal part of the shared culture of proletarian America. By appropriating the nation's sacred music, he was attempting to displace the same value onto his alternative ideology. Religion itself might be nothing more than "pie in the sky," to quote Hill's most famous phrase, but his own music was a secular hymnal, a testament of faith in the cause of worker solidarity.[34]

The transactions between received forms and radical designs are finally more complex than Hill intended. If his lyrics radicalize familiar tunes, so did those tunes domesticate his radical politics. To put it another way, his songs tended to dissolve into what they opposed, ultimately reinforcing rather than threatening the interconnected religious-political traditions he rejected. In the end, his songs are only songs, the mementoes of martyrdom and a defeated cause. As Kenneth Patchen himself writes in the closing lines of "Joe Hill Listens," with an utterly unintended irony:

> Let them burn us, hang us, shoot us,
> Joe Hill
> For at the last we had what it takes
> to make songs with.

In short, Joe Hill's ballads drifted toward the same ideological cul-de-sac that lies at the end of the debate over aesthetic form in the 1930s. In the early years of the century, and again in the Depression decade, dissent is entangled in a variety of affirmations that ultimately diffused revolutionary energies.

The tension is exacerbated in Patchen's "Joe Hill Listens" by the poem's clamorous insistence that it was Hill, and not his demagogic enemies, who was the genuine patriot:

> but Joe
> We had something they didn't have:
> our love for these States
> was real and deep.

---

[34] In the introduction to his fictionalized biography of Joe Hill, *The Preacher and the Slave*, Wallace Stegner refers to the I.W.W. as "a militant church" (Boston: Houghton Mifflin, 1950), p. vii.

In Patchen's reconstruction of Hill, the call to revolution subsides into a nationalist lyric, a love poem in which a sexualized geography becomes the object of the radical lover's attention:

> This land
>   is our lover. How greenly beautiful
> Her hair; her great pure breasts
>   that are
> The Rockies on a day of mist and rain.
> We love this land of corn and cotton,
>   Virginia and Ohio, sleeping on
> With our love, with our love . . .
>   How green is her hair,
>   how pure are her breasts; the little farms
>   nuzzling into her flanks
>   drawing forth life, big rich life . . .[35]

Like his appeal to a more genuine patriotism, Patchen's conception of gender is grounded in a traditional set of attitudes. "Joe Hill Listens" implies, quite correctly, that underneath the debates between Right and Left in the 1930s lay a cluster of shared assumptions that dulled the edge of dissent; the demand for transformation co-existed with demonstrations of fundamental continuity.[36]

This continuity exhibits itself in another dimension of the proletarian literary paradox (if it deserves that term): the revolution might be welcomed as the overthrow of all conventional cultural assumptions, but radical writing tended to behave in a rigorously conventional way. Almost without exception, proletarian poets and novelists conformed to the most familiar literary precedents. The future might be "undreamed of," to quote *Culture and the Crisis* again, but its utterance was inscribed in strictly familiar vocabularies and forms. Metrics and rhyme schemes, characters and plots, were typically undemanding and simplified. The innovations of modernism, which had been reshaping literary expression on both sides of the Atlantic for a quarter-century, are conspicuously absent from most of the decade's radical writing.

The omission is, of course, calculated. For the majority of radical theorists, the principal task of committed writers was to make their work

---

[35] Kenneth Patchen, "Joe Hill Listens to the Praying," in *The Collected Poems of Kenneth Patchen* (New York: New Directions, 1968), pp. 45–49.

[36] Another example of the shared attitudes that tied left-wing dissidents to mainstream culture can be found in their nearly universal response to homosexuality. With few exceptions, the Left joined in condemning or pitying homosexuals as deviants, criminals, or perverts.

broadly accessible, especially to the working class who made up their intended (though they were not the actual) audience. An elaborate, self-regarding technique would exclude the masses. "Proletarian Realism" was the phrase Michael Gold coined to describe what was needed. Form should follow the function of arousing an oppressed and generally slightly educated people: technical devices were to be regarded as means to the end of revolutionary inspiration.[37] The best fiction would serve as a transparent lens, effacing itself in order to frame and clarify the reality of class struggle.

Aside from its naiveté, this point of view was attended by two ironies. First, it implied a dependence upon an uncomplicated realism which contemporary science and history were both deserting as inadequate. As we have already seen, the relativizing of history that figured so prominently in the twenties and thirties was accompanied by – indeed, was at least a response to – similar tendencies in science. Amid the indeterminacies of quantum mechanics and the postulations of uncertainty, the stability of the historical object seemed increasingly irrelevant and even delusory.[38] In short, the proletarian commitment to the aesthetic and political future was threatened by its accommodation to an obsolete epistemology.

The second irony that entangled the Marxist devotion to received literary forms lay in the unwitting but inevitable ideological consequences that follow from technical choices. Put simply, the proletarian writers embraced antagonistic and even antithetical assumptions when they told their tales of anti-bourgeois revolution within the conventions of bourgeois culture. They aspired to escape from the prison house of the past,

---

[37] Of course, most of the radical writers rejected not just modernism but any literature encumbered by claims of high artistic value – as do their self-appointed radical descendants. Egalitarian logic demanded the rejection of all elite cultural products, whether contemporary or ancient. Recalling the reading she did in her impoverished childhood, for example, Agnes Smedley makes this laboriously sardonic comment: "The nearest I ever came to the classics was a large volume of something called 'poetry.' Because it was printed on very thin paper, it quite naturally hung from a string in a privy. A man by the name of Shakespeare seemed to have written it but I could make neither head nor tail of it." Smedley, *Battle Hymn of China* (New York: Alfred A. Knopf, 1943), pp. 5–6.

[38] For just one example of the influence of new scientific conceptions upon historical practice, see Roy F. Nichols, "History Teaching in This Intellectual Crisis," *The Historical Outlook* (November, 1933), pp. 357–363. Published four years after the Crash, the essay mentions the Depression just once, and then only to emphasize its ultimate insignificance. The "crisis" of the title refers instead to intellectual dislocations precipitated by recent scientific theories, in particular relativity: "With our Newtonian world thus being destroyed around us it is evident that we are in the midst of an intellectual crisis which, so far as thinking goes, dwarfs the present economic unpleasantness" (p. 357).

but the elementary and urgent need to be understood (by people who, to add a further irony, had no interest in their work) kept the door locked against their own intentions.

Language itself worked against them. Meridel Le Sueur might welcome the literary uses of what she called "native language," but that language was co-extensive with the map of inequality that Le Sueur and other radicals were trying to re-draw.[39] As Jonathan Chance, the central character of Josephine Herbst's *Rope of Gold*, realizes: "It would take a new language" (p. 7) to describe revolutionary aspirations; such a language, however, could not simply be willed into being, and its absence continually bedeviled radical cultural ambitions.

The dilemma was exacerbated by the uncomfortable literary compromises that most radical critics negotiated. Insofar as the revolutionary aesthetic received official codification, it did so in the anthology, *Proletarian Literature in the United States*, published in 1935, and edited (of course) by a committee: Granville Hicks, Michael Gold, and Isidor Schneider, among others. The volume's introductory essay was written by Joseph Freeman, an earnest, veteran radical who had long and somewhat poignantly tried to subordinate his literary taste to revolutionary requirements.[40]

Freeman's intellectual gymnastics offer revealing evidence of the problem he and his allies faced. While insisting that art is "an instrument in the class struggle," he nonetheless conceded that art also depended upon special and even mysterious talents: "Whatever it is that makes an artist, as distinguished from a scientist or a man of action, is something beyond the power of anyone to produce deliberately" ("Introduction," *Proletarian Literature*, pp. 9, 11). By acknowledging that "a Comintern resolution in rhyme does not make proletarian poetry" (p. 16), by confessing that much of proletarian literature had in fact been downright crude, by saluting the search for "perfection of form" (p. 18), Freeman and his colleagues surrendered their revolutionary ambitions as hostage to inherited categories and values. In effect, they offered voluntary assent to the oppressive cultural legacy they so strenuously condemned.

---

[39] The phrase comes from a speech Le Sueur delivered at the first American Writers Congress, in April, 1935.

[40] In his memoir, *American Testament*, Freeman tells of the experiences that led him from bourgeois respectability to radical commitment. Though published in 1936, the book ends with the election of Herbert Hoover. That distance conferred a retrospective authority on Freeman's revolutionary stance, and also accounts for the grimly self-satisfied tone in which he condemns the philistines, bohemians, and liberals of the twenties.

Tensions between political aspirations and the constraints imposed by imaginative conventions pervaded most of the radical writing of the thirties decade, from Michael Gold's *Jews Without Money* (1930), to Tom Kromer's *Waiting for Nothing* (1935), to the stories and poems included in *Proletarian Literature*. Alan Calmer, who served on the anthology's editorial board, made something like this point in an essay, "The Proletarian Short Story," which appeared in *New Masses* in July, 1935.[41] Calmer judged only a handful of proletarian stories to be distinguished (he mentions the work of Albert Halper, Albert Maltz, and James T. Farrell).

The more typical fiction was unimpressive: "There is still nothing in sight that looks like a proletarian *Winesburg, Ohio*, or a revolutionary *In Our Time*" (p. 17). Calmer's examples declare his literary affiliations. In his view, radicals write badly because they "are unconcerned with literary tradition" and especially because they ignore the experimentation that is such a potent dimension of contemporary literature (p. 17). He argues that too many of them rely upon formulas, in particular the "conversion" plot, in which a bourgeois character is suddenly made radiant with proletarian wisdom. "The conversion ending has become a revolutionary equivalent of the Cinderella formula: the protagonist is abruptly transformed from a passive, ignorant individual into a highly class-conscious activist, in the same way the homespun heroine is changed, with a wave of the wand, into a beautiful princess" (p. 17).[42]

Whether or not Calmer's analysis seems correct in its details, it is undeniably the case that adherence to conventional canons of judgment diverted proletarian energy into patterns of consensus that transcended and therefore nullified differences of politics. Consider a few examples. In Robert Cantwell's "The Hills Around Centralia," set in Washington state's timber country in 1919, two Wobblies flee from a lynch mob that includes several boy scouts, mere children who have been pumped full of patriotic zeal. The story is told primarily from the viewpoint of one of the

---

[41] Alan Calmer, "The Proletarian Short Story," *New Masses* (July 2, 1935), pp. 17–19. There were a few experimental exceptions to the proletarian generalization. Calmer himself mentions the stories of Jack Balch, who deployed a form of stream-of-consciousness in the story, "Take a Number and Take a Seat," and Louis Mamet, who combined narrative with dramatic dialogue in "The Machine." Other examples of what might be called "proletarian experimentalism" include Robert Cantwell's *Land of Plenty* (1934), and Edward Dahlberg's *From Flushing to Calvary* (1932).

[42] Apparently, Cinderella's appeal was ubiquitous: Walt Disney's animated version of the story was released in 1939, and enjoyed considerable commercial and critical success. It almost goes without saying that Disney's straight, un-ironic version of Cinderella, in which an impoverished waif is suddenly made secure and wealthy, had obvious relevance for a Depression audience.

boys, who stumbles into the Wobblies in the woods and must reluctantly listen to a patient, monosyllabic explanation of the radical cause. By using the frightened boy as his central figure, Cantwell creates a melodrama of initiation and education. The lecture also offers a revisionist history of American labor's struggles. Similarly, Tillie Lerner's "The Iron Throat" includes a six-year-old girl, Mazie, whose simple questions serve as a mechanism to elicit a partisan view of US history. By using children as their focus, both Cantwell and Lerner suggest that the radical version of America's past is virtually self-evident – child's play, in fact.

The most prominent figures in the reconstructed left-wing history of the 1930s were unquestionably Sacco and Vanzetti. Though quite recent in chronology – part of the near past of the 1920s – the trial and execution of the two immigrants had taken on an historical aura. Indeed, in a sense their deaths drew a line separating past from present: Josephine Herbst wrote that the 1930s actually began on August 22, 1927, the day Sacco and Vanzetti died. The event resounded through the politics, the literature, and the art of the Depression decade.[43] Although they had been committed to anarchism rather than collectivism, their conviction for murder was interpreted by the Left as an episode in the American class struggle. Electrocuted in the midst of international protests on their behalf, Sacco and Vanzetti became enduring symbols of the heroism of protest against injustice.[44]

In the dozen or so years between their deaths and the end of the thirties, the Sacco and Vanzetti case was re-enacted in over a hundred poems, as well as a large number of stories, novels, and plays.[45] The poems included Edna St. Vincent Millay's "Fear," Witter Bynner's "The

---

[43] In her memoir, "A Year of Disgrace," Herbst wrote: "So far as I was concerned, what had been the twenties ended that night." Cited in Winifred Farrant Bevilacqua, *Josephine Herbst* (Boston: Twayne Publishers, 1985), p. 95. In 1935, Malcolm Cowley marked the eighth anniversary of the execution with a poem estimating the consequences of the episode for the entire "intelligentsia." In Cowley's opinion, it was "obvious" that the radical commitments of writers and artists in the 1930s could be traced back to Sacco and Vanzetti. See "Echoes of a Crime," *New Republic* (August 28, 1935), p. 79.

[44] The most striking demonstration of the long shadow cast by the Sacco and Vanzetti case on the American imagination is perhaps Katherine Anne Porter's *The Never-Ending Wrong*, written largely in the 1930s, but published in 1977 as a grim, unrevoked protest to mark the fiftieth anniversary of the execution.

[45] See G. Louis Joughin and Edmund M. Morgan, *The Legacy of Sacco and Vanzetti* (Chicago: Quadrangle Paperbacks, 1964 [1948]), especially "Part III: The Legacy to Literature." Originally published twenty years after the events, this book contains the fullest inventory of literary responses the case elicited in the 1930s.

Condemned," and Countee Cullen's "Not Sacco and Vanzetti." Upton
Sinclair's *Boston* (1928) was the first of the novel-length treatments of the
case; it was followed in the 1930s by Nathan Asch's *Pay Day* (1930),
Bernard De Voto's *We Accept With Pleasure* (1934), and long sections of
John Dos Passos's *The Big Money* (discussed below). Among the plays
based on the case, the most significant were probably *The Male Animal*
(1939), by James Thurber and Elliott Nugent, a satiric comedy which
invokes Sacco and Vanzetti as virtually self-evident instances of American
intolerance, and Maxwell Anderson's *Winterset*, which won the first New
York Drama Critics Circle Award in 1936.[46] Even texts that were
ostensibly apolitical weighed in. In a passage quoted in an earlier chapter,
the volume on Massachusetts in the American Guide series gave a summary of the Sacco and Vanzetti case that state officials found far too
sympathetic to the executed anarchists.

In 1936, in response to the celebrations of Harvard's tercentenary, six
alumni, including Heywood Broun and Quincy Howe, organized a
protest against Harvard's former President, A. Lawrence Lowell. Lowell
had served on the independent commission that had examined and
ratified the guilty verdict.[47] The alumni published 5,000 copies of a
pamphlet, *Walled in This Tomb*, which condemned Lowell as an example
of "the incredible and destructive twists of men's minds – even the mind
of a president of Harvard University" (Joughin and Morgan, *Legacy of
Sacco and Vanzetti*, pp. 348–349).[48]

Several years earlier, Anderson had collaborated on a short play called
Gods of the Lightning (1928), an angry piece of agit-prop that was banned
in Boston and closed after two dozen performances in New York. When
he returned to the Sacco and Vanzetti case in *Winterset* eight years later,
Anderson accepted the challenge of transforming recent politics into what
the preface to the printed version of the play calls "tragic poetry." Written
in verse, the play's action is compressed into a single evening, in a

[46] The movie version, which was adapted by Anderson for RKO in 1936, starred Burgess Meredith
recreating the role of Mio that he had played on stage.
[47] Governor Alvan T. Fuller's decision to name an Advisory Committee reveals the almost
unprecedented scale of the public outcry provoked by the case. Along with President Lowell, who
acted as the unofficial chair of the panel, the other members were Samuel W. Stratton, President
of the Massachusetts Institute of Technology, and Robert A. Grant, an affluent lawyer and
novelist.
[48] Hitchhiking through Ohio in the late twenties, Younghill Kang was picked up by a man who said
that "he had graduated twice from Harvard, and was ashamed of it. That damned committee who
executed Sacco and Vanzetti!" *East Goes West: The Making of an Oriental Yankee* (New York:
Charles Scribuer's Sons, 1937), p. 376.

tenement neighborhood under the Manhattan Bridge. Mio Romagna has devoted his life to proving the innocence of his father, Bartolomeo, an immigrant anarchist who has been executed for a murder he did not commit.

In an implausible but dramatically intense set of encounters, all the principals gather: the murderers, Trock and Shadow, their accomplice, Garth Esdras, his rabbi father and his sister Miriamne, and the corrupt judge who presided over the case and now, half-deranged, wanders the streets. In a mock trial directed by Mio, the truth is established; however, in the play's final scene Mio and Miriamne, who have fallen in love, are murdered by Trock. While this ending might seem to demonstrate again that justice is hostage to force, Anderson insists on a more elevating message. Miriamne's father, in the play's last speech, assures the bystanders that righteous conviction transcends death:

> Oh, Miriamne,
> and Mio – Mio, my son – know this where you lie,
> this is the glory of earth-born men and women,
> not to cringe, never to yield, but standing,
> take defeat implacable and defiant,
> die unsubmitting.[49]

Winterset, in other words, unlike *Gods of the Lightning*, is less interested in exposing the evils of the capitalist judicial system than in sanctifying the system's victims.

In common with most Americans, John Dos Passos was rather slow to respond to the Sacco and Vanzetti case. Once he engaged himself, however, he became a leading figure in the defense effort, visiting both men in their prison cells, and raising funds for the legal appeals. After writing about the case for the *New Masses*, Dos Passos published a pamphlet that was circulated by the defense committee in the spring of 1927, *Facing the Chair: The Story of the Americanization of Two Foreign-born Workmen*. In August, when the citizens' panel advised Alvan Tufts Fuller, Governor of Massachusetts, against granting a new trial, Dos Passos published "An Open Letter to President Lowell," in which he declared that the case "has become part of the world struggle between the capitalist class and the working class." As the date for the execution approached, Dos Passos joined the picket line, which included William

---

[49] Maxwell Anderson, *Winterset* (Washington, DC: Anderson House, 1935) p. 133.

Gropper, Edna St. Vincent Millay, Paxton Hibben, Michael Gold, Katherine Anne Porter, and Grace Lumpkin.

The tragedy of the American experience, in Dos Passos's appraisal of it, lies in the distance between democratic myth and oppressive reality. In their beliefs as well as in their unwarranted deaths, Sacco and Vanzetti embody that tragedy, which haunts the three volumes of *U.S.A.* They also exemplify, more completely than any of the trilogy's other characters, the failure of American history to move forward.

Like most of Dos Passos's work in the twenties and thirties, *U.S.A.* does not reach very far back into the American past for its subject matter; the three novels represent the first three decades of the twentieth century. The panoramic scope of the books is more evidently geographical than temporal. However, making use of cross-references and allusions, Dos Passos inserts the nation's more recent events in the context of its longer history, thus creating a standard of judgment and appropriating America's past for contemporary radical purposes. As Jean-Paul Sartre put it, in a gnomic but celebrated phrase, time in Dos Passos's trilogy is neither "fictional" nor "narrative," but "historical."[50] In effect, one thing simply follows another, with the inexorable rhythm of a predetermined sequence.

Form follows facts. The events of *U.S.A.* lead toward the catastrophe of the execution with the same irreversible and accelerating fatality that marked the case itself. The final pages of *The Big Money* (1936), the final volume of the trilogy, transcribe both the events and the emotions of those who worked to prevent the death of Sacco and Vanzetti. The narrative of Mary French reproduces the furious activity of the defense committees and the despair that followed their failure to prevent the execution. The late Newsreels include headlines that punctuate the grim march of the case, counterpointed with fragments of songs, including the "Internationale," which represent the ideals of the protestors more accurately than those of the anarchist immigrants.

In the forty-ninth and fiftieth sections of Camera Eye, Dos Passos coordinates history, politics, and language in support of his most fundamental thematic statement. The two sections are organized around an extended historical analogy, in which the recent immigrants, Sacco and

---

[50] Jean-Paul Sartre, "John Dos Passos and *1919*," *Literary and Philosophical Essays* (New York: Macmillan, 1970), p. 95. Cited in Harry B. Henderson, III, *Versions of the Past: The Historical Imagination in American Fiction* (New York: Oxford University Press, 1974), p, 243.

Vanzetti, are likened to the nation's original settlers, the immigrants of
the seventeenth century:

walking from Plymouth to North Plymouth...this is where the immigrants
landed the roundheads the sackers of castles the kingkillers haters of oppression...[51]
    and now today
       walking from Plymouth to North Plymouth suddenly...you see the
Cordage...the Plymouth Cordage this is where another immigrant worked
hater of oppression who wanted a world unfenced[52]

Historical roles are reversed. The "lawyers district-attorneys collegepre-
sidents Judges" (p. 444) who trace their descent from the earliest colonial
families are discredited; these avatars of legitimacy are in fact America's
"betrayers." Brilliantly exploiting the xenophobia that created the context
of hate around the case, Dos Passos turns such pillars of established
authority as Judge Thayer and President Lowell into the "strangers," who
have invaded the country and "bought the laws" (pp. 468, 469). In their
place, Sacco and Vanzetti are identified as the true "founders" of
Massachusetts.

    Throughout his meditations on Sacco and Vanzetti, Dos Passos laid
heavy stress on the integrity of their language. Their truth stands as a
rebuke to the "ruined words worn slimy in the mouths of" repressive
political leaders. The words of the two immigrants recover whatever
historical validity may remain to American values. The two men, murdered in their struggle to reclaim the country for its own people, renew
"the old words of the immigrants" (p. 444). Beyond that, Sacco and
Vanzetti serve as a model for Dos Passos's own task as a writer: "pencil
scrawls in my notebook the scraps of recollection the broken halfphrases
the effort to intersect word with word to dovetail clause with clause to
rebuild out of mangled memories unshakably (Old Pontius Pilate) the
truth" (p. 444).

    This might serve as a shorthand description of Dos Passos's method in
U.S.A., and it discloses the centrality of Sacco and Vanzetti to the trilogy's
design. In the prefatory essay he wrote in 1938, when the three novels were
published in a single volume, Dos Passos declared that "mostly U.S.A. is
the speech of the people." More than any other of its biographical or
fictional figures, Sacco and Vanzetti define the trilogy's chief point of

---

[51] In describing the Puritans as haters of oppression, Dos Passos reveals the selective and romantic
character of his historical imagination.
[52] John Dos Passos, *The Big Money* (New York: New American Library, 1979 [1936]), p. 444.

Illustration 14. Ben Shahn, "The Passion of Sacco and Vanzetti"

imaginative intersection, where history and language join together: "the men in the deathhouse made the old words new before they died" (p. 444).

Left-wing painters also endeavored to anchor contemporary protest in a heroized past. The most famous example is probably Ben Shahn, who in 1932 created what are probably the most famous radical images of the twentieth century: a series of gouache and tempera panels mourning the deaths of Sacco and Vanzetti. Titled collectively "The Passion of Sacco and Vanzetti," the panels portray the two anarchists as noble victims of judicial murder. In the final image, they lie in their open coffins, over which three figures loom: the members of the so-called "Lowell Committee," the advisory group that recommended against clemency.

As an immigrant from a parochial background, Shahn had been struck by discovering how much history – "an American history and a world history" – he didn't know.[53] Combining national and Biblical stories, Shahn responded to the Sacco and Vanzetti case with frankly religious intensity. Not surprisingly, he claims descent from one of Europe's greatest religious painters: "I was not unmindful of Giotto, and of the simplicity with which he had been able to treat of connected events – each complete in itself, yet all recreating the religious drama, so living a thing to him."[54] A secular Jew, Shahn nonetheless likened Sacco and Vanzetti to the self-sacrificial Christ. As he said in another interview: "I got to thinking about the Sacco-Vanzetti case...Ever since I could remember I'd wished that I'd been lucky enough to be alive at a great time – when something big was going on, like the Crucifixion. And suddenly I realized I was!"[55] The title rubric, "Passion," refers of course to Christ's condemnation and death.[56]

Sacco and Vanzetti were not Shahn's only historical subjects. In 1931, he had commemorated the Dreyfus Affair in thirteen watercolors. In 1933, he reached back into America's radical past to celebrate Tom Mooney. Less visible in the 1930s than Sacco and Vanzetti, Mooney was still a hero on the Left. A California labor leader who opposed American entry into World War I, he had been convicted in a bombing that killed ten and left

---

[53] Cited in Howard Greenfeld, *Ben Shahn: An Artist's Life* (New York: Random House, 1998), p. 14.
[54] Cited in Kenneth W. Prescott, *Prints and Posters of Ben Shahn* (New York: Dover Press, 1982), p. vi.
[55] Cited in John D. Morse, ed., *Ben Shahn* (New York: Praeger, 1972), p. 15.
[56] Perhaps the most unexpected visual tribute to Sacco and Vanzetti was a bas-relief displayed for the first time in 1937, on the tenth anniversary of the executions. The sculpture is the work of Gutzon Borglum, more famous for the colossal presidential heads he carved into Mount Rushmore.

forty wounded during a Preparedness Day parade in San Francisco in July, 1916. Shahn's pictures are part of the campaign that insisted on Mooney's innocence: after spending over twenty years in jail on perjured testimony, Mooney was pardoned in 1939. Shahn studied the case in newspaper files and photo archives, and worked quickly to produce a series of fifteen small gouache studies and one larger painting in tempera. While the critical reception was generally hostile, Diego Rivera, the radical Mexican muralist whose work exerted widespread influence on US painters throughout the decade, wrote that "Ben Shahn's series on the Mooney case is even stronger and of finer quality than his Sacco–Vanzetti paintings" (Greenfield, *Ben Shahn*, p. 87).

As Shahn's rhetoric demonstrates, both literary and visual evocations of Sacco and Vanzetti also exemplified the left-wing attempt either to demolish or appropriate America's religious heritage. Religion makes up a substantial portion of that circumambient culture in which all American discourse is situated, a widely internalized set of communal assumptions that lies far beyond the reach of merely "rational" opposition. Along with nationalism and popular conceptions of heroism, religion has done much to shape American perceptions of both past and present events. The radical argument with traditional values that is recorded in the proletarian literature of the 1930s included recurrent and predictable attacks on religion. The core insight here, though often labeled Marxian, was in fact a commonplace of social criticism in the nineteenth and early twentieth centuries: Christianity, which had served for generations to buttress oppression, must be demystified as a prelude to liberation.

At the same time, left-wing resistance to religious traditions co-existed with an effort to appropriate religion for the radical cause. Beyond denouncing religious beliefs as simple bad faith, left-wing writers also tried to translate them into politically more congenial terms. The translations were sometimes deliberate, sometimes inadvertent. The difference hardly matters. Some writers on the Left may have taken comfort from Emile Durkheim's positivist diagnosis: the mysteries of religion, Durkheim argued early in the century, "cannot play the same role in the future as [they] did in the past."[57] However, at some level, most of the Left understood that received ideologies are nearly ineradicable: resistance eventually shaded into some version of negotiation.

[57] Emile Durkheim, *The Elementary Forms of the Religious Life*, Karen E. Fields, trans. (New York: The Free Press, 1995 [1912]), p. 432. In the next sentence, Durkheim added the shrewd observation: "However, religion seems destined to transform itself rather than disappear."

In his essay, "Religion as a Cultural System," Clifford Geertz describes the secular significance of religious ideas: "Religious concepts spread beyond their specifically metaphysical contexts to provide a framework of general ideas in terms of which a wide range of experience – intellectual, emotional, moral – can be given meaningful forms."[58] Geertz's comments on the organizing power of religious belief are relevant to the whole cluster of traditional attitudes with which radical literature struggled.

In Pietro Di Donato's *Christ in Concrete* (1939), the working men of the story become in some analogical way Christ, even as they abandon their Catholic faith. That sort of pious translation occurred throughout the decade. John Steinbeck's novels frequently dramatize the divided radical response to religion. Jim Nolan, the principal communist spokesman in the debates that punctuate *In Dubious Battle* (1935), translates his Roman Catholicism into Marxism. Steinbeck declared that his personal sentiments differed from Nolan's, and resembled those of the more vaguely humanitarian Doc Burton. Whatever Steinbeck's personal affiliations, Nolan's displaced religious vocabulary accurately suggests how religious beliefs were often recast in secular terms in order to enlarge the domain of oppositional politics.

Put simply: a radical message may find a more congenial audience if it is domesticated and familiarized by association with the sacred. The Christlike Jim Casy of *The Grapes of Wrath* (1939) exemplifies the same strategy. Casy is, of course, less dogmatically Marxist than Jim Nolan, but his proletarian demands for justice define him as a kind of secular saint. And the novel's sensational last scene, in which Rose of Sharon nurses a dying man with the breast milk that cannot feed her own stillborn child, is an enormously sentimental gesture toward the centuries of devotion that have attended the Madonna and Child in Western art.[59]

The heroism of Sacco and Vanzetti is often defined in traditional religious terms. Quite a few of the poems written about the two men present them as martyrs in a sacred cause, sometimes even as contemporary Christs. Jeanette Marks's poem, "Two Crucified," E. Merrill Root's "Eucharist," and Clement Wood's "Golgotha in Massachusetts," all narrate the execution of the two anarchists as a modern crucifixion. Despite the rigor with which both Sacco and Vanzetti opposed organized

---

[58] Clifford Geertz, "Religion as a Cultural System," in Michael Banton, ed., *Anthropological Approaches to the Study of Religion* (New York: Praeger, 1966), p. 25.
[59] Dorothea Lange's "Migrant Mother (1936)," which also derives much of its emotional impact from its deliberate appropriation of the Madonna's iconography, has already been mentioned.

religion of any kind, the thick texture of religious associations in their portrayals prove the desire of radicals to clothe dissent in the dignity of mythic regalia.

As radicals re-told America's story, the "visible saints" were not the Puritan settlers and their descendants, but the disenfranchised evangels of protest. Certain coincidences were noted with sardonic relish: the Statue of Liberty was dedicated in 1886, the year the Haymarket anarchists died;[60] Sacco and Vanzetti were electrocuted in August, 1927, just three months after Charles Lindbergh's triumphant solo flight across the Atlantic. Each mythic event was annulled by its counter-statement.

As the representation of Sacco and Vanzettti in *U.S.A.* correctly implies, transactions between past and present in left-wing writing in the 1930s were multi-dimensional. The proletarian demand for a "new" literature co-existed, uncomfortably but inevitably, with back-looking loyalties and allegiances. Rebellion and deference intermingled in poems and novels that tried to escape the confines of traditional values while at the same time conferring traditional marks of high status on their proletarian subjects. There was usually more of Emerson than of Marx in these negotiations.

In a poem called "To the Museums," Isidor Schneider used the buildings and their contents as a metaphor for this cultural duality. The poem's speaker advises revolutionary workers not to tear down the museums but to take them over: "Come to the museums. On all the gates, the pillars, put up posters: 'Workers enter here. Claim what is stored here. It is yours.'"[61] In the four stanzas of the poem, Schneider encourages the workers to re-label the masterpieces of Western painting – landscapes, nudes, Madonnas – and thus to gain possession of the heritage that has been denied them.

Rather than simply divorcing radical ambitions from the cultural achievements of the past, proletarian literature tried to seize history and culture and put them in the service of revolution. This theme received one of its most elaborate statements in "Thalassa, Thalassa," by James Neugass, a poem that endeavored to resolve what might be called the dilemma of cultural inheritance. The four stanzas of the poem are

---

[60] Henry David's landmark volume, *The History of the Haymarket Affair, a Study in the American Social-Revolutionary and Labor Movements*, was published in 1936, on the fiftieth anniversary of the bombing and trial.

[61] Isidor Schneider, *Comrade: Mister* (New York: Equinox Cooperative Press, 1934), n. p.

organized by a contrapuntal movement across time; the classical Greek past and the proletarian present are linked together in an act of mutual revelation and revision.

The poem's epigraph is a quote from a communist press dispatch describing a successful strike by Greek seamen in the harbor of Buenos Aires: "With the assistance of revolutionary trade-unions on shore [the men] won all demands." The opening lines of the poem swerve away from the militant expectations of the epigraph, presenting what seems to be a leisurely imitation of Homeric verse:

> Mariners, seabirds, sailing-ships of the lustrous early annals,
> And the prow-scarred waves, and the seas, wine-dark to jewel-bright,
> Known of all suns and moons and winds and weathers and waves:
> Bravers of dragon'd watery abysses beyond the Pillars of Hercules...

And so on, in ten long, slowly moving lines, complete with familiar Homeric formulas. The "star-steerers," with their cargoes of "spices, gods, feathers and strange barbaric trophies," are apostrophized in the stanza's final line: "O mariners, seabirds, Greeks!"

The second stanza opens with the predictable proletarian rebuttal: "Perhaps and maybe: that was a long time ago. Ask the professors." The present reality of Greek seamen on strike replaces the legends. An obsolete diction is deployed ironically to emphasize the irrelevance of classical literature's accounts of heroism: the men who went out on strike are the "crews of twenty-fives argues named for gods and owners' wives."

However, Neugass wants to rehabilitate the ancient tales, not merely dismantle them. In a sequence that epitomizes the proletarian response to history, the third stanza of "Thalassa" returns to ancient Greece, but this time presents the ancient heroic scene from the point of view of the ordinary seamen who manned the ships that Homer and other poets sang of:

> And in the old days, yearned after by poets and schoolmasters
>   Well, maybe it wasn't all amber and beryl, or "ivory and apes";
> What were the Boeotian words for "crimp," "fink," and "doghouse"?
>   . . .
>   shipped out to sea to fetch home gems,
> Velvets, wines, whores for the temples and slaves for the vineyards:
> Butchered by State enemies, on the decks of floating meat-markets
>   . . .
>   Well, maybe it wasn't all milk and honey, all culture and art.

In other words, what would the Trojan War look like if the story were told by one of the common sailors or soldiers who died at sea or on the beach? The poem intends the question to be at once subversive and affirmative. In effect, Neugass forges an alliance between past and present by erasing the apparent sharp contrast between classical heroes and contemporary labor militants. Reaching back and forth across two millennia and more of history, Greek sailors have joined together and "pitched overboard their lying history" (Freeman, ed., *Proletarian Literature in the United States*, pp. 176–177).

The poem's title presents a compressed version of its argument. Though Neugass offers no annotation, the phrase "thalassa, thalassa" is a quotation from Xenophon's *Anabasis*.[62] In the fourth book, Xenophon tells of the sufferings of his Greek soldiers on their overland hard march through hostile Asia Minor toward the Black Sea. After weeks of skirmishing and struggle, the troops finally reach the high ground that gives them a view of the sea: "When the first men reached the summit and caught sight of the sea there was loud shouting . . . Xenophon thought it must be something very important; he mounted his horse and took Lycios with his horsemen, and rode forward to give help. Soon they heard the soldiers shouting 'The sea! The sea!' [Thalassa! Thalassa!] and passing the word along."[63] It is "one of the most vivid passages in Greek historical writing," a principal text in the history of courage, solidarity, and survival.[64] By invoking the episode in his title, Neugass binds together two narratives, apparently disparate and unconnected, and in so doing reinterprets both past and present. Xenophon's anonymous soldiers merge with Neugass's striking sailors; between them they rescue a reconstructed and legitimate past, on which an acceptable model of proletarian heroism might be constructed. At the same time, "Thalassa" once again discloses the limits of the radical imagination: it is the presence of the past that confers value.

In their essay, "Recent Problems of Revolutionary Literature" (1935), William Phillips and Philip Rahv attacked the intellectual sabotage of "leftists" who "make a mockery of" cultural continuity by "combating all

---

[62] As with much so-called proletarian writing, Neugass's use of Xenophon raises the question of audience: how many working-class readers, or readers of any class in the 1930s, for that matter, would have recognized the reference?

[63] Cited with alterations from W. H. D. Rouse, *The March up Country: A Translation of Xenophon's Anabasis* (Ann Arbor: University of Michigan Press, 1974 [1947]), p. 107.

[64] Peter D. Arnott, *An Introduction to the Greek World* (London: Macmillan, 1967), p. 12.

endeavors to use the heritage of the past."[65] That charge, as the examples in this chapter should have made abundantly clear, is at best inadequate. Marx came closer to the facts of the case when he wrote, "the tradition of all past generations weighs like an alp upon the brain of the living."[66] Searching for an aesthetic strategy that would forward their political commitments, writers on the Left in the 1930s engaged in a complex, sometimes contradictory argument with the past, marked in turns by acts of repudiation, revision, and restoration.

[65] William Phillips and Philip Rahv, "Recent Problems of Revolutionary Literature," in *Proletarian Literature in the United States* (New York: International Publishers, 1935), p. 370.

[66] Karl Marx, *The Eighteenth Brumaire of Louis Napoleon* (New York: International Publishers, 1963 [1852]), p. 5.

Epilogue: The world of tomorrow and the world of yesterday

What was once a swamp in Flushing, Long Island – the "valley of ashes" of *The Great Gatsby* – had been transformed into a place of miracles. The inspirational symbolism of the New York World's Fair of 1939–1940 was calculated and timely. Fully ten years after the Crash, the nation's crippled economy continued to resist the solutions of the New Deal. The Fair, mainly intended to generate revenue for the city, turned into one of the great public events of the decade. For a few hours at least, visitors could leave behind the dreariness of unemployment and class struggle and enter an ideal world of rational planning in which social problems found elegant solutions. As conceived by the corporate leaders of General Motors, General Electric, Kodak, among others, America's future would be orderly, clean, lily-white, and free of smog and slums.

It was called "The World of Tomorrow," but in fact the World's Fair brought the past and future together, often in unexpected ways. While the Fair was famous for its predictions of the technological marvels that lay in store in the decades to come, it was officially conceived as a celebration of the 150th anniversary of Washington's inauguration in New York. The Fair counseled hope, but the hope was rooted in nostalgia: like its sleek, modern buildings, America would rise out of stagnation and discover a prosperous carefree future – a future, as we shall see, that bore some striking resemblances to the past.

Visitors to the Perisphere – one of the Fair's two iconic buildings, along with the Trylon – stood on two rotating platforms that circled "Democracity 2039." The city of the future would be small in scale, set in wooded preserves, with machinery subordinated to human use. This romantic conception of urban living obviously descended from the theories of such writers as Ebenezer Howard, whose influential *Garden Cities of Tomorrow* (1902) inspired several generations of planners.[1] Upon inspection, the city as foreseen by Howard and the designers of Democracity was less urban than suburban, despite disclaimers to the contrary. It was a dream of the past decked out in the deceptive glamor of the future.

This version of the city was also codified in a documentary film created for presentation at the Fair. Produced by the American Institute of Planners, with an "original outline" by Pare Lorentz, commentary by Lewis Mumford, and a musical score by Aaron Copland, *The City* pasted together a sequence of contrasting images that underscore the failure of the contemporary city and the need to re-build on a smaller, greener scale.[2] The film's opening section is set on the Sias Farm, established in 1791, a place that exemplifies the virtues of community and self-reliance. Mumford's text, read by Morris Carnovsky, directs us to admire the clean water, the stability, the mutual responsibility, and the neighborliness of Sias Farm and the small town nearby. These are people who for generations have achieved "lasting harmony between the soil and what we built or planted there." Even death is subsumed in the overflowing sentimentality, portrayed here as repose that follows years of tranquility.

Abruptly, the film shifts from a blacksmith shop to a modern factory. The camera lingers over smoke and slag, harshly lit expressionist landscapes of despair in which men are dwarfed by the fiery wasteland in which they are obliged to labor. The scene then moves to the makeshift shacks in which the workers' families do their best to eke out lives in the midst of dirt and deprivation. "There must be some way out," the narrator insists. Next, in a rushing staccato voice, over images of skyscrapers and crowded city streets, of children playing on dangerous streets, of mass feeding in greasy canteens and mass commuting on crowded subway cars, of limitless automobile congestion and universal anxiety and anger:

Follow the crowd. Get the big money. You make a pile and raise a pile. That makes another pile for you! Follow the crowd. We've reached a million! Two million! Five million! Watch us grow. Going up. It's new. It's automatic. It dictates, records, seals, sterilizes, stamps and delivers in one operation without human hands. What am I bid? What am I offered? Sold! Who's next? The people, yes! Follow the crowd. To the Empire City, the Windy City, the Passion City! The people, yes!

---

[1] *Garden Cities of Tomorrow* was the second edition of Howard's *To-Morrow: A Peaceful Path to Real Reform*, originally published in 1898. Lewis Mumford wrote the introductory essay for a 1946 edition of the book.

[2] After overestimating *The City* as "one of America's greatest social documentaries," Martin J. Medhurst and Thomas W. Benson provide a valuable close reading of the film's structure in "*The City*: The Rhetoric of Rhythm," *Communications Monographs* (March, 1981), pp. 54–72.

Then, in a much quieter voice: "The people, perhaps."

With its allusions to Dos Passos and Sandburg, and its brittle contempt, the passage turns its back on the reality of the contemporary city, and rejects the idea that urban problems might be solved in the framework of large urban concentration. The modern city is nothing more or less than "disorder turned to steel and stone," the city of dreadful night so feared by the Victorians. The inhabitants are named Mr. and Mrs. Zero – here an allusion to the main character in Elmer Rice's once-famous play *The Adding Machine*.

The City proved to be "one of the most popular attractions" at the Fair.[3] The consequences would be serious and far-reaching. As the film's final section makes clear, the solution that the American Institute of Planners proposes for urban problems is to abandon the city and start over. The screen is filled with images of neatly manicured lawns and flower gardens; tree-lined streets and sun-filled small workshops, as the narrator tells us that this is what the new city will look like: "green cities...built into the countryside," ringed with trees and fields and gardens. Like many utopian fantasies, the future coalesces with the past: the city of tomorrow will recreate the small town of the past.

"This is no suburb," the narrator insists, though suburb is exactly what this is. Anticipating the postwar suburb, every face is white, and men and women pursue their rigorously separate vocations in workplace and home. In an eerie way, Mumford's *The City*, which was his revenge against the city, did foresee the fate of American cities in the second half of the twentieth century: hollowed out by a conspiracy of highways and suburbs, abetted by racism and outsourcing.

Mumford's script for *The City* could have been inferred from his earlier work, especially the two books he published in the thirties, *Technics and Civilization* (1932) and *The Culture of Cities* (1938); in the estimate of one scholar, these "count among the most celebrated social-historical critiques of the thirties."[4] Influenced by Ebenezer Howard, by Patrick Geddes, and by the apocalyptic vision of Oswald Spengler, *The Culture of Cities* lamented the rise of the highly centralized, high-density, high-rise modern metropolis, with its indifference to green space and human scale. Frank Lloyd Wright also contributed his portion to his friend Mumford's baleful views. "The value of this earth, as man's heritage, is pretty far gone

---

[3] Donald L. Miller, *Lewis Mumford: A Life* (New York: Weidenfeld & Nicolson, 1989), p. 366.
[4] Daniel T. Rogers, *Atlantic Crossings: Social Politics in a Progressive Age* (Cambridge, MA: The Belknap Press of Harvard University Press, 1998), p. 397.

from him now in the cities centralization has built," Wright declared in the opening sentence of his slipshod but provocative commentary, *The Disappearing City* (1932). "The properly citified citizen has become a broker dealing, chiefly, in human frailties . . . a slave to her instinct."[5]

Combining planning principles with a selective and romantic view of medieval cities, Mumford argued for a rehabilitation of contemporary urban living as garden cities that would accommodate and even encourage connectedness and community. The alternative, the continued and untrammeled growth of urban concentrations into Megapolis, would lead inevitably to decay, decline, and tyranny. Without major changes, "our cities, blasted and deserted, will be cemeteries for the dead: cold lairs given over to less destructive beasts than man."[6]

The Culture of Cities earned Mumford an appearance on the cover of *Time* magazine, and elevated him to a position of unprecedented influence. The handful of "greenbelt" suburban towns laid out by the Resettlement Administration reproduced some of Mumford's ideas. Acknowledging the strength and historical reach of his argument, it should at the same time be noted that his pessimistic view of the modern city also ratified deeply cherished American attitudes. Consequently, his work provided intellectual cover for the decades of political neglect that followed, which left many American cities underfunded and overburdened with the care of the poor.

The counter-argument came more than two decades later, in Jane Jacobs's urban manifesto, *The Death and Life of Great American Cities* (1961). Jacobs defended the city from "the Decentrists," as Mumford and his planning allies were called. These theorists "hammered away at the bad old city. They were incurious about successes in great cities. They were interested only in failure. All was failure. A book like Mumford's *The Culture of Cities* was largely a morbid and biased catalog of ills."[7] Mumford's dyspeptic conception of the American city was rooted in a long history of phobia, reaching back at least to Thomas Jefferson and forward to the Southern Agrarians.

[5] Frank Lloyd Wright, *The Disappearing City* (New York: William Farquhar Payson, 1932), p. 3. One of the book's most striking illustrations, a panoramic shot of New York's skyline under a cloudy sky, is captioned "Find the Citizen."

[6] Lewis Mumford, *The Culture of Cities* (New York: Harcourt, Brace and Company, 1938), p. 11.

[7] Jane Jacobs, *The Death and Life of Great American Cities* (New York: Random House, 1961), p. 20. On Jacobs's debate with Mumford, see Alice Sperberg Alexiou, *Jane Jacobs: Urban Visionary* (New Brunswick, NJ: Rutgers University Press, 2006), pp. 70–75.

The argument over the city intensified in the 1930s. As unemployment spread, poverty increased and also became more visible: the bread line was an indelibly sorrowful emblem of the decade. Mumford was one of several theorists who dreamed dreams of garden cities that would magically do away with the crowding, noise, and dirt of urban life.

The federal government offered ideological support for the city's enemies. The government, which had long taken an official interest in the countryside – the Country Life Commission had presented its famous report to President Theodore Roosevelt in 1911 – undertook its first investigation of city life in the late 1930s. The Research Committee on Urbanism published its findings under the title *Our Cities, Their Role in the National Economy*, in 1937. The report acknowledged that cities were the centers of transportation, culture, finance, and industry, and reached the sophisticated conclusion that urbanism was a marker of "national maturity." At the same time, cities emerge from the document mainly as problematic: the assertion that suicide rates in "urban places of 10,000 population and over has been about 50 percent higher than in the smaller cities and rural areas" serves as a lurid symbol of the pathologies of modern urban life.[8]

The Fair featured another urban prophecy, this one, alas, a truer forecast, on daily display in "Futurama," designed by Norman Bel Geddes for General Motors. This exhibit, as young David Altschuler recalls in E. L. Doctorow's fictionalized book of memory, *World's Fair*, "was everyone's first stop."[9] Futurama offered its visitors a ride across an entire idealized continent, knit together by fourteen-lane superhighways on which traffic flowed with swift efficiency, by-passing cities and reinforcing the idea that cities were the world of the past, not the future. In its salute to the highway and the automobile, General Motors envisioned the world it would then spend the next several decades creating, hand-in-glove with government subsidy and sponsorship. By no coincidence, the Pennsylvania Turnpike opened in August 1940, just a few months before the Fair closed. It was the first long-distance freeway in the nation, and it would become the first section of the interstate highway system.

The Fair's simultaneous appeal to past and future, whether by design or inadvertence captured the conflicted imagination of the 1930s. The

---

[8] [C. A. Dykstra, *et al.*,] *Our Cities: Their Role in the National Economy* (Washington, DC: United States Government Printing Office, 1937), pp. 10–11.

[9] E. L. Doctorow, *World's Fair: A Novel* (New York: Random House, 1985), p. 292.

multi-lane highways of Futurama promised the land of tomorrow, but they also beckoned America's citizens toward the simplicities and pieties of the past: of westering wagons, the frontier, the open road. In 1936, a few years before the Fair opened, that mythic road had been deployed as the climactic image in two of the decade's major works. At the end of Dos Passos's *U.S.A.*, the anonymous Vag stands beside a road that leads nowhere. He is hungry and homeless, ignored by the speeding cars as he tries to hitch a ride, invisible to the passengers on the silver plane that soars over his head. At the same moment, Charlie Chaplin incorporated the road as the final image in his great film, *Modern Times*. The Tramp and the Gamine (Chaplin and Paulette Goddard) have bounced from one indignity to another, but in the film's last scene they walk arm in arm down an open road. While Dos Passos's Vag is mocked by the road's archetypal but bankrupt history, Chaplin's Tramp embraces its call to a new life. As the preceding chapters have demonstrated, the culture of the thirties enacted that debate over the meaning of the past and its symbols in countless novels, non-fiction books, plays, poems, and paintings.

Appendix: Literary prizes and bestsellers

For the first thirty years, all but one of the Nobel Prizes in literature went to Europeans. (The exception was India's Rabindranath Tagore, the 1913 laureate.) In 1930, Sinclair Lewis became the first American to win the prize, an honor that had been denied to Henry James and Mark Twain, among others. Lewis's selection was controversial, but it signaled a new international attitude toward American letters, a recognition that American writers had earned the European esteem so long denied them. In fairly rapid succession, two other Americans also won in the thirties, Eugene O'Neill (1936) and Pearl S. Buck (1938).

The Pulitzer Prizes had established themselves from the first awards in 1917 as the country's preeminent accolade in journalism and literature. These were the Pulitzers awarded in the 1930s:

1930

Novel	*Laughing Boy*, Oliver Lafarge
Drama	*The Green Pastures*, Marc Connelly
History	*The War of Independence*, Claude H. Van Tyne
Biography or autobiography	*The Raven*, Marquis James
Poetry	*Selected Poems*, Conrad Aiken

1931

Novel	*Years of Grace*, Margaret Ayer Barnes
Drama	*Alison's House*, Susan Glaspell
History	*The Coming of the War 1914*, Bernadotte E. Schmitt
Biography or autobiography	*Henry James*, Charles W. Eliot
Poetry	*Collected Poems*, Robert Frost

1932
Novel   *The Good Earth*, Pearl S. Buck
Drama   *Of Thee I Sing*, George S. Kaufman,
                                            Morrie Ryskind, and Ira Gershwin
History   *My Experiences in the World War*, John J.
                                            Pershing
Biography or autobiography   *Theodore Roosevelt*, Henry F. Pringle
Poetry   *The Flowering Stone*, George Dillon

1933
Novel   *The Store*, T. S. Stribling
Drama   *Both Your Houses*, Maxwell Anderson
History   *The Significance of Sections in American
                                            History*, Frederick J. Turner
Biography or autobiography   *Grover Cleveland*, Allan Nevins
Poetry   *Conquistador*, Archibald MacLeish

1934
Novel   *Lamb in His Bosom*, Caroline Miller
Drama   *Men in White*, Sidney Kingsley
History   *The People's Choice*, Herbert Agar
Biography or autobiography   *John Hay*, Tyler Dennett
Poetry   *Collected Verse*, Robert Hillyer

1935
Novel   *Now in November*, Josephine Winslow
                                            Johnson
Drama   *The Old Maid*, Zoe Akins
History   *The Colonial Period of American History*,
                                            Charles McLean Andrews
Biography or autobiography   *R. E. Lee*, Douglas S. Freeman
Poetry   *Bright Ambush*, Audrey Wurdemann

1936
Novel   *Honey in the Horn*, Harold L. Davis
Drama   *Idiot's Delight*, Robert E. Sherwood
History   *A Constitutional History of the United
                                            States*, Andrew C. McLaughlin

Biography or autobiography	*The Thought and Character of William James*, Ralph Barton Perry
Poetry	*Strange Holiness*, Robert P. Tristram Coffin

1937

Novel	*Gone with the Wind*, Margaret Mitchell
Drama	*You Can't Take It With You*, Moss Hart and George S. Kaufman
History	*The Flowering of New England 1815–1865*, Van Wyck Brooks
Biography or autobiography	*Hamilton Fish*, Allan Nevins
Poetry	*A Further Range*, Robert Frost

1938

Novel	*The Late George Apley*, John Phillips Marquand
Drama	*Our Town*, Thornton Wilder
History	*The Road to Reunion, 1865–1900*, Paul Herman Buck
Biography or autobiography	*Andrew Jackson, 2 volumes*, Marquis James
Biography or autobiography	*Pedlar's Progress*, Odell Shepard
Poetry	*Cold Morning Sky*, Marya Zaturenska

1939

Novel	*The Yearling*, Marjorie Kinnan Rawlings
Drama	*Abe Lincoln in Illinois*, Robert E. Sherwood
History	*A History of American Magazines*, Frank Luther Mott
Biography or autobiography	*Benjamin Franklin*, Carl Van Doren
Poetry	*Selected Poems*, John Gould Fletcher

1940

Novel	*The Grapes of Wrath*, John Steinbeck
Drama	*The Time of Your Life*, William Saroyan
History	*Abraham Lincoln: The War Years*, Carl Sandburg
Biography or autobiography	*Woodrow Wilson, Life and Letters. Volumes* VII *and* VIII, Ray Stannard Baker
Poetry	*Collected Poems*, Mark Van Doren

Bestsellers are harder to document accurately than prize winners, but here is a composite list that probably comes close to an accurate record of the decade's bestselling novels and non-fiction books (I list only the top five for each year):

1930: FICTION

Cimarron, Edna Ferber
Exile, Warwick Deeping (British)
The Woman of Andros, Thornton Wilder
Years of Grace, Margaret Ayer Barnes
Angel Pavement, J. B. Priestley (British)

1930: NON-FICTION

The Story of San Michele, Axel Munthe (Swedish)
The Strange Death of President Harding, Gaston B. Means and May Dixon Thacker
Byron, André Maurois (French)
The Adams Family, James Truslow Adams
Lone Cowboy, Will James

1931: FICTION

The Good Earth, Pearl S. Buck
Shadows on the Rock, Willa Cather
A White Bird Flying, Bess Streeter Aldrich
Grand Hotel, Vicki Baum (Austrian)
Years of Grace, Margaret Ayer Barnes

1931: NON-FICTION

Education of a Princess, Grand Duchess Marie (Romanian)
The Story of San Michele, Axel Munthe (Swedish)
Washington Merry-Go-Round, anonymous [Drew Pearson and Robert S. Allen]
Boners: Being a Collection of Schoolboy Wisdom, or Knowledge as it is Sometimes Written, compiled by Alexander Abingdon; illustrated by Dr. Seuss
Culbertson's Summary, Ely Culbertson

1932: FICTION

The Good Earth, Pearl S. Buck
The Fountain, Charles Morgan (British)
Sons, Pearl S. Buck
Magnolia Street, Louis Golding (British)
The Sheltered Life, Ellen Glasgow

1932: NON-FICTION

The Epic of America, James Truslow Adams
Only Yesterday, Frederick Lewis Allen
A Fortune to Share, Vashni Young
Culbertson's Summary, Ely Culbertson
Van Loon's Geography, Hendrik Willem Van Loon (Dutch-American)

1933: FICTION

Anthony Adverse, Hervey Allen
As the Earth Turns, Gladys Hasty Carroll
Ann Vickers, Sinclair Lewis
Magnificent Obsession, Lloyd C. Douglas
One More River, John Galsworthy (British)

1933: NON-FICTION

Life Begins at Forty, Walter B. Pitkin
Marie Antoinette, Stefan Zweig (Austrian)
British Agent, R. H. Bruce Lockhart (British)
100,000,000 Guinea Pigs, Arthur Kallet and F. J. Schlink
The House of Exile, Nora Waln

1934: FICTION

Anthony Adverse, Hervey Allen
Lamb in His Bosom, Caroline Miller
So Red the Rose, Stark Young
Good-Bye, Mr. Chips, James Hilton (British)
Within This Present, Margaret Ayer Barnes

1934: NON-FICTION

While Rome Burns, Alexander Woollcott
Life Begins at Forty, Walter B. Pitkin
Nijinsky, Romola Nijinsky (Hungarian)
100,000,000 Guinea Pigs, Arthur Kallet and F. J. Schlink
The Native's Return, Louis Adamic

1935: FICTION

Green Light, Lloyd C. Douglas
Vein of Iron, Ellen Glasgow
Of Time and the River, Thomas Wolfe
Time Out of Mind, Rachel Field
Good-Bye, Mr. Chips, James Hilton (British)

1935: NON-FICTION

North to the Orient, Anne Morrow Lindbergh
While Rome Burns, Alexander Woollcott
Life with Father, Clarence Day
Personal History, Vincent Sheean
Seven Pillars of Wisdom, T. E. Lawrence (British)

1936: FICTION

Gone with the Wind, Margaret Mitchell
The Last Puritan, George Santayana
Sparkenbroke, Charles Morgan (British)
Drums Along the Mohawk, Walter D. Edmonds
It Can't Happen Here, Sinclair Lewis

1936: NON-FICTION

Man the Unknown, Alexis Carrel (French-American)
Wake Up and Live!, Dorothea Brande
The Way of a Transgressor, Negley Farson
Around the World in Eleven Years, Richard Patience and Johnny Abbe
North to the Orient, Anne Morrow Lindbergh

1937: FICTION

Gone with the Wind, Margaret Mitchell
Northwest Passage, Kenneth Roberts
The Citadel, A. J. Cronin (British)
And so – Victoria, William Vaughan Wilkins (British)
Drums Along the Mohawk, Walter D. Edmonds

1937: NON-FICTION

How To Win Friends and Influence People, Dale Carnegie
An American Doctor's Odyssey, Victor Heiser
The Return to Religion, Henry C. Link
The Arts, Hendrik Willem Van Loon (Dutch-American)
Orchids on Your Budget, Marjorie Hillis

1938: FICTION

The Yearling, Marjorie Kinnan Rawlings
The Citadel, A. J. Cronin (British)
My Son, My Son!, Howard Spring
Rebecca, Daphne du Maurier (British)
Northwest Passage, Kenneth Roberts

1938: NON-FICTION

The Importance of Living, Lin Yutang (Chinese-American)
With Malice Toward Some, Margaret Halsey
Madame Curie, Eve Curie (French)
Listen! The Wind, Anne Morrow Lindbergh
The Horse and Buggy Doctor, Arthur E. Hertzler

1939: FICTION

The Grapes of Wrath, John Steinbeck
All This, and Heaven Too, Rachel Field
Rebecca, Daphne du Maurier (British)
Wickford Point, John P. Marquand
Escape, Ethel Vance [Grace Zaring Stone]

1939: NON-FICTION

Days of Our Years, Pierre van Paassen (Dutch-Canadian-American)
Reaching for the Stars, Nora Waln
Inside Asia, John Gunther
Autobiography with Letters, William Lyon Phelps
Country Lawyer, Bellamy Partridge

1940: FICTION

How Green Was My Valley, Richard Llewellyn (British)
Kitty Foyle, Christopher Morley
Mrs. Miniver, Jan Struther [Joyce Anstruther] (British)
For Whom the Bell Tolls, Ernest Hemingway
The Nazarene, Sholem Asch (Polish)

1940: NON-FICTION

I Married Adventure, Osa Johnson
How to Read a Book, Mortimer Adler
A Smattering of Ignorance, Oscar Levant
Country Squire in the White House, John T. Flynn
Land below the Wind, Agnes Newton Keith

Without pretending to more precision than the numbers allow, note that about one quarter of the bestselling novels were by foreign authors, most of them British. (I've excluded mystery writers, which would tilt the results even further: Agatha Christie was a major bestseller in the USA throughout the thirties.) The consensus opinion is that, across the entire decade, *Gone with the Wind* was the bestselling novel, followed by *Anthony Adverse*, *The Good Earth*, and *The Grapes of Wrath*, in that order.

Index

8/11

DATE DUE